A Governor's Story

To the workers of Michigan and America
who are finding their way in a time
of extraordinary challenge and change

A GOVERNOR'S STORY

The Fight for Jobs and America's Economic Future

· · · · · · · · · · · · ·

DISCARD

JENNIFER GRANHOLM
and
DAN MULHERN

PublicAffairs
New York

PublicAffairs books are available at special discounts for bulk purchases
in the U.S. by corporations, institutions, and other organizations. For more
information, please contact the Special Markets Department at the Perseus
Books Group, 2300 Chestnut Street, Suite 200,Philadelphia, PA 19103, call
(800) 810-4145, ext. 5000, or e-mail special.markets@perseusbooks.com.

Book Design by Linda Mark

Library of Congress Cataloging-in-Publication Data
Granholm, Jennifer.
  A governor's story : the fight for jobs and America's economic future /
Jennifer Granholm and Dan Mulhern.—1st ed.
    p. cm.
Includes bibliographical references and index.
ISBN 978-1-58648-997-7 (hardcover)—ISBN 978-1-58648-998-4 (ebook)
1. Granholm, Jennifer. 2. Governors—Michigan—Biography. 3. Women
governors—Michigan—Biography. 4. Michigan—Politics and government—
1951- 5. Michigan—Economic policy. 6. Social problems—Michigan—History—
21st century. 7. United States—Politics and government—2001–2009. 8. United
States—Politics and government—2009- 9. United States—Economic
policy—2001–2009. 10. United States—Economic policy—2009- I. Mulhern,
Daniel Granholm. II. Title.
F570.25.G73A3 2011
977.4'043092—dc23
[B]
2011017332

First Edition
10 9 8 7 6 5 4 3 2 1

CONTENTS

Photo Insert on text between pages 172–173

SEVEN MONTHS OF FREEFALL

A Michigan Timeline: December 2008–June 2009

January 7:
Michigan unemployment office reports more than a million calls per day from newly unemployed workers. Phone systems cannot handle volume of calls.

February 10:
GM announces another 3,400 salaried job cuts, 90% in Michigan.

January 21:
The Bureau of Labor Statistics reports that Michigan's unemployment rate jumps a full percentage point in one month.

February 17:
GM and Chrysler submit new restructuring plans to Obama administration, asking for $21.6 billion more to stave off bankruptcy.

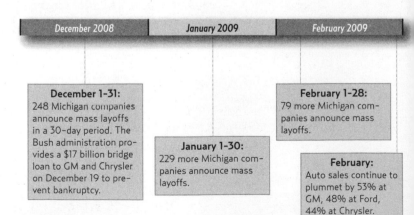

December 2008 | January 2009 | February 2009

December 1-31:
248 Michigan companies announce mass layoffs in a 30-day period. The Bush administration provides a $17 billion bridge loan to GM and Chrysler on December 19 to prevent bankruptcy.

January 1-30:
229 more Michigan companies announce mass layoffs.

February 1-28:
79 more Michigan companies announce mass layoffs.

February:
Auto sales continue to plummet by 53% at GM, 48% at Ford, 44% at Chrysler.

May 1:
Chrysler announces suspension of production at all United States and Canadian plants.

May 5:
Governor slashes another $350 million in mid-year cuts from state budget.

May 7:
GM announces a $6 billion 1Q loss.

March 4:
Long lines of unemployed people are observed outside unemployment and state welfare offices.

March 5:
Unemployment in Michigan jumps to 25-year high, up 1.4% since December. A record number of state residents sign up for Medicaid.

April 2:
Published reports show 109,000 more people left Michigan in 2008 than moved in, highest outward migration in nation. The state loses a family every 12 minutes.

May 13:
Detroit Public Schools emergency financial manager Robert Bobb asks the federal government to put the school district under a "special presidential emergency declaration" to allow district to receive emergency funding.

March 9:
Budget crisis causes Pontiac public schools to lay off entire staff.

April 13:
Michigan sixth in nation in foreclosures.

March 11:
Michigan Senate Fiscal Agency shows state tax receipts for February down by 31%. Sales tax collections show "steepest monthly decline during the past 25 years."

April 16:
Unemployment jumps again more than 60%.

May 15:
State Revenue Estimating Conference reports Michigan will take in $1.72 billion less than initially estimated; governor and lawmakers must make another round of deep budget cuts.

April 28:
GM announces accelerated plans to close 16 more auto plants as part of restructuring effort.

March 29:
President Obama announces 30 days to bankruptcy for Chrysler, 60 days for GM.
  GM CEO Rick Wagoner forced to step down.

April 30:
Chrysler files for bankruptcy.

May 20:
Michigan's unemployment rate rises to its highest mark since late 1983, highest in the nation.

June 1:
GM files for bankruptcy, the largest bankruptcy in U.S. history.

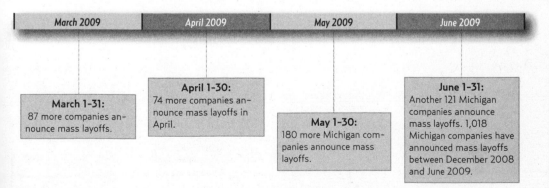

March 2009	April 2009	May 2009	June 2009

March 1-31:
87 more companies announce mass layoffs.

April 1-30:
74 more companies announce mass layoffs in April.

May 1-30:
180 more Michigan companies announce mass layoffs.

June 1-31:
Another 121 Michigan companies announce mass layoffs. 1,018 Michigan companies have announced mass layoffs between December 2008 and June 2009.

It wasn't supposed to be like this.

INTRODUCTION

THIS IS THE STORY OF MICHIGAN DURING MY YEARS AS GOVERNOR. It's the story of one of the largest, most economically significant states in the Union as we hit rock bottom—then slowly, painfully, began to climb back toward recovery, resuming growth and, in my last year in office, enjoyed the most improved job creation rate of any state. There are clear reasons for the shocking decline of Michigan, its eventual rebirth, and the hopeful signs of growth the state is now experiencing. In these pages we've sought to explain those reasons and show why they matter deeply to everyone in America.

For Michigan is no aberration. Rather, it is a harbinger of what can happen and indeed *is happening* across this country. America is struggling to rise beyond what many call a "jobless recovery" while also being plagued with other economic woes—a chronic energy shortfall, crumbling infrastructure, inadequate systems of health care and education, and unrelenting fiscal deficits. Michigan has been ground zero for all these problems.

Cities, states, and the entire nation are grappling with unprecedented budget shortfalls, but before them, Michigan tackled eight straight years of gigantic budget deficits, cut a greater percentage from its budget than any state in the country, and balanced the budget every year.

Governments at every level are struggling to define fair new labor practices that respect the dignity of workers while recognizing new economic realities, but in Michigan we found ways to work with unions both private and public to define tough yet reasonable concessions that have made economic progress possible again.

Businesses around the country are striving to rebound from the worst economic crisis since the Great Depression, but Michigan's most important employers have already lived through the largest bankruptcies in American history and emerged with new life and hope for a better future.

For a decade, Michigan has been America's main laboratory for experimenting with adaptations to the new economic realities. In the process, we have learned a lot. We tested solutions that some governors are now proposing, sometimes discovering that they didn't work because they were built on assumptions that were once largely true but are now dangerously wrong. Chastened by the experience, we shifted to different solutions that are now bearing fruit. In the chapters that follow, we'll recount our eye-opening experiences for the benefit of citizens, policy experts, business leaders, and elected officials everywhere.

If there's a central message we hope readers will take away from this book, it is that today we face an extraordinary battle for America's future, especially the future of the middle and working classes. It's a battle that demands a greater level of fresh, creative thinking than any crisis we've faced in decades.

Had I magically been able to read this book eight years ago, I would have been stunned to discover some of the things I was forced to do by the dilemmas I faced as governor. I made cuts in long-cherished social programs that some loyal Democrats considered unconscionable. I disappointed many of our party's traditional allies, from public employee unions to educators to arts organizations, with tough demands for belt-tightening, flexibility, and increased self-reliance. And if I had it to do over again, I would make many of the same choices—except that I would make them sooner. I made plenty of mistakes, too, and we learned from them. And the overarching lesson was that many of our old views of the world simply don't match reality anymore.

In Michigan, we've had to change. And the nation has to change, too.

The most important mind-set shift we now require is a break with the conventional wisdom about economic growth. After three decades of conservative ascendancy, global competition is confronting us with the hard fact that pure laissez-faire, free-market theory no longer works. Recent experience shows that tax cuts, deregulation, and a hands-off approach to government don't amount to a magical formula for jobs, profits, and prosperity.

The evidence is plentiful, but one data point stands out above the rest: 42,000 manufacturing plants throughout the United States closed in the last decade, many of them in Michigan. This massive disappearance of manufacturing jobs has taken place *despite* a steady decrease in business taxes and regulation.

Why? There are many reasons—but chief among them is the fact that countries like China, India, and Brazil are offering cheap labor, government loans and subsidies, and many other inducements to American companies eager to cut costs and boost their profits by offshoring their production facilities. And manufacturing is only one industry that can and will move. If corporations can essentially ship massive factories on boats to China, creating enormous capital investments there, what makes us think they can't and won't move software development teams, call centers, design studios, research units, legal staffs, printing companies, and many other operations?

Of course they can. Of course they are.

In a world where governments on every continent are quite consciously and publicly fighting to attract capital and jobs, only the U.S. government has been forced by ideological restrictions to compete for those jobs with its hands tied behind its back.

And because, in the real world, the laissez-faire dogma that politicians feel forced to defend is so clearly unworkable, they compound the problem with hypocrisy. Both Republican and Democratic governors commit the supposedly unpardonable sin of "intervening in the market" every single day. They structure tax incentives, breaks, credits, and regulatory waivers to lure businesses to their states' borders. The result is state-versus-state competition rather than a national effort to win the race against global competition. Michigan may be able to beat Indiana, North Carolina, and Texas in head-to-head battles over auto supply factories or solar research facilities, but individual states are not equipped to outcompete Mexico, China, and Korea when the governments of those nations enter the fray.

It's time to inject a major dose of realism into our national economic debate. That's why the last chapter of this book focuses on the policy initiatives we need to see from Washington—the kinds of programs that will defend our national interests, create and retain jobs, support essential industries, and encourage the technological innovation that will drive economic growth in the twenty-first century. We need a uniquely American, globally competitive approach to economic growth.

Abandoning rigid right-wing economic thinking doesn't mean returning to old-fashioned liberal approaches. Again, Michigan offers a test case. The new Michigan now emerging has been through a profound identity crisis and is adapting to the new global realities. Scores of thousands of Michigan's workers, having been buffeted by harsh economic storms, are retooling themselves for new careers and developing the high-tech skills the knowledge economy demands. Our auto industry, rapidly adapting to the clean energy demands of a changing planet, is now posting profits and expanding its workforce for the first time since 2000. With the United

Auto Workers leading the way, organized labor is pioneering new cooperative approaches that make work more creative and companies more flexible and competitive, while protecting the rights and dignity of workers. Clean tech companies by the hundreds are setting up shop in Michigan, where they will lead the way to an America that is energy self-sufficient and less reliant on environmentally destructive fossil fuels.

None of these people and organizations is looking backward or trying to re-create "the good old days" of Michigan's storied past. They're advancing boldly into a new, uncharted future—and doing so with confidence, imagination, and determination.

There's much more work to be done. Michigan's economic battles are far from over. But we've found a path to progress that is starting to work—and it's a path that can enable America to prevail in the coming decades as well. That's the larger significance of our story—and the real reason that we hope people everywhere will read and heed the lessons of Michigan.

America can prevail in the decades ahead. This book is our prayer that it will.

·   ·   ·   ·   ·

A WORD ABOUT THE STYLE AND FORMAT OF THIS BOOK. IT'S NOT a conventional autobiography but rather, as the title makes plain, a governor's story—a chapter in the history of Michigan, its challenges during difficult times, and one leader's efforts to surmount those challenges, along with the larger lessons we take from these experiences.

Dan and I wrote this book together because we lived through the story together. We are best friends, with deeply shared values, equally combative minds, and a mutual devotion to our family, state, and country. We brought very different perspectives to our journey together, and we hope they enrich this account. Dan insisted that the book be written in Jennifer's voice, and she insisted that he be listed as coauthor. Like all the other important projects we've undertaken in our lives together, this book has been a true partnership, which has enriched the process enormously for each of us.

Finally, please note that many of the accounts in these pages include conversations among the key participants. These dialogues are re-created from our best recollections. They are not verbatim records of the language, but they are accurate in substance and spirit.

Jennifer Granholm and Dan Mulhern
May 2011

chapter 1

THE BOUNCE

ELECTION NIGHT, TUESDAY, NOVEMBER 5, 2002. DAN'S WHOOPING drew me into the bedroom of our Marriott Hotel suite, where he was trampolining on the bed, reaching for the high ceiling with each bounce. He'd been adrenaline pumped and sleep deprived for days, but our nonstop, twenty-four-hour, pre-election Time-for-a-Change bus tour across Michigan had obviously pushed him over the edge.

"Oh yeah! We did it!" he yelled as he bounded high in the air, arms flapping. "You won! We won! You won!"

"You're crazy," I said.

"You *won*, Babe!" Bounce. "All that killer work!" Bounce. "You did it!" Bounce. "Can you believe it?"

"No," I said. My eyes moved to my papers on the desk. "But I suspect I'm going to need that victory spee . . ."

"*Suspect?*" he yelled.

"Yes, and I'd love for you to look it over when you're done jumping for joy, you nut."

"Who's the nut?" Bounce. "You need to *savor* this moment!" At the apogee of his next jump, he swept his arms toward the floor-to-ceiling windows. Seventy floors below, the lights of Detroit and, on the horizon, Windsor, Ontario, spread out in a glittering panorama. "It's"—bounce—"*a-may-*zing!"

I flipped through the pages of my speech for a final time. I was numb. Yes, it was really happening. Within the hour I'd travel to the ballroom downstairs, step to the podium in front of supporters and the TV cameras, and accept what I knew would be the biggest job I would ever hold: governor of Michigan—the eighth largest state in the country, an economy bigger than that of Saudi Arabia or Greece, an opportunity for me to serve in a way that I had never imagined.

I finished tweaking my acceptance speech and joined family and friends in the adjacent suite, where they were huddled around TV screens at opposite ends of the big room. Election results from around the state were rapidly piling up. One network had already called the race. As more friends and family members arrived, the volume of noise in the hotel room kept rising. Finished with bouncing but still hypercharged with excitement, Dan came in and began circling the room, swapping hugs and victory shouts with one person after another.

The chief members of my political team, Dave Katz, Jill Alper, and Rick Wiener, pulled me aside. "Jennifer," Rick said, "you've got this won. It's ten forty-seven. The eleven o'clock news is about to start. It's time to go downstairs and declare victory."

I shook my head. "Not until I hear from him."

"He'll call," said Dan. "If Dick Posthumus is anything, he's a gentleman."

As if on cue, the phone rang. "Shh! Quiet down, everybody!" someone hissed. Our five-year-old son, Jack, was the closest. He picked up the phone.

"Hello?" he said. He listened for a moment, his eyes growing wide, then held out the receiver. "It's Dick!" he yelled, provoking badly muffled laughter from the giddy crowd.

Pressing my finger to my lips to hush the group, I took the phone and turned toward the sparkling Detroit skyline. Behind me, the room turned stone quiet, TVs muted, as everyone listened.

"Congratulations, Jennifer," the lieutenant governor said. "I'll be giving my concession speech in a few minutes. You ran a great race."

"Thank you," I said. "You ran a good race, too. You're a class act. I really appreciate the call, and I wish you only the best." I slowly put down the phone.

"That's it," I said, turning to everyone. "Dick Posthumus just conceded. So thanks to you all—"

Hoots and hollers drowned me out. Young staffers in white Granholm-for-Governor T-shirts, bleary-eyed from months of work on four hours of sleep a night, exchanged hugs and high fives with gray-haired politicos whose last winning gubernatorial race had been when Dan and I were still in law school. Dan's swarm of siblings, nieces, cousins, and friends clinked longneck bottles and wine glasses.

I pulled away from the throng and moved back into the bedroom, quickly changed into a blue suit, grabbed my speech, and followed the crowd out of the suite to the elevators. Leading the way was the confident and brassy Colleen Pobur, her head adorned with walkie-talkie headphones. Colleen and I were friends from our days working in Wayne County government. I love her gusto for life—the way she swears, smokes cigars, and calls football plays better than any man I know. We always joke that we're bossy broads, and tonight Col was in her bossiest glory. Behind her I herded Kate and Cece, our daughters, aged thirteen and eleven, looking wide-eyed, thrilled, and bewildered. Colleen, eyes dancing, gave them high fives. "We got *some* party for you, girls!" she crowed.

We emerged on the ballroom level, passed swiftly through a series of unmarked doors, and snaked our way through a huge industrial kitchen where I exchanged quick hugs with grinning waiters and waitresses in their tuxedo uniforms. "You did it, Ms. Granholm!" one shouted as they waved and hooted. Narrow service corridors led us to a dark backstage space just behind a heavy curtain that stretched across the ballroom stage. The air trembled with the muffled din of celebratory music and excited voices.

Nervously, I peeked through the slit in the curtain at the pandemonium on the other side: balloons, bunting, deep blue Granholm and Cherry signs, TV cameras crowded together on a platform in the middle of the room, and hundreds of people—schoolteachers in ball caps, firefighters in yellow T-shirts, store clerks, factory workers, social workers, senior citizens, pastors, and moms with their daughters holding handmade signs with messages like "You go, GRRRL!" They'd worked to elect a governor who promised to invest in education and health care, a woman they believed would heal an aching state by stopping Michigan's economic slide.

I sold that vision, and I bought into it, too. I was determined to fix the problems of the state that had put its faith in me.

I glanced at Kate, peeking out through the curtain with me and grinning in her braces. I flashed back to the time when First Lady Hillary Rodham Clinton had come to Detroit to speak to a women's rally at Cobo Center, just two blocks from where we were now. Five-year-old Kate and I were lucky enough to have front-row seats that night. I was a federal prosecutor and a working mom who wanted her daughter to see an inspiring role model. As the curtain parted, I lifted Kate up for a better look. Just at the moment Hillary emerged, Kate rose above the crowd, and hearing the thunderous applause, she stared at me, eyes wide, and asked, "Mom, are they clapping for *me*?"

Tonight, they *would* be clapping for Kate, and for all of us. She would go from the front row to the stage, a part of history in the making.

Colleen signaled the moment. From behind the curtain, Larry Tokarski, affectionately nicknamed "Cecil B. Tokarski" for his showman's flair in planning events, introduced me, using his best booming "voice of God" delivery: "Ladies and gentleman, Michigan's forty-seventh governor!" and we pushed through the curtains as the funky "Celebrate good times, come on!" blared over the sound system. A sea of exuberant people surged against the stage.

Arms up, I tried to quiet the hollering, but the happy crowd ignored me. It was their victory, too. Little Jack was waving. Kate and Cece were laughing and grinning. Dan's brothers and sisters and their kids were jammed in behind us on the small stage. Dan began shaking the hands of friends in the crowd just inches away. My running mate, Lieutenant Governor–elect John Cherry, and I raised our hands into a V for victory, and the people in the crowd went wild, applauding, bouncing, waving signs, and chanting. I managed to get through the victory speech only by shouting over them.

The excitement was understandable. Most of my supporters knew it was a fluke that I'd been elected governor at all. I wasn't even from Michigan. I'd been born in Canada and raised since the age of four in California's San Francisco Bay area, far from the factories and farms of the Midwest. My dad, Victor Ivar Granholm, is a gentleman and a Republican, a stoic Swede who never raises his voice. I have never once heard him utter a swear word, falsehood, or complaint. My mom, Shirley Dowden Granholm, is a pragmatic, earthy Newfoundlander whose mildly scatological humor causes my dad to laugh out loud daily. When I was little, my mom encouraged me, "Spread your wings and fly!" But she also gave me three specific pieces of advice: "Don't talk about yourself—nobody wants to hear it—don't ask strangers for money, and don't wear your dress-up clothes every day." With that guidance, I have no idea how I ended up running for office.

As a child, I was a gifted student, but by my teen years I was unfocused and restless in class. Eventually, that restless side took charge. At nineteen, I took off from our family home in San Carlos and drove eight hours south to Los Angeles in a yellow Ford Courier pickup truck to try my hand at acting. One of the thousands of young blonde wannabes in Hollywood, I took classes at the famous American Academy of Dramatic Arts and dreamed of becoming the female Lawrence Olivier. But those were the days of *Three's Company* and *Charlie's Angels*, and the cattle-call auditions for pretty girls willing to show off their assets and the vapid encounters with seedy agents and producers left me disgusted and angry.

Meanwhile, I was supporting myself as a lowly clerk in the customer service department at the *Los Angeles Times* and as a tour guide on the back lots at Universal Studios. Increasingly disillusioned with acting, I spent the summer of 1980 on the patio behind the office at Universal Studios, cherishing the moments between tours when I could read political philosophy and civil rights history, marinating in me a growing desire to change the world. I canvassed door-to-door for independent presidential candidate John B. Anderson. I became a naturalized U.S. citizen. But with no college degree and no credentials, I knew I could be nothing more than a two-bit player in life or politics. I fled Los Angeles, determined to make up for lost time. I was twenty-one, in focus, and on a mission to become educated.

I was admitted to the University of California at Berkeley and dove right in, reborn as an avid student with a voracious appetite for knowledge. I had part-time jobs but was obsessed with politics and civil rights, and I was hell-bent on getting straight As. (Dan still teases me about my irritation with the professor at the University of Bordeaux, France, who, during my junior year abroad, marred my transcript with an A-minus.) I emerged in 1984 with dual degrees in political science and French, the first person in my family to graduate from college.

As an educational late-bloomer, I felt my future explode wide open when I was accepted to Harvard Law School. I remember pulling the large envelope with the Harvard return address out of my mailbox, hands shaking so hard I had trouble tearing the envelope open. I dumped the contents onto a nearby desk and felt my heart racing as I read and reread the acceptance letter through moist eyes, not quite believing it was true.

My life's direction changed forever at Harvard, where I met Dan. He had been a religious studies major at Yale and had considered becoming a priest before deciding to attend Harvard Law. I was one of a band of idealistic students protesting Harvard's investments in companies doing business in apartheid South Africa. Dan courted me during an overnight sit-in outside the Harvard president's office, in between chants of "Derek Bok! Get the word! This is not Johannesburg!" Later I was among the students disciplined by Harvard for protesting the presence of a South African diplomat on campus. ("Don't get kicked out of Harvard, for Pete's sake," my mom warned, "after all the work you did to get in!") In my third year, I was elected editor in chief of the *Harvard Civil Rights–Civil Liberties Law Review*. None of this deterred Dan.

He'd been born and raised in a large Irish-Italian Catholic family in the working-class town of Inkster, Michigan, and three months after we met, we were engaged. But not before I thoroughly cross-examined him. I told him honestly that I could never emulate Mary Mulhern, his wonderful, self-sacrificing mom, who had given her life to raising seven children. With me, family life would have to be fifty-fifty: I'd cut the lawn, he'd cook, I'd do the dishes, and raising kids would be a joint project. He passed the grilling.

What drew me to Dan were his gentleness, his heart, and his passion for the poor. I loved that after Yale he'd taught theology and then spent a couple years running an inner-city youth center in New Orleans. I loved that he didn't care about making money but wanted to serve people instead. I loved that he would leave fresh lilacs or wax-paper-pressed fiery New England leaves and lyrical notes in my law school mailbox. And I loved that he was a music-loving jock who cooked a mean pot of jambalaya.

Dan intended to make a difference. He had plans to enter politics, with a dream of one day becoming governor of Michigan. I planned to be a civil rights lawyer, maybe one day a professor or judge. I thought we'd make a great team.

While preparing us for marriage, Father John MacInnes, a thirty-five-year-old assistant chaplain at St. Paul's Catholic Church in Cambridge, helped us think about the future of our relationship. In our last meeting, he asked Dan, "What if, eight or ten years from now, the Democratic Party comes to Jennifer and says, 'We want you to run for an open Senate seat. You're smart, electable, and this is a great time for a woman candidate.' How would you feel about that, Dan?"

I laughed out loud at the thought, but Dan considered the question seriously. "I think I'd probably feel jealous," he said at last. "I'd have some adjusting to do. But if Jennifer felt like she was being called to run, I'd support her a hundred and ten percent." Although the idea seemed ridiculous to me at the time, the answer typified the noble and soulful Irishman I'd come to love.

In spite of our many similarities and deep connections, Dan and I are behavioral opposites. I love in him the things I lack in myself. He stops to smells the roses (and to jump on the bed); ever future-focused, I can't stop pressing forward. We noticed those differences as early as our honeymoon in Ireland. My plan was to see every inch of Ireland (and we got pretty close), but Dan got me to slow down and savor the experience. He'd coax me to park our rented car just to climb a beckoning hill or to linger at a pub just to see if some local musicians would show up and

jam. Between the two of us, we created the perfect honeymoon—
and experienced Ireland in ways we'd never have done without
each other.

Over the years, our understanding of our differences has deepened. I've come to see that by nature I'm just not introspective. I
am someone who does, not someone who ponders. I've always believed that through diligent effort I could battle my way through
anything. I gain a sense of accomplishment through activity—
making lists, checking things off, getting things done. I've never
seen a personal counselor, never been in therapy, and for the most
part this life strategy has worked for me.

Early in our marriage, it frustrated Dan that I wasn't more self-
reflective. It took years of honest tussle for him to see I'd never
become like him: introspective, intuitive, and eager to find the
deeper emotional and spiritual truths in life's challenges. Those
weren't my strengths or my way.

Eventually, we learned to accept and appreciate our divergent
natural tendencies, deep personal imprints that are largely im-
mutable. I came to understand and feel enriched by Dan's reflec-
tiveness, and he's come to accept and appreciate my need to
continually get things done.

In 1986, our postwedding plans puzzled people: "He's from Detroit, you're from San Francisco, and you're moving to—Detroit?
Are you crazy?" But when I married Dan, I married Michigan, with
its sky-blue waters; its green, cathedral-like forests; and its generous, resilient, down-to-earth people. Dan and I both felt deeply
that if we wanted to make a difference, to have an impact, to raise a
family, and to be connected to a real community, Michigan was the
place for us to be.

Young idealists as we were, we quickly immersed ourselves in
a series of worthy causes, from homelessness to school reform.
Armed with his law degree, Dan went to work in downtown Detroit for Wayne County and was soon named director of youth

services. His interest in politics led him to manage the election campaign of Congressman Sander Levin and then run Levin's local office. Later, Dan spent six years as vice president for advancement at his alma mater, University of Detroit Jesuit High School, giving something back to the historic institution where Dan's own values had originally been inculcated.

I worked as a successful federal prosecutor and then, beginning in 1994, as Wayne County corporation counsel, where I led the law department of Michigan's largest county. I was thoroughly happy, immersed in a challenging mix of policy, practice, and management, with a personal reputation that extended only as far as our small circle of activists, and with three spunky young kids who kept me hopping outside the office. But in 1998, when Frank Kelley, Michigan Attorney General, shocked political followers by announcing his retirement after thirty-seven years on the job, our young political buddies—David Katz and Mike Duggan; our wonderful boss, Ed McNamara; and the politically savvy Tom Lewand Sr., a former Democratic Party chair—began prodding me to "go for it."

Once again I laughed at the idea. "Are you crazy?" I asked. Attorney general (AG) wasn't a country commission or a State Senate seat. It was a statewide office, the slot on the ballot under the gubernatorial line, and I'd never run for office at any level. I took a lot of convincing. Dan was the natural candidate—state oratory champion, president of the Yale Debate Association, and a gifted writer, teacher, and thinker. I didn't care to speak in public unless I was arguing before a jury. Suddenly we faced the challenge Father MacInnes had proposed hypothetically years before. What should we do?

Dan and I debated the question at length. He urged me to think about this opportunity as the big chance for public service with a potential impact on millions of people that we'd both been dreaming about. He assured me that he'd take care of our kids, then eight, seven, and one. Finally, during a five-hour drive to a reunion with our law school friends in Chicago, he offered the clinching argument: "Politics is about timing. A chance like this may never come your way again." Given that the campaign would last only four months, he argued, it was an ideal opportunity—one I didn't dare pass up.

So I leaped. Seven other candidates, all men, and none with my prosecutorial and civil law experience, vied for the spot. I built my campaign around a promise to fight for everyday people. "I'll take your case!" I told ripped-off consumers. "I'll take your case!" I told environmentalists eager to protect the waters of the Great Lakes. "I'll take your case!" I told parents who wanted to guard their children against online predators, and seniors who needed protection from financial con artists. I won the Democratic nomination and subsequently became Michigan's attorney general.

In my new job, I happily wielded the hammer that flattened culprits who preyed on the innocent. I prosecuted child pornographers, privacy and identity pirates, gas gougers, and those who'd fleeced seniors and vulnerable people through scams and rip-offs. I was young, idealistic, fiercely earnest, and I had a ball.

Dan, innately entrepreneurial, had by then started his own successful business—Mulhern Hastings Group—doing leadership training and consulting. He was in demand and thriving, making good money and feeling that his gifts were being fully used.

Then, seemingly overnight, new and old friends began urging me to run for governor.

"C'mon," I protested, "it's ridiculous. I just got here," meaning the Attorney General's Office. Our three kids were still young—Jack was not even in kindergarten—and there was much more for me to do as the state's top advocate. Dan's business had taken off, and our lives were full. Yet term limits meant that Governor John Engler would be leaving in 2002. The door was open. Michigan's economy was crumbling, people were hurting, and our schools were still failing. With the flight of manufacturing jobs to other regions and countries, Detroit and smaller cities across the state were rotting at their economic core. I strongly felt we needed leaders who would fight for education, economic revival, and the needs of everyday citizens.

Because I had real doubts about running for governor, Dan and I invited our close friend Dave Katz to our house to weigh the pros and cons.

The minuses: I was young, had served just a single term as AG, and would be running against much more experienced politicians. I would also be a "first," which had both positive and negative sides. "I put the vast experience of your opponents in the plus column for you, Jennifer," Dave said. "You'll get an LG [lieutenant governor] like John Cherry who knows the legislature. But you're new. Your ideas are new. You've shown that as AG. You fought cybercrime when most people probably couldn't even find the on switch to a computer. It's old versus new, yesterday versus now. And being a female? A mom? Are you kidding? Who are they going to relate to?"

I shared another minus that had worried me: Our baby, Jack, was just shy of four years old. Should a mom be "abandoning" her children to run for office?

"You've got Dan on your side," Dave pointed out. "He's said he'll be the primary parent. If people raise it as an issue, we'll remind them that Engler has triplets who've spent their entire eight years in the governor's mansion. What kind of double standard would that be? He can have triplets, but a woman can't serve? I *know* you wouldn't put up with that!" The argument fired me up. Women voters would love that fight, and so would I.

As for the issue of experience, I had some achievements we could talk about. I'd had a 98 percent conviction rate as a prosecutor, had served as head of the state's largest civil law firm as corporation counsel for Wayne County, and had reduced budgets and state payouts for lawsuits by over 75 percent.

Dave added, "And you got 2,000 people to volunteer to become mentors to kids. And prosecuted bad nursing homes."

Dan was ready to close down the debate. "Jen, I don't think you like it, but nobody's going to care a whole lot that you're a better manager and executive than your opponents. They're going to care that you're a real person, like them. You can relate to them. You'll fight for them and their families. That's a winning story."

With that conversation, I was in.

The primary race was top-caliber tough. Former Governor Jim Blanchard pounded me from the middle. Former Congressman David Bonior hit from the left. I was the progressive pole in between. They had the backing of traditional Democratic forces, including the mighty United Auto Workers (UAW), which backed the staunchly liberal Bonior. My advantage was that I was different: younger, female, with a fresh voice. Voters sensed that Michigan was facing new challenges in a global world and needed innovative thinking about how to respond, and it was time for a woman. Implausibly, I won an upset victory over the two political veterans and emerged the Democratic nominee. I felt as if I'd gone fifteen rounds with Muhammad Ali *and* Joe Frazier.

Time was bringing big changes to Michigan, and Democrats were ready for change.

The general election offered a classic contrast. My opponent, sitting Lieutenant Governor Dick Posthumus, promised a return to good times. His boss, Governor Engler, had entered office twelve years earlier promising to execute a classic Republican agenda. He privatized many state functions, fought the teachers unions, and cut taxes. Many on the left saw Engler as a mean-spirited bully, but he basked in the glow of a national economic boom during the Clinton years. Sky-high sales of American sport utility vehicles, not yet challenged by foreign brands, drove the auto industry, and with it the Michigan economy, toward full employment; at one point in the late 1990s, a mere 3.2 percent were jobless in our state.

But by Engler's eleventh and twelfth years, unemployment and voter uneasiness were rising. Owing to globalization, improved productivity, and technological change, factories were cutting jobs or moving them to low-wage countries. The unemployment rate in Michigan climbed to 6 percent, and with the economy faltering and tax receipts diving, the state budget was badly out of balance. Posthumus promised that the Engler formula of tax cuts would soon take hold again, but those promises were looking threadbare.

I ramped up my campaign of hope and change, promising higher levels of citizen engagement, a deep commitment to urban revitalization, and the creation of a more diverse knowledge economy. I never talked about the fact that I was the first female attorney general and would be Michigan's first female governor. I ran as a no-nonsense prosecutor who would be a tough governor fighting to improve the lives of Michigan families.

Above all, I promised to focus on creating an educational system that offered excellence to all children. My education priorities would have a familiar ring even today: First fix Michigan's looming budget problems; then invest in early childhood education; shrink class sizes; reform urban schools to meet new, higher standards; elevate the profession of teaching; give every child access to a college prep curriculum; hold college tuition down; and provide scholarships for all achieving children. Educational improvement was critical to holding and attracting good-paying jobs and restarting growth in our state.

Posthumus emphasized his conservative credentials and his Michigan roots, which he claimed would enable him to serve our state better than a relative newcomer with past connections to "Berkeley, Hollywood, and Harvard." And worse yet, born in Canada! The whisper campaign suggested, *She's not one of us.* But my campaign attracted widespread support from college graduates and laborers, small business owners and entrepreneurs, independents and moderate Republicans. Voters who hadn't pulled the Democratic lever in years signed on.

I won with 52 percent of the vote. But in other Michigan races, my fellow Democrats didn't fare so well.

A few minutes after my victory speech in the hotel ballroom, Genna Gent, our efficient, whip-smart communications director, pulled me into a small side room to brief me on the rest of the night's results. With her short blonde hair and her sassy glasses, Genna is a combination of stately beauty and nonstop brains, with depth rare for her age and a Gen-X edginess that occasionally jolted the rest of us. "The good news," she said, "is that you won. The bad news is that nobody else did."

"What do you mean?" I asked.

"You'll be the lone Democrat in a sea of Republicans. It looks like the Michigan House and Senate will stay Republican. Every statewide office, every branch of government will be Republican. Except you."

"What about Butch?" My good friend Butch Hollowell was the Democrat running for secretary of state.

"Lost," she said.

"And Gary, too?" Gary Peters was the Democrat running to replace me as attorney general.

"Lost," she said. "Same with the Supreme Court. I'm guessing that we're gonna have some battles on our hands, especially with a billion-dollar budget gap to fix."

"Wow, that's really unfortunate. Really, really unfortunate." We stared at each other in silence for a moment, each imagining the battles ahead. In the ballroom next door, we heard the band start up again. I straightened up and said, "Well, it is what it is. Maybe it won't be so bad. Now that the election's over, maybe people will be pragmatic and find ways to work together."

Colleen, with her walkie-talkied ears, poked her head through the door. "What in blazes are you two gabbing about with those sour mugs at a time like this? We got a party out here!" She pulled me back into the noisy ballroom, and we were swallowed up by a swarm of happy celebrants.

Next morning, I opened the hotel room door and saw the *Detroit Free Press* on the floor. There was my picture, holding my hands aloft in victory. The four-inch headline didn't need an exclamation point: "SHE'S THE BOSS."

I was thrilled, of course—but more importantly, I was ready to get to work. There was plenty to do, and the widespread ticket-splitting by voters meant that none of it would be easy.

I hit the phones, assembling the team. Dan went to see Rick Wiener, whom I had asked to be my chief of staff. Dan wanted Rick's opinion on whether he should drop any of his consulting clients. Rick went over those that were clearly off-limits: the state, of course; city governments and agencies; probably schools (a disappointment for Dan, who had a successful "leaders of learning" program for school principals that he loved); regulated companies like utilities and probably hospitals; and heavily grant-funded nonprofits.

After fifteen minutes, Dan threw up his hands. "Rick," he declared, "there isn't a Michigan client who is *not* touched by the governor's office." Dan decided then and there that the cleanest and most ethical path would be to shutter his business while I served as governor. With a mixture of wistfulness and excitement, he went from successful business owner to an entirely new role: Michigan's first First Gentleman.

· · · · ·

AS IF TO CRUELLY TEST THE METTLE OF A NEW GOVERNOR, Michigan holds its inauguration ceremony on January 1 on the open steps of the Capitol. In 2003, it was a bone-snapping zero degrees when I raised my hand to take the constitutional oath. I'd asked Damon Keith, a civil rights icon and federal judge, to swear me in. I had clerked for "The Judge" out of law school, and we'd grown so close that he customarily introduced me to people as his "fourth daughter." I put a hand on our family Bible, and The Judge led me through the oath, clause by clause, in what became a call-and-response duet, his voice growing in enthusiasm and climbing an octave as he reached the final clause, "So help me God." As I repeated the words, our frozen breaths braided together, rising aloft, the crowd erupted, a nineteen-gun salute cracked the icy air, and people shuffled toward shelter as fast as their deep-chilled bodies would allow.

My folks had flown in from California. Dad, ever the taciturn Swede, insisted he was fine in his beige trench coat and his fishing hat, in spite of what Mom repeatedly called "this ridiculous weather." Dan, the kids, and I hunched our shoulders to our ears and quick-stepped the hundred yards from the Capitol to a black Mustang convertible—how my heart sank when I saw that open car—for the quarter-mile ride to the convention center for indoor songs and speeches, including a rousing "Star-Spangled Banner" from Michigan's own Queen of Soul, Aretha Franklin.

We wanted an inauguration that would reflect the inclusive administration we planned, and so we turned it into an extended series of people's events at museums and gathering places all over Michigan. Thousands stood in line to get their children's pictures taken with the new governor. I instructed kids in Grand Rapids or in Marquette way up in the Upper Peninsula not to "give me a dead fish" but to look me in the eye and offer a strong handshake. "We have high expectations of kids in Michigan," I always added.

After one of those receptions, Dan told me, "You know, some of those little girls look at you in a special way. It's like they're looking into a mirror of possibility. They don't see you. They see themselves thirty years down the road." But the most humbling and inspiring moments at these inaugural events would come when a woman in her eighties or nineties would advance to the front of the line, take both my hands in hers or touch my cheeks, and say, "I never thought I would live to see this day."

At the same time, the receptions were haunted by the ghosts of Michigan past and the reality of Michigan present. Especially in Southfield, Flint, and Detroit, the receiving lines included folks who'd recently moved from assembly lines to unemployment lines. A Detroit man spoke for thousands: "We're counting on you to bring the jobs back," he said, his voice shaking, his hands draped like wings about his son and daughter.

"I won't let you down," I assured them with a confident voice, determined. "We'll get those jobs back." Each time I spoke those words, the weight of responsibility on my shoulders grew—as did my impatience to tackle the job I faced.

Back in the state capital, Lansing, I adorned my new office with books and images of my heroes: a photo of Mother Teresa, another of Judge Keith, a sculpture with faces of Mahatma Gandhi and Dr. Martin Luther King, *Profiles in Courage* by John F. Kennedy, Benjamin Thomas's *Abe Lincoln: A Biography*, Hillary Clinton's *It Takes a Village*.

I also framed and hung on the wall a wrinkled bit of paper I'd found in the bushes in front of our house the summer before, in the midst of the gubernatorial campaign. My schedulers had mercifully given me two whole hours to tend to my beloved but bedraggled garden. While weeding, I grabbed a green and white scrap of paper that had blown beneath a shrub—a Chemlawn receipt for fertilizer treatment. I was about to ball it up and toss it in a refuse bag when I spotted scribbled writing on it. My name jumped off the page. It said: "Ms. Granholm, don't forget the little people."

I'd saved that anonymous note as a reminder of what elections are all about: the problems of those who don't have a voice. It was time, finally, to go to work for them.

· · · · ·

WITHIN DAYS, KEY STAFF AND I MET FOR OUR FIRST OFFICIAL full-blown discussion of the state budget. I was eager to tackle my first crucial challenge as governor and confident that cutting the deficit was manageable so long as we applied enough ingenuity, intelligence, and determination to the problem. It wouldn't be easy, but, in the words I'd quote in my first State of the State speech three weeks later, "Only challenge produces the opportunity for greatness."

As I walked into the meeting room, Mary Lannoye greeted me. "You might want to get some coffee, Governor—black."

"I'd suggest something stronger," Jay Rising said with a sardonic chuckle.

Mary Lannoye had agreed to stay on as my budget director. A serious Michigan State University fan, tall, athletic, with her gray-brown hair always pulled back in a no-nonsense ponytail, Lannoye had been budget director for two counties before serving as state budget director for Governor Engler. She knew everyone in Lansing and could track every penny in the $42 billion, 55,000-person enterprise that was the state of Michigan. Her deputy, Nancy Duncan, had knowledge equally broad and deep. Both were steely-eyed professionals. They had prepared stacks of revenue and expenditure spreadsheets, with recommendations for cuts.

I'd appointed Jay Rising state treasurer. A lawyer and former deputy treasurer under James Blanchard, the last Democratic governor, Rising was a whiz kid. Now in his late forties, he looked twenty years younger. He was well known for his financial acumen and his ability to devise innovative solutions to intractable problems. Jay, we joked, could explain any solution to a group of legislators and leave them so awed and confused they felt compelled to vote yes.

The budget mess we faced was no surprise. In the last two years of Governor Engler's administration, the state economy had begun one of its dreaded cyclical turns. For one hundred years,

Michigan had been driven by the auto industry. When the country flourished, more people bought cars and spurred our automakers to full capacity. Parts suppliers charged great premiums, workers took home checks fattened with overtime pay, and stockholding employees and families watched their nest eggs grow. The rest of the economy benefited. People renovated their homes, took vacations, spruced up their wardrobes, and went out to dinner. Thousands were able to rent or purchase cottages and maybe even a boat "up north" on Lake Superior, Huron, Erie, Michigan, or our 11,000 inland lakes.

Then the inevitable downturn would come. When the national economy slowed, demand for cars slackened, especially for the big, costly vehicles that produced most of Detroit's profits, such as Continentals, Cadillacs, and Challengers. Autoworkers were laid off, and the ripple effects were felt all over the state. In the past, of course, we'd always bounced back eventually. The boom-or-bust cycles were exasperating, but Michigan was unfailingly resilient, and the good times had been good enough to enable millions of working people to enjoy a comfortable middle-class life, even without a college degree. The bounty included a healthy state government that provided essential services for Michiganders at every income level—education, health care, infrastructure, parks, the arts, and much more.

The latest economic downturn had a new twist. "Here's the deal," Jay said as he showed graphs to the team. "People aren't buying cars, we're in a national recession, so tax revenues are down. That's no surprise. But on top of that, the Republicans who controlled things around here for a decade effectively built a new state tax structure—and built it when economic conditions were at their peak and with economic assumptions that were unimaginably rosy."

"Let's get specific," I said. "The basic budget assumes a 3.5 percent unemployment rate and income tax revenues that correspond to that number, but we're already at, what, 6.3 percent?"

"That was December, Governor," Jay said. "I just heard that the preliminary estimates for January are 6.5, and it looks like 7 percent is possible before summer."

"And the national unemployment rate?" I asked.

"Comes out tomorrow and will probably stay around 6 percent."

"Wonderful," said Kelly Keenan, my legal counsel and seasoned political veteran. "Engler took credit for tax cuts that made everyone happy, and we're left holding the bag. Now we've got to fix everything they broke . . . and to do it with no money. These guys got out of town just in the nick of time."

"You're not kidding," Jay said. "On top of the rosy assumptions, they also adopted more tax cuts that will roll in automatically over the next few years, with no offsetting revenue increases to pay for them. The business tax rate is scheduled to drop each year until business taxes go away altogether. We have a massive structural deficit projected to worsen for all of this year and into the next." He reviewed the numbers: a midyear deficit of $285 million for the current fiscal year and a projected deficit for the next fiscal year that had almost tripled in the past two months and was now around $1.7 billion.

"A parting gift that keeps on giving," Kelly said.

This was the problem we had to get under control in the budget we were scheduled to present in just a month. Its sheer scope was staggering. Nancy and Mary together had forty years of budgeting experience; neither had ever seen anything this bad.

I thought back to the promises I'd made. "Okay, we'll make cuts. But what about early childhood education?" I asked. "I made it a huge priority in my campaign. Those programs can make a lifelong difference for kids. Surely we can figure out a way to fund them."

Mary shook her head. "Maybe next year," she said glumly. "Take a look at these spreadsheets."

A pall crept slowly over the room. State sales taxes fund our schools, and when they shrink, the law *requires* us to make immediate, midyear cuts to return to balance. The school aid fund was deep in the red. Cuts in the middle of the school year would mean schools couldn't spread the reductions over the entire year but would have to cut twice as deep. And the longer we waited, the worse it would get. A knot was forming in my stomach.

"Welcome to office, Governor," said Jay. "As the first official act of this new Democratic administration, we have to slash public education."

Lieutenant Governor John Cherry, a savvy veteran of twenty years in the state legislature, spoke up. "Maybe it's not a complete disaster," he offered. "It provides you an opportunity to demonstrate you're a tough, no-nonsense leader who'll do what has to be done. Besides, the economists are all predicting this recession will be over later this year. We'll be on the rebound, and you'll be able to restore the cuts in your next budget. Right?" He glanced over at Jay.

Jay nodded cautiously, reading the charts prepared by Treasury Department experts. "The economists are predicting a rebound after this quarter. We should see steady growth after that into next year, tens of thousands of jobs filled. Even David Littmann, Comerica Bank's chief economist, who's normally a pessimist, is saying, 'The economic fundamentals have never been stronger.'"

"We'll do what we have to do. Maybe it's a good time to come into office," I suggested hopefully. "Start the year slow, ramp up, and finish strong." The team murmured its agreement.

Reassured by the prospect of a rebound in the third quarter, I swallowed my first dose of bitter medicine. On January 15, 2003, after championing education as my top priority, my first official act was to inform every Michigan school district that the School Aid Fund was almost $200 million in the red. Already six months into their fiscal year, schools would have to cut millions out of their spending.

My Scandinavian stock means I expect stormy weather as a natural part of life. My parents wonderfully taught me never to brood or feel self-pity in times of trouble but to move on and do what I could to make things better. Dan and I shared a mantra picked up from his friend Joe Caruso: *Accept, adjust, advance.*

But starting my term this way was troubling. I later shared a little of my disappointment with Dave Katz, who had been through the grinder with me and run my gubernatorial campaign and whose unfailing optimism always lifted my spirits.

"I'm inheriting a mess, Dave. We don't have money to do *anything* we talked about. Can you believe this?"

"Governor, don't worry," Dave said. "Manage well, start to diversify, and as things bounce back later this year, you'll reap the credit for the turnaround."

I deeply wanted to believe him—that we would ride the wave of an economic rebound and ultimately be able to keep our promises to the voters. But I needed to hear him say it again. "You really think so?"

His blue eyes were unwavering. "I guarantee it," he said confidently.

chapter 2

PLAYING DEFENSE

THE REALITY WOULD PROVE TO HAVE LITTLE RESEMBLANCE TO the neat, uplifting scenario Dave Katz and I had sketched. Life in the governor's chair quickly turned out to be less about enacting my agenda and more about managing a cascading series of crises.

Early in the year, I became embroiled in tense budget negotiations with the Republican legislature. The previous administration had bequeathed to us a series of unwanted gifts, some of which we were still discovering as we studied the state's ledgers in greater detail and as the recession deepened. Governor Engler and his team had burned through the state's $2 billion "rainy day fund" in an effort to get out of town without making major cuts. At the same time, they made tax cuts that were scheduled to take effect year after year during *my* term.

Conservative dogma, increasingly dominant since the 1980s, asserted that tax cuts would automatically rejuvenate a flagging economy by freeing up capital for private companies to invest in growth. But with the contracting economy layered on top of reduced tax rates, state government revenue was nose-diving. We had to find a way to pull out of a $1.7 billion hole, representing nearly 20 percent of a general fund budget of approximately $9 billion.

As we worked to wrangle this problem in an uneasy partnership with Republican leaders in the state legislature, the ticking of a new time bomb suddenly became much louder.

On April 8, I was stuck in traffic on my way to Bosch, an auto supplier in Farmington Hills, where I was scheduled to meet with its CEO, Kurt Liedke, about the possibility of expanding the company's headquarters in Michigan. I referred to these economic development meetings as "playing offense"—I figured Michigan needed to play two parts offense to every one part defense, and I asked the scheduling division to allot my time accordingly. Today I was cursing the traffic jam under my breath when my Blackberry began buzzing with a call from Treasurer Jay Rising.

"It's confirmed," Jay said when I answered his call. "The DMC is about to implode."

The Detroit Medical Center was the biggest health care system in the state. It consisted of nine "safety net" hospitals serving many of our poorest and most vulnerable citizens. Its facilities included women's and children's hospitals as well as one of the most active trauma centers in the country. It was no secret that the DMC's budget relied on Medicaid reimbursements that failed to cover costs, meaning that the DMC provided enormous amounts of absolutely vital but uncompensated care. The system's CEO, Dr. Arthur Porter, had been threatening hospital closings and massive layoffs and had begun publicly demanding a state-funded rescue.

I glanced at my watch. "I've got ten minutes," I said to Jay. "Give me the big picture."

"We've got to bail out the DMC," Jay said, matter-of-factly. "The rest of the health care system will not be able to absorb their collapse. If they go down, they'll take everyone down with them."

"What are you saying? They're too big to fail?" I asked, unwittingly using a description that would later become all too familiar.

"You could say that, Governor," Jay replied. "I'll send you a graph that shows the amount of indigent care they provide and one showing their finances. They've been duct-taping the thing together for years. But if we let them go under, the suburban hospitals will be next. All the poor people that DMC helps without getting paid for it will flood other hospitals' emergency rooms. It's an absolute mess."

"How much do they need to survive?" I asked.

"Fifty million," he said.

I groaned. "You've got to be kidding me. Where the heck are we going to get that?"

My mind was racing. It was obvious that letting the DMC collapse wasn't a viable option. But the problem was much more complicated than even the budgetary constraints we were under. The DMC was poorly managed, and both Dr. Porter and other board members had already come under increasing scrutiny and criticism. The attacks reinforced the worst racial and ethnic stereotypes peddled by Detroit-bashing politicians, mostly Republican legislators from the suburbs and smaller communities. Why, they asked, should the "good citizens" of Michigan bail out "*their* hospital system"—an inner-city network that served mainly minority-group members? The implications behind this "us versus them" attitude were repugnant to me, but the underlying problems were real and had to be dealt with.

"Okay, Jay," I said. "So I'm not interested in throwing good money after bad. I need to understand the problem—how the DMC got into this situation and how we can be sure they won't be back in the soup next year. I'll be back in Lansing by two o'clock.

You'll have to take me through it step-by-step. If we decide to ask for a bailout, we'll have to make a damn persuasive case, given what we're up against." I rung off as my car pulled into the Bosch parking lot, three minutes late for our meeting.

I knew that a bailout of the DMC would rip wide open the already-gaping hole in our general fund budget. My counterparts in the ongoing budget battles were experienced Republican legislators. Senate Majority Leader Ken Sikkema was a pre-term-limits legislator who'd been in office a third of his life—sixteen of his fifty-two years. Ken was Harvard educated, and rumor had it he had once been a Democrat. But those roots were long severed; his Twenty-eighth Senate District put him squarely among the Grand Rapids, Westside Republicans, and he was a hard-right fiscal and social conservative. Ken was tightly wound. I had difficulty imagining him smiling and waving in a parade or serving up Coney dogs at a picnic with constituents. But he was dependably honest. When he gave his word, it stuck.

Even though Speaker Rick Johnson, fifty years old, was only in his fifth year in office, he had the air of a seasoned dealmaker. He possessed an easy sense of humor and a ruddy round face, and he looked like the longtime farmer and agricultural booster that he was. I could easily imagine him in a cornfield in overalls perched on a John Deere tractor. In Lansing he was well known for working a room, backslapping, and downing a beer with the guys after work.

We made an unlikely trio—but we were the three entrusted by the state of Michigan with the responsibility to, somehow, come up with a budget that 10 million citizens could live with. We met frequently in my conference room at the Capitol, sometimes in pairs, sometimes including the full "quadrant" of legislative leaders, which included the Democratic minority leaders from the two houses. The meetings often grew tense, sometimes loud, because no one in the room—including veteran staffers—had ever had to make cuts this deep. At one early meeting, Sikkema had yelled and cursed at Mary Lannoye and Nancy Duncan and barred Tim Hughes, my legislative director, from walking onto the Senate floor, furious that I had publicly called the Republicans' spending proposals "fiscally irresponsible." (He publicly apologized for the tirade after it was leaked to the press.) Every day the Lansing news services reported the latest episodes in the soap opera under leak-fueled headlines like "Showdown at the OK Corral" and "Parties Take Off the Gloves on Budget."

The issues were complicated. None of us wanted to increase sales, property, or income taxes. I wanted to delay (or "pause") the scheduled cut in the income tax rate, and after much posturing, the Republicans agreed. Sikkema and Johnson went after state employees, trying to roll back already-promised raises; I agreed to negotiate concessions. I wanted to close some corporate tax loopholes to avoid cuts to health care, but Sikkema and Johnson pushed back. We agreed to make tough cuts to higher education, revenue sharing, adult education, and more. I made both symbolic and substantive reductions: I conspicuously presented my budget to the legislature printed on leftover stationery from former Governor Engler, and in meetings we reused Engler's printed cork coasters (we just flipped them over to reveal their blank sides). I brought my sack lunch to work from home every day. I sold off state planes and vehicles, cut boards and commissions, froze hiring, consolidated departments, and announced that I would return 10 percent of my salary to the state treasury each month. Each side proposed and the other rejected innumerable additional ideas for spending cuts and revenue enhancements. Nevertheless, the budget gap loomed discouragingly wide.

I held back on the bailout request for the DMC. I knew it would be a very tough sell politically, especially as there wasn't a Republican district within miles of the DMC's hospitals. I asked Mary to look for a chit I could trade at the appropriate moment. What would be worth $50 million to Sikkema and Johnson? That's the kind of political horse-trading on which human needs—in this case, health care desperately required by tens of thousands of seniors, children, and people with disabilities—often depend.

At the same time, I knew it would be political and financial idiocy to bail out the DMC without insisting on significant reforms. Over two months, I issued executive orders and tasked a team of outside experts with recommending restructuring, oversight, and ethics changes at the DMC. I appointed Janet Olszewski, director of the Department of Community Health, to head a regional authority to identify solutions to the problem of too much concentrated uninsured care falling upon one system. I encouraged the chair of the DMC's board of directors to fast-track a search for a new CEO and to establish a new ethics policy for the system. A state finance team tore through the DMC's books, and our higher education advisors worked to find support for the DMC in its relationship with Wayne State University's medical school. Janet Olszewski's Medicaid team was told to scour every line of available federal funding. Then on June 16, I met with Detroit Mayor Kwame Kilpatrick and Wayne County Executive Bob Ficano to secure their support for a DMC bailout. And through it all, my political team worked hard to keep lines of communication open to ensure the move wouldn't be seen as another attack by white leaders on Detroit and on Dr. Porter.

And then I slipped the DMC back into my pocket.

The day after my meeting with the mayor and the county executive on the DMC, Teresa Bingman was buzzed into my office. Teresa was a composed, smart lawyer who was the liaison with law enforcement.

"Gov, we have another hot one. A riot in Benton Harbor. Started last night." She held up a newspaper as she strode to my desk. The headline read, "House Burned, Police Vehicles Vandalized During Benton Harbor Riot."

"Is it under control now?" I asked.

"No. It's getting worse. MSP is there now." That was the Michigan State Police, directed by Colonel Tadarial J. Sturdivant.

"Okay, get the colonel on the phone so I can be briefed on the latest."

Two hot early summer nights had kindled riots and fires in Benton Harbor, a small community on the eastern shore of Lake Michigan with a population of 12,000, a stunning 25 percent unemployment rate, and deep racial divisions. Benton Harbor was Michigan's poorest city. Predominantly black, it looks across the St. Joseph River to the city of St. Joseph, a prosperous, predominantly white community. Although they are called the "twin cities," they couldn't be less alike, profoundly separated by race and class. Once home to foundries, boatyards, and appliance factories, Benton Harbor had seen most of its jobs migrate to cheap labor sources abroad. These were economic blows produced by the same kinds of national, even global trends that were hurting the rest of Michigan, with the added complication of racial injustice and the achievement gap that continues to separate white and black a century and a half after the abolition of slavery.

Now violence had been triggered in Benton Harbor by the death of Terrence Shurn, a young black motorcyclist fleeing white officers in a high-speed chase. Young people had taken to the streets, launching bricks, sticks, bottles, and Molotov cocktails; burning down a home; and damaging several police cars. After police used tear gas to break up a crowd of about three hundred, some of the protesters had shot at police, yelling, "Kill the cops; it ain't over!" Benton Harbor's mayor, Charles Yarbrough, had publicly pleaded with his citizens, "The burning must stop, the rocks must stop, people must stop being hurt."

With its combustible combination of race, a police shooting, and mob violence, the story hit the national news. A phalanx of national news teams was now rushing into town. News helicopters flew overhead. The ticker at the bottom of the news networks streamed, "Race Riots in Michigan."

I quickly moved three hundred officers from the Michigan State Police and surrounding jurisdictions onto the streets of Benton Harbor, declared a state of emergency, and imposed a 10:00 PM curfew for children under the age of sixteen. By the third night of the uprising, state and community efforts aided by cooling summer rain showers had dampened the unrest. I flew to Benton Harbor and stood on the steps of community leader Reverend James Atterberry's Brotherhood of All Nations Church of God in Christ to address the citizens and the media, urge calm, and promise that my administration would help.

A sitting governor hadn't come to the town in decades. Citizens were eager to tell me their stories and anxious to know whether we would bring real help. I found myself falling in love with this small, fragile community. Some advisors were urging me to ensure continued calm by sending the National Guard into Benton Harbor, but I became convinced that the presence of outsiders in military uniforms would send the wrong signal to the community and exacerbate the problem. Instead, we needed to partner in order to improve Benton Harbor through strategic investment in physical and human capital.

At my first cabinet meeting after the riots, I asked every state department head to personally visit Benton Harbor and see what she or he could offer. That same week, we created an inclusive local committee called the Governor's Benton Harbor Task Force. Its charge was to make recommendations to address the underlying causes of the violence. After much work and input, the final Task Force report, issued four months later, called for more job training, better educational opportunities, good housing, affordable health care, improved policing, and more youth recreation programs.

We rallied our team to implement the recommendations, and Benton Harbor rallied with us. I declared Benton Harbor our first City of Promise, so designated under a program that would channel targeted state assistance to communities in greatest need. In partnership with the people of Benton Harbor, we developed educational and vocational programs and infrastructure projects. Congressman Fred Upton, a Republican, helped secure federal grants to build new, affordable housing and to put more police officers on streets and in schools. Over time, we nearly doubled the number of officers in the Benton Harbor Police Department, and crime was eventually cut in half.

We also invested in projects to encourage long-term growth and civic improvement. The school district opened three career academies for high-school students featuring smaller classes and work-relevant studies. We invested in job training and adult education, new housing, and infrastructure. We also began a large signature development project slated to employ Benton Harbor residents—the Harbor Shores residential and commercial project, with two hotels, an indoor water park, a conference center, marinas, a Jack Nicklaus golf course, refurbished public beach access, and, later, another eight hundred single-family homes and condominiums. Whirlpool would ultimately invest $85 million and open its new corporate headquarters downtown.

As the summer of 2003 continued, the promise of most of these efforts lay in the future. But by setting them in motion, we'd at least restored a measure of calm to the community and created an atmosphere in which positive change could begin.

Meanwhile, I had the rest of the state to think about, including the still-unsolved budget crisis. By July, the Republican leaders and I had sketched the outlines of a deal. But there was still one important piece missing: the DMC bailout. Sikkema and Johnson had surely been waiting for me to broach the topic. When I put this final request on the table, they mounted a fine display of indignation.

"Governor," Sikkema said, his face red with outrage, "I don't see how you can raise this issue at the last minute. If the DMC's been managed so poorly, maybe we should just let it fail."

"Besides," Rick Johnson said, feigning exasperation, "I can't muster a single vote from my members to send yet more money into Detroit."

Both men raised the "good money after bad" argument, and I outlined the steps we were taking to secure strict oversight, new leadership, and greater accountability at the DMC. I also explained how the fall of the DMC would impact health care costs and delivery for nearly half the state. Saving the DMC was the right thing to do—in human terms and in prudent management terms. But as a matter of political reality, I knew my task came with a price tag: Sikkema and Johnson had to be able to tell their caucus members they'd fought against the bailout, and they needed some kind of trophy to show for their reluctant capitulation.

After another round of their indignant pushback, I asked, "So what do you need to get the votes?"

"Our number one priority is preserving Merit Scholarships," Sikkema replied.

I knew this was coming. The scholarships had been established by the prior administration to reward and support students who scored well on the state standardized tests. In the negotiations, I had been holding out on funding them even though I wanted them, too, sensing that this would be their ask for the trade. These were the final steps of the budget Kabuki. Thankfully, the Bush administration had just approved fiscal stabilization/stimulus funds for the states to stoke the nation's climb out of recession and to prevent state cuts from further damaging the recovery. Thus, Sikkema, Johnson, and I knew we could squeeze out enough money to keep the Merit Scholarships alive *and* preserve the DMC.

"Deal," I said, holding out my hand. Sikkema shook it, followed by Johnson.

The DMC board did as it had promised. Members selected a new CEO, Mike Duggan, who, though new to health care, was known for his tough management expertise and political smarts.

We put in place an oversight committee and reporting deadlines to ensure high standards of ethics, transparency, and tough, disciplined leadership. And the first year after the government bailout and restructuring, DMC reported a multi-million-dollar surplus.

By July 15, the 2004 budget deal was done. It was barely half a year since my inauguration, and we'd already survived three major crises—the budget, the DMC crunch, and the Benton Harbor riots. Time, I thought, to get back on offense.

· · · · ·

WHILE I WAS DEFUSING CRISES IN MY DAY JOB, DAN AND THE kids were struggling to hold things together on the home front. There, too, things just weren't working out precisely the way they were supposed to.

In June, the kids had just finished school—eighth grade, sixth grade, and kindergarten—in our old neighborhood in Northville, a Detroit-area suburb. So now we could finally move into the governor's residence, some eighty miles away in Lansing.

The good news was that the commute was over. The bad news was that the official residence was a disaster zone—quite literally. "My advice," my predecessor John Engler had said when we joined him for lunch there during our transition into office, "is to knock this place down." We didn't find it quite as hopeless as Engler had. But it definitely needed an enormous amount of work. Among other problems, it had only one child's bedroom.

We raised private dollars for an addition and renovation. But when construction began in the spring, the contractors found asbestos, lead, PCBs, mercury, and black mold in various parts of the house. Our family move-in day, June 15, turned out to be the same day the demolition crew moved in to strip the place down to its studs.

I slept in the only inhabitable room in the torn-up residence, a bedroom above the decommissioned kitchen. Dan and the kids were temporarily exiled to the governor's summer residence on Mackinac Island. This spectacular, one-hundred-year-old, ten-bedroom "cottage" perches atop a cliff above the Straits that connect Lake Michigan with Lake Huron, separating the state's Upper and Lower Peninsulas. The island is ringed by an eight-mile paved trail and is home to rustic paths, parks, shops, bikes, horses—and no cars. It's a summer paradise.

But I was separated from my family by a 200-mile, four-hour drive. I did my best to get away to Mackinac for a weekend here or there. After one three-week stint eating my dinners at a picnic table in the garage in Lansing and missing the family badly, I was looking forward to a long weekend on the island in mid-August. A gorgeous Michigan summer was getting away too quickly. I couldn't wait to get up there.

I spoke with Dan on Wednesday night, August 13. "It'll be great to see you tomorrow," he said. "I'm only sorry you can't kick back with us for a whole week. Lord knows you deserve a break."

"No kidding," I said. "Can you believe how many things have fallen apart since the inaugural?"

"Things will even out," he consoled. "But on some level, aren't you loving this? You get off on dealing with these crises, don't you?"

But I could fix minicrises all day and never get to the major change we need. I was tired of talking about the crises. "Hey," I asked, "what's the weather supposed to be like up there this weekend?"

"Hot," he said. "Eighties all weekend." The hotter the better, I thought, imagining basking in the sun on the cottage's long porch.

I woke up at 4:30 the next day with the predator-like focus one gets with just one day of work left in the office. Determined to do a week's work in a day, I scanned my scheduling book and made my mental lists. I was in the office early and hit the key tasks hard—working to close the deal on an economic development director, looking over the state's financial numbers, reading reports on education, jobs, housing . . .

Then suddenly at 4:15 PM, the lights went out and my computer screen went black. I opened my office door and saw Genna Gent, our communications director, walking through the waiting area to check out the nonfunctional ceiling lights. We looked at each other, and she just shrugged. "Odd," she said. The entire second floor had gone dark.

Sergeant Norm Lipscomb of the Michigan State Police's Executive Protection Unit was stationed outside my office. He picked up his cell phone to call the emergency team at the state police. Within moments he reported back gravely, "They're telling me it's a massive power outage. Michigan and a bunch of other states have gone dark."

It was less than two years since the attacks on the World Trade Center. My first thought was the same as everyone's: terrorism.

I called Dan. The power was working on Mackinac Island, and they hadn't heard the news reports about the blackout. I told him I couldn't possibly leave the office. "Of course," he said, sounding disappointed. "Then we're coming home. The girls are going stir-crazy. We all miss you." He hung up the phone and set about packing up two girls, their two friends, one babysitter, and our little guy, Jack.

I used my cell phone to summon key people to my office, illuminated now only by daylight through the tinted windows. Teresa Bingman, Genna, and Rick Wiener gathered and began making calls to the utility regulators, our homeland security advisor, and our state police command. Rick, who is a pacer anyway, was making loops around my cavernous office while talking on his cell phone. Meanwhile, Genna, Teresa, and I staked out different corners of the room to make our separate calls.

Within an hour, we pieced together the news. A massive power fluctuation in New York had crashed power systems across Ontario, the Northeast, and the Midwest. Forty-five million Americans—5.4 million in Michigan—had lost electricity. No one knew the cause or the prospects for a quick recovery, although terrorism was beginning to appear unlikely. I ordered the activation of the state's Emergency Operations Center (EOC), about ten minutes from the Capitol building in Lansing, and summoned every department head to report there immediately.

I saw that I'd missed a call from Dan and hit his speed dial. His voice was gloomy. "We were all set to jump on the ferry until we heard that there's no power between here and Lansing. We've got power here, so we might as well just stay."

"I'm sorry, Babe," I said.

"Whatcha gonna do?" came his attempt at stoicism. I could feel his sadness as he let me go. "You're doing what you need to be doing. Call me if you get a chance."

Accept, adjust, advance. I was off to the EOC.

The Emergency Operations Center is a technology-filled room nested in a large, barricaded building shielded by intense security. Within thirty minutes, the members of my cabinet and their deputies had occupied their designated seats in the semicircle of four rows of desks, each outfitted with a computer and phone. The walls were covered with electronic maps and reports, while the front corners of the room were filled with flat-screen televisions broadcasting news updates of the crisis. I was positioned in front of the room alongside the EOC director.

For the next day and a half, I played the role of an orchestra conductor, experiencing the incredible complexity of this crazy organization called a state. Each department head worked a phone and computer, and every thirty minutes we passed a microphone around the room to let each director share information and requests for immediate help. We checked on prison security, hospitals, banks, police departments, water supplies, schools, restaurants, mental health facilities, universities, museums, border crossings, stadiums, and more, each profoundly affected by the loss of power.

I declared a state of emergency to request help and facilitate the moving of people and goods where they were most needed. Starved of electricity, water systems around metropolitan Detroit began to fail; I ordered bottled water and portable toilets delivered to community centers where people had gathered. The electrical failure caused a small explosion to rock the Marathon Oil refinery in Melvindale, near Detroit; I ordered the evacuation of households within a mile of the facility and shut down traffic on nearby Interstate 75. Around the state, senior citizen centers and hospitals were without running water or electricity; I ordered the National Guard to deliver water trucks and portable generators. Local law enforcement requested help in darkened cities; I ordered the state police to coordinate law enforcement.

I stayed at the EOC until 2:00 AM, when the state had gone to bed, and I returned with coffee and donuts by 7:00 on Friday morning—as did the rest of our team, exhausted, bleary-eyed, but intensely focused. The work continued until Saturday morning as power began to click back on in one community after another. By the end of that day, normal services had been restored.

The blackout was the most intensely focused crisis of my first year in office but also, in an odd way, the most manageable. It required, above all, disciplined, centralized leadership. There was no ambiguity about who was in charge. Lines of responsibility were clear; pettiness and ego were set aside. I'm proud to report that there was no looting in Michigan and just one death indirectly attributable to the blackout (from an indoor generator emitting carbon monoxide). The crisis and the teamwork it demanded cemented new bonds among my cabinet heads and key department leaders.

"If we have to have a crisis, that's the kind of crisis I like," I joked with Dan when I called him on Saturday evening.

"Yep," he agreed, chuckling. "Quick. Controllable. And everyone obeys your commands. Just the way you like it."

"Very funny. Glad to see you've got your sense of humor back."

Ultimately, we learned the cause of the blackout: High demand for electricity had overloaded the grid that distributes electricity to the eastern United States. As circuit breakers tripped at generating stations from New York to Michigan and into Canada, millions of people were affected.

"What's the lesson here?" I asked Peter Lark, chair of Michigan's Public Service Commission, the body that regulates utilities and electricity lines.

"It's pretty simple, actually," Peter told me. "We've failed to invest in the power grid. Now the facilities are old, deregulation has removed responsibility for investment, and the infrastructure has become enormously fragile."

I sighed. "A lesson about the wisdom of deferring maintenance and investment in basic infrastructure—"

"—I think you mean the stupidity of deferring it," injected Peter.

Each of the crises I faced during my first year in office—the vast state budget deficit, the implosion of the DMC, the riots in Benton Harbor, the blackout—was symptomatic of deeper, systemic stresses. Each involved the failure to maintain and invest intelligently in our human and physical infrastructure. For decades, we'd preferred to pretend that the systems we relied upon to make life worthwhile could be wholly self-correcting and self-supporting—from the hospitals that provided us with health care to the schools that educated us, from the industrial base that created our jobs to the energy grid that powered our cities, and, ultimately, the structure of government itself and the bipartisan comity that made it work for us. Now those decades of neglect were taking their toll—first in small, chronic failures, then in massive, catastrophic breakdowns.

· · · · ·

NATIONAL CRISES CAN AFFECT EVERY TOWN AND STATE IN AMERICA, adding more painful layers to a governor's daily work. During my first year in office, President Bush took our nation into war in Iraq. And so began eight years of the most important, and saddest, job any governor has: calling the families of fallen soldiers to thank them for their service and to grieve with them over their loss.

Sherry Hicks, my assistant and right hand for my years as corporation counsel, attorney general, and governor, was deeply sensitive to the importance and difficulty of these phone calls. She insisted that the scheduling unit block out sufficient time per call, guarded my office door against visitors, and made sure I had everything I needed before I picked up the phone: a memo about each soldier's career, life, and family; my Bible; and a box of Kleenex.

There were some things I said in every condolence call. I promised that flags across the state would be flown at half-staff on the day of the funeral and that the flag from the state Capitol would be delivered to the family as a keepsake. I pledged that the beloved son or daughter, husband or wife—now a Michigan hero—would never be forgotten. And I always thanked the parents of soldiers for raising a hero. Beyond that, the calls were as varied as the families of the fallen. Some shared stories of a soldier's childhood, his or her youthful dreams, and the patriotism that led to military service. Others talked about e-mails or phone calls received from overseas, often sharing stories of the civilian lives touched by American servicemen and -women or praising fellow troops. Many openly wept on the phone with me, a stranger, and I wept with them.

That first year, I had to make 22 of these heartbreaking calls. Over my two terms in office, the number grew to 205.

· · · · ·

IN THE MEANTIME, IN THAT SUMMER AND FALL OF MY FIRST YEAR in office, I was crisscrossing the state to meet onsite with diverse employers, such as SBC, Pfizer, and the small businesses in our university incubators called "Smart Zones." I also met with dozens of Michigan manufacturers as part of our "Manufacturing Matters" agenda, first by holding a statewide summit that developed specific state and federal policy recommendations and then by visiting the businesses onsite. I visited Tower Automotive in Traverse City to celebrate its new site. I visited Smurfit Stone in Ontonagon, in our Upper Peninsula, and listened to its plans for growth. I held a roundtable at American Axle in Detroit, a key supplier to General Motors. Its CEO, Dick Dauch, who grew up on a farm and had hands as big as shovels, boldly proclaimed great confidence in being able to manufacture in America . . . even though the company was having a little trouble with China's unfair trade practices. I was encouraged by the bullishness of Michigan's CEOs even through the challenges of the recession.

"Glad I made it for the second half," I puffed as I clambered over the bleachers to sit next to Dan at Kate's JV basketball game. "Just got back from Saginaw—another manufacturing roundtable. We'll just get through this rough patch," I said, half apologizing for my schedule, half explaining my hope for the economy. "Now that the explosive crises are behind us, hopefully we'll have some clear sailing."

We cheered Kate on as she furiously backpedaled to defend against a 3-on-2 break. "I'd love to see Kate get a chance to score, but she's playing some pretty awesome defense right now," Dan said.

I watched as Kate grabbed the ball for an instant, only to have it knocked out of her hands. "I'd still rather be playing offense," I replied.

chapter 3

A DIFFERENT KIND OF CRISIS

BY THE FALL OF 2003, IT WAS CLEAR THAT BOTH THE ECONOMY and the state budget were getting worse. State tax revenues were plummeting. "Where the hell is the rebound?" I asked the economic experts during the September cabinet meeting. None of them had an answer.

The budget I had signed into law wasn't going to hold. I had to negotiate more budget cuts—another $920 million on top of the $1.7 billion we had agreed upon just a few months earlier. We had punched new holes to tighten our belt, but the shrinkage wasn't nearly enough. What more could we do?

I couldn't cut still deeper into basic state services without the support of the people. So in October, I set out on a statewide "budget tour" to gather citizen input on the new round of cuts.

I visited eleven cities, touching every region and media market of the state, the details orchestrated brilliantly by my communications advance teams and my savvy, hands-on spokeswoman, Liz Boyd. We held televised one-hour sessions with TV stations serving as hosts. Local community groups or media outlets invited forty to seventy-five people to participate, representing a bipartisan cross-section of the population. Area legislators from both parties attended.

Each audience member was given a hand-held electronic clicker to use in selecting from lists of options. I guided the audience through the choices we faced: Should we cut funds for public K–12 education or adult education or release prisoners thirty days earlier? Should we reduce grants to arts organizations, health care options for senior citizens, or scholarships to private colleges? Eliminate the guard towers at the prisons or cut mental health services? Trim the number of police officers in local communities through cuts to revenue sharing or reduce the economic development dollars available to attract jobs? These are the kinds of nitty-gritty real-world choices that state executives and legislators have to wrestle with—the thorny realities behind easy-sounding generalities like "cutting waste" and "making government smaller." Voters seldom confront such hard and specific choices. We tallied the votes of our town hall participants in real time and displayed them on live TV in each region. Home viewers were invited to e-mail their votes as well. I brought back the results to the legislative leaders who were negotiating the budget with me.

I was surprised at the degree to which citizens in every corner of the state agreed on several specific priorities. They wanted to keep funding for health care and K–12 public education intact. If we had to cut, they preferred cuts to higher education, private scholarships, prisons, adult education, and the arts. I took their advice. Although they didn't like having to cut worthwhile programs, the citizens understood the need and had helped to make the decisions—democracy at work.

I dreaded bearing the bad news to some of the groups that had been most instrumental in getting me elected. I had to place unions, adult education providers, colleges, cities, and the arts under the budget cleaver. I was particularly anxious when I spoke before the annual meeting of ArtServe Michigan, an important arts advocacy group in Lansing, to explain why we had to slash state funding for its programs by 50 percent, a loss of about $12 million per year. I assured audience members, "These cuts will be restored when the economy bounces back." I was relieved when they responded, not with boos or catcalls but with a standing ovation—an illustration of the fact that, even in our brittle and polarized climate, people appreciate honest talk that respects their role as citizens.

But even as the bad economic news mounted, we continued to look ahead to the recovery we'd been promised. Each January, Michigan inhales a lungful of optimism at the annual brag-fest, the North American International Auto Show, in Detroit. Like Michigan governors before me, I would attend the charity preview to get an advance peek at the new models and the concept vehicles that represented the fantasies of auto company engineers and car lovers alike. Michigan royalty would be out in full force. The CEOs of the Big Three automakers—General Motors, Chrysler, and Ford—and their major suppliers would be converging with thousands of other VIPs in the massive Cobo Center for a black tie gala, celebrated amid buffed cars and buff spokesmodels.

Dan and I got decked out in unaccustomed finery and headed for the show. On the way, I read through a collection of clippings on the state of the auto industry. A report from the global accounting and consulting firm KPMG indicated the "worst is behind the industry" and reported that the consensus among one hundred executives surveyed was that peak profits exceeding the record year of 2000 would come between 2004 and 2006. I read excerpts to Dan in the car. "From their lips to God's ears," Dan responded.

Dan and I hit the show floor, and with state police clearing the way and schedulers tugging my arm, we navigated from Japanese reporters to potential German investors to the elaborate stands where Channel 4 reporters were covering the event live. We barely had time to scan the space-age concept cars or to watch the Jeeps literally climbing the walls. We kept missing the champagne pours and found ourselves whispering to each other, "Who's that?" each time a gaggle of well-wishers grabbed us for a photo op. If Dan and I felt odd in tux and gown, it was even odder to see our friends from the United Auto Workers similarly garbed.

"Rebound" was the word on everybody's lips. The atmosphere was upbeat, energetic, thoroughly bullish. It was impossible not to believe that the economy was ready to surge forward. The new vehicle models looked magnificent, and they wouldn't be towing just workers' aluminum fishing boats or executives' cabin cruisers and catamarans. They'd also be pulling the whole Michigan economy.

Of course, the foreign competition wasn't standing still. We passed the Toyota exhibit where pride of place went to the Prius, only the second import to win Motor Trend Magazine's coveted "Car of the Year" award. (The Infiniti broke through in 2003.) With its ultra-advanced hybrid engine, the Prius boasted an astonishing fuel economy rating of sixty miles per gallon in the city.

"It's kind of scary," Rick Wiener muttered. He didn't have to say more.

We reached the General Motors VIP area. GM CEO Rick Wagoner, who'd been piloting the company through rough waters since 2000, greeted us, as did a coterie of his tuxedoed execs. They repeated the same refrain echoing around the hall: "The worst is behind us. The future will be incredibly competitive. But we're ready for it."

"How far are we behind Toyota when it comes to green cars?" I asked.

"Governor, you have to see our technology," Rick told me. He and United Auto Workers Vice President Richard Shoemaker walked us through a series of slick displays highlighting

GM's environmental initiatives. We got a high-level tutorial in hybrid engines and hydrogen fuel cells. The intelligence and energy being poured into these projects were palpable, and I felt more hopeful.

We moved on to the Ford exhibit, where Bill Ford, the company's CEO and great-grandson of Henry Ford himself, was jazzed about the new Mustang. A year earlier it had debuted as a jaw-dropping concept car; now it was available in showrooms, the most talked-about car at the show. It seemed everyone had a story about his or her '65 Mustang (some were still driving theirs), and Bill Ford was thrilled to be presiding over the rebirth of a classic that he, too, had owned as a young man. But he became even more fervent when we asked about green technology. "The Escape is coming next year," he bragged. "A hybrid with the power to tow. It's a real car."

The auto show naturally represents the most hopeful face of the industry and, in turn, of our state. Dan and I left the gala feeling more upbeat than we had in weeks. But it didn't take long for the mood to dissipate.

Late that month, newspapers released two sets of numbers that pulled in different directions. A public poll put my approval rating at a ridiculously high 77 percent. My team was publicly stoic ("We don't pay attention to polls") but inwardly giddy. At the same time, auto sales were falling and Michigan's unemployment rate was climbing ominously. We'd lost 30,000 manufacturing jobs over the course of 2003. I hoped that my honeymoon with the voters would last just a while longer as we waited for the economic cycle to catch up.

· · · · ·

THE VOICE OVER THE PHONE WAS GRIM. "GOVERNOR, I HAVE some troubling news." It was Jim Donaldson, vice president of the

Michigan Economic Development Corporation. "We've got another crisis. Electrolux is threatening to leave Greenville and move to Mexico."

"How many jobs?" I asked.

"Twenty-seven hundred," he said.

"Wow! Remind me—what's the population of Greenville?"

"Eight thousand. That includes kids, grandparents. The town has grown up around the factory," Donaldson said.

"Okay," I said, thinking out loud. "We can save it. We'll just have to convince them to change their minds." Even as we spoke, I started typing an e-mail to assemble my executive team. I told Jim, "We'll make them an offer they can't refuse."

For a century, Greenville—forty minutes northeast of Grand Rapids, in Montcalm County, near the center of Michigan's Lower Peninsula—had been home to the world's largest refrigerator plant. Now the plant was in the hands of a Swedish appliance conglomerate, Electrolux. All the local businesses depended on Electrolux. The coffee shops welcomed Electrolux workers for breakfast in the morning. The grocer, the cleaners, the barber, the dentist, the newspaper, and Huckleberry's, the local watering hole, were all in business because the town's citizens cashed checks from Electrolux. The other main employers in town were minor auto parts plants owned by Federal-Mogul and Tower Automotive, and suppliers of Electrolux. The company's announcement that it planned to move the plant to Mexico was like a bomb detonated at the heart of downtown. The assault was puzzling, too, because the plant was profitable and the company had invested $110 million in a new assembly line as recently as 2001. I couldn't imagine they'd walk away from all that.

"Time to fight back," I told the local leaders in the Greenville community center as we formed a SWAT team that we nicknamed the Nitty Gritty Committee. It included Mayor Lloyd Walker, City Manager George Bosanic, UAW regional director Don Oetman and his local union officials, Montcalm Community College president

Don Burns, the president of the chamber of commerce, and a host of federal, state, county, and local officials. We broke up into teams to tackle individual challenges. We sent two representatives to Electrolux's U.S. headquarters in Boston. Three were assigned to assess the costs of a new plant. Another calibrated the impact of tax incentives. And four worked on a training plan for the company's workers.

We devised a blockbuster stack of incentives for the company, starting with waiving its taxes for the next twenty years. We offered help in financing the building of a new factory and millions in grants to train their employees. The United Auto Workers, representing the employees, offered over $30 million in wage, benefit, and hiring concessions. The pile of incentives totaled more than $750 million over twenty years. We stacked these bargaining chips and slid the pile across the table.

We were proud of our efforts and felt sure we had a good chance of reversing the company's decision.

At a meeting on January 15, the team presented the pile of incentives to the company. The company assessed our offer for all of seventeen minutes.

"It's a valiant effort," their spokesman said and acknowledged the enormous amount of work that had gone into it. "One of the best incentive offers we've ever received. But we've got to cut costs, and we can pay $1.57 an hour in Juarez. There's nothing you can do to make up for that."

There's nothing you can do.

We were devastated. In the days to come, in one postmortem conversation after another, we went over our offer again and again. What else could we have offered? But we knew the answer: Our pockets were empty. We had nothing else to give.

Meanwhile, the news broke in Greenville. When the first shift came in out of the ten-degree chill on the morning of January 16, 2004, Electrolux called all the employees together and announced the decision to move the plant to Mexico.

The layoffs would soon begin. Two hundred eighty married couples working in the plant would be losing both jobs. The same would happen to the many Electrolux workers who were married to Electrolux suppliers. The Greenville plant was to wind down gradually, shrinking over the course of a year as the assembly lines were moved south. Electrolux planned to use the workforce in Michigan to work out the bugs in the new line before shipping it off to Mexico. Carving their own caskets.

I watched the news reports from Greenville. Workers were stunned—rumors of the incentive package had given them hope, and now their hopes were crushed. News camera crews followed workers trudging out of the plant, capturing their reaction: tears, anger, numbness, grief. Reporters interviewed local business owners, who were fearful for their future. They interviewed Greenville's genteel Mayor Walker, who proclaimed, "NAFTA [North American Free Trade Agreement] is just killing the industrial strength of this country." And the cameras were there the following morning when workers showed up for their shifts on time, many with American flags pinned to their lapels.

The month after Electrolux's announcement, I attended a gathering of the Democratic Governors Association in Washington, DC. A crew of new governors was present, and we were taking turns giving reports on the progress in our states to the assembled group of lobbyists and fund-raisers, who were standing around, drinks in hand. The mood was upbeat and casual. No one had prepared remarks. Governor Gary Locke of Washington, chairman of the association, introduced me. "Jennifer's an upcoming Democratic star. She has a 77 percent approval rating—tops in the country! Tell them what a great job you're doing in Michigan, Jennifer."

My head and heart were still in Greenville. I was among friends, and I recounted the story.

"In Michigan," I said, "we are the fallout of these unenforced trade agreements. The average guy is left without a job, maybe without a pension, and as a final insult he trains his foreign replacement before he hands in his ID badge. And there's nothing we can do about it. Nothing. This isn't about tax policy. It's not about regulations. It's about whether we are going to make things in America."

A stunned, uncomfortable silence filled the room.

Governor Locke cleared his throat, stood up, and said, "Okay, then! Now let's hear about Governor Napolitano's successful first year."

As Janet Napolitano took the floor, Locke draped an arm over my shoulder and steered me a few feet away from the group. "My God, Jennifer," he whispered sympathetically, "that's a terrible story. What's the answer? There has to be some hope for manufacturing in this country."

"I wish I knew, Gary," I said, looking down at the floor.

He shook his head. "It's an American tragedy." He paused for a moment, and we listened to Napolitano eloquently describing her plans for full-day kindergarten in Arizona. Then Locke nudged me, and I saw a twinkle in his eye. "Hey, just a suggestion," he whispered, "but next time I ask you to brag about what you are doing, maybe you should focus on one of your successes."

In early 2005, Wal-Mart opened a superstore in Greenville. Some of the workers who'd lost their jobs at Electrolux went to work at the new Wal-Mart. Their Electrolux jobs had paid $15 an hour, bolstered by health and pension benefits. Their Wal-Mart jobs paid $8 an hour and provided virtually no benefits. Nevertheless, they felt lucky to have these jobs. The closing of the Electrolux plant had given Montcalm County the highest unemployment rate in Michigan, a particularly dismal fact in the state with the highest unemployment rate in the nation.

It was the story of the national economy in a nutshell: an American manufacturer and the jobs it generated, vanished from a city in the heartland and replaced by a global retailer selling products made mostly overseas.

The month the last refrigerator came off the Greenville assembly line, the workers invited me to a picnic they ruefully dubbed "The Last Supper," held at a large arena called Klackle's Orchard Pavilion. A rock band played as hundreds of former Electrolux families ate from box lunches, clustered around small round tables with checkered tablecloths. Buddies from the assembly line asked one another, "So, what are you going to do?" Most often the answer was "I don't know" or a helpless shrug.

As I approached the first table I saw, a lean man with forearm tattoos and a baseball cap intercepted me, nudging forward his two young daughters, who looked about ten and twelve years old. "Governor," he said, his hands on their shoulders, "these are my beautiful girls. I'm forty-eighty years old, and I've worked in this plant for thirty years. I went from high school to factory. My father worked here. My grandfather worked here. My whole life, all I've ever known is how to make refrigerators." Then he opened his palm and placed it over his chest, his brown eyes intense, desperate. "So, Governor, tell me, who is ever gonna hire me?" I caught the expectant gaze of his daughters, young eyes wondering how the governor was going to fix their daddy's problem. I talked about starting over, about Montcalm Community College, and about faith, but for him and so many like him, I had no satisfying answer.

Other workers joined the conversation. Within a few minutes, a line snaked through the pavilion, between and around tables— hundreds of laid-off workers wanting to tell me their stories, wanting me to understand their pain. As governor, I'd called the families of fallen soldiers and attended the funerals of police officers, all heroes too young to die. But this was different—a mass grieving, a legion of the walking wounded in the wake of an economic tornado. How could this happen? they asked. And what do we do now?

I stayed until 6:00 in the evening, long enough to speak with every worker in that line.

I'm not usually an emotional person. I invariably choose action over sadness. But back at the governor's residence that night, I wept for those workers, those families, that little town. And, I guess, maybe I wept for me, too, wondering how I could give the people of Michigan a fighting chance in an Electrolux world.

"This crisis is different." I said to Dan. "It's not just the usual economic cycle. The Michigan economy is going through a structural change. These jobs are *gone*."

My mind raced, searching for solutions. There were hundreds of thousands of people like those Electrolux workers in towns large and small all across Michigan. We had seven times more manufacturing jobs per capita, largely automotive, than any other state. I could fill stadiums with these workers who were too young to retire and too old, they thought, to start over—a generation of workers between the ages of thirty and sixty who were left naked, exposed by the global shift of manufacturing jobs to low-wage countries.

"We're going to use every tool we have to help Michigan," I said to Dan. "But this is not, I guarantee you, not going to be Greenville's epitaph."

Clearly, direct battles against Latin America or China on the cost-cutting front were futile. Our tax-incentive offers had fallen pitifully short of what the Electrolux executives could save by hiring workers in Mexico. An entirely new approach was required.

"Let's get some experts in here," I said to Lisa Webb Sharpe, our cabinet secretary, at our next 8:00 AM executive team meeting. "I need some advice from people who've been analyzing this problem. Economists and economic developers—experts from inside and outside state government."

"I'm on it," Lisa said, as she pulled out her Blackberry.

"Let's pull together a cabinet retreat—or a series of them—so our whole team can tackle this thing," I added.

"Got it," she said, already thumbing at the keyboard. "Consider it done."

At lunchtime, I headed upstairs, blue canvas lunch bag on my arm. Dan's office was two floors directly above mine. "Okay, so we're post-Electrolux," I blurted as I hurried through his door. "Are you okay if I talk this through out loud?" Without waiting for an answer, I began pacing the room. "Is there any future for traditional manufacturing in America?" I started, posing questions as much to myself as to Dan. "And especially for building cars? We're more dependent on the auto sector than any other state. Can we reasonably hold onto any of it?"

"It's scary as hell," Dan said, following me with his eyes. "And I hate to say it, but we can't go head-to-head on manufacturing with Mexico and China, no matter what our tax structure is. Can we?"

"No," I said. "That's the brutal truth from Electrolux." Not a day had passed that I hadn't remembered those words: *There's nothing you can do.* I stopped pacing and plopped down at the table, where Dan was unpacking his lunch. "Head-to-head on cost, we lose," I said, crunching a carrot. "So we need other ways to balance the field. We've got to find advantages that counterbalance the impossible wage differential."

"Right." Dan responded, assuming his business-consultant posture. "So here's what I'd say. Assess the state as though it's a business. What strengths does Michigan have that can still be exploited—or transformed into an advantage for the future?"

"We're one step ahead of you," I said. "I just asked Lisa to set up off-site cabinet retreats and call in some economic experts." I unwrapped my tuna sandwich and took a bite. "My gut tells me that because of Michigan's bones—our lakes and geography, our quality of life, our universities—we'll be all right in the long term. But what do we do *now?* The workers at places like Electrolux can't wait for the long term."

"Involve them in the process," he said. "Challenge them. Support them. But give the work back to the people." Dan smiled. "I know you want to fix the problem. That's your style. And you're the best fixer I've ever known. But what can you fix?"

"Well, let's see. How about America's nonexistent trade policy enforcement?" I offered sardonically.

"Not your lane."

"Lifting the health care and retirement burdens off U.S. manufacturing?" I continued.

"Not your lane," he repeated.

"Making American cars the best in the world again?" I said in a mocking tone, knowing full well these were fixes outside of my control.

"Still not your lane," Dan replied. "I get your frustration, Jen. You're dealing with businesses, unions, and workers who are stuck in a world that's gone. You want to help them—especially the workers. But the hard truth is that even with fairer trade, those workers don't have the skills they need for the careers of tomorrow. They either have to retrain for new jobs or face a seriously diminished quality of life. It's their work, too, and you have to give the work back to them."

I gazed out the window from Dan's fourth-floor office. The flags over the Capitol were hanging limp beneath a steel-gray sky. Most of the people Dan was talking about had never gone to college. Twenty or thirty years ago, they didn't have to. Now I was going to ask them to go and sit next to some nineteen-year-old in a college class? It was an entire generation of workers facing a terrible dilemma not of their making.

Then something in me locked into gear. Dan occasionally gave me specific advice, but more often he gave me a broader perspective—and that helped. Now I needed to get moving. We had no time to waste.

Lisa Webb Sharpe rolled out the cabinet retreats with a rich mix of inside and outside experts—economists from the Brookings Institute, from our Treasury Department, from think tanks and universities in Michigan. The cabinet and our key executive team members took three separate days over the course of several months to get away from the daily buzz of the office, once at the governor's residence in Lansing, once in a large conference room at Michigan State University, and once at an aeronautics conference room at the state hangar at the airport. We considered advice from a business council I'd convened. We studied historical data and economic trends, and brainstormed, probed, and debated. Gradually, a consensus began to emerge.

Michigan needed to focus on two priorities: educating our citizens and diversifying the economy. And in the meantime we had to protect people from falling through a fraying safety net.

On education, we'd already begun the planning process. I'd appointed a bipartisan commission led by Lieutenant Governor Cherry to design a road map for doubling the number of college graduates in Michigan. The commission worked throughout 2004 and published a detailed road map for reaching that goal. One of the most important of its nineteen recommendations was making sure that every child in Michigan took a college prep curriculum. This would be the first step toward a far-reaching shift in public and individual attitudes toward education, the kind of change we absolutely required to compete in the twenty-first century.

At the same time, diversification of our economy was equally crucial. Overreliance on any single sector, even one as large and powerful as auto manufacturing, left us vulnerable to long-term decline. That meant building specific new sectors based on our existing competitive advantages. Our opportunity analysis and the advice of our experts helped us identify several promising prospects:

- Life sciences: Michigan's strong university system gave us access to leading research facilities and a steady stream of top-flight graduates, for whom careers in pharmaceuticals and biotechnology could be an attractive lure to remain in the state.

- Clean energy: Michigan boasted both a strong tradition of manufacturing excellence and a favorable geography for the generation of renewable energy, thanks to our proximity to the enormous natural resource of the Great Lakes.
- Homeland security and defense: Owing to the continuing fallout from 9/11, both of these were growth areas. The power of veteran senator Carl Levin on the Armed Forces Committee could help ensure that Michigan got its share of this work.
- Advanced manufacturing in fields like robotics, nanotechnology, and materials sciences: Michigan's track record in science, engineering, design, and manufacturing gave us a measurable advantage in all these growing fields.

We would later expand the list to include opportunities in tourism and the film industry.

We also needed to diversify inside the auto industry by attracting more research and development centers and pursuing international auto companies and suppliers. We loved America's Big Three, but they no longer dominated the global auto industry as they had in the 1940s and 1950s. We needed to recruit companies from other countries that wanted to do business in America, making it easy for them to select Michigan as their home base. Manufacturing in China and Mexico might be cheaper, but the United States still represented one of the world's biggest and most affluent consumer markets. Proximity to those tens of millions of customers was one of the remaining advantages we had to find a way to exploit.

The other innate strength lay in our state's human talent. At one of our retreats, an economist reminded us that Michigan had more engineers—in fact, more sheer brainpower—associated with the car industry than all the other states combined. That made a huge difference in an industry that manufactured the most techno-logically advanced, mass-produced product in the world—one that combined an astonishing 10,000 parts into a seamless, power-ful whole. We needed to use our IQ advantage to attract compa-nies to Michigan—and try to maintain and increase that collective IQ by creating training opportunities for the thousands of less-skilled workers who'd been left jobless by the industry exodus.

I came home from the final retreat energized. I found Dan sit-ting at the kitchen table with our seven-year-old Jack, helping him with his math homework. I danced around the table, arms swaying triumphantly. "Woo hoo!" I crowed. "We're on the march!"

Jack grinned, happy for the distraction from the multiplication tables.

"I take it the governor has a clear strategy?" Dan inquired, peering at me over his reading glasses.

"Not just a strategy—it's a plan of attack! We're going on offense!"

Jack loved anything that smacked of battle. "Like an army on horseback?" he demanded, eyes aglow.

"You got it, Jack! Instead of being the victim, we're going to be the predator. Instead of being the dinner, we're going to be feasting!"

Jack thrust a fist in the air. "Instead of retreating, you're going to hunt them down and chew their bones!"

"Well, something like that," I laughed. "And we're not backing down!" I turned to Dan. "No more fearing globalization. We're going to take advantage of it. We're going to travel the world and lure companies back to Michigan. We're gonna turn our biggest threat into an opportunity!"

I liked the sound of it.

Now all we had to do was turn it into reality.

We tasked the Michigan Economic Development Corporation to ramp up its research and identify the ripest opportunities to attract job-creating companies to Michigan. Germany stood out like a banner headline at the top of the MEDC's list.

Michigan had been startled in 1998 when Chrysler merged with Daimler-Benz, the premier German auto company that produced the Mercedes. Michiganders weren't sure what to think. We loved the idea that such a world-renowned corporation would want to partner with Chrysler, and we were glad Chrysler now had access to the capital, engineering prowess, world-class nameplate, and world markets that Daimler-Benz could offer. On the other hand, in every merger one company and its leaders tend to dominate, and it was clear from the beginning that, "merger of equals" press releases notwithstanding, the Germans were the heavyweight. Chrysler execs left in a steady stream. Profits sagged. The media demoted GM, Ford, and Chrysler from the Big Three to the Detroit Three. By 2000, Toyota had muscled its way into the top three global ranking, and its eleven-year-old Lexus marque had become the world's leading luxury auto brand. Auto show hype had faded. The slippage was palpable.

That same year, Daimler dispatched Dieter Zetsche to run its ailing Chrysler division. I liked Zetsche. He was a charming and eccentric engineer, tall and balding, with an oversized white mustache, twinkly eyes, and lanky frame. He also had a quirky sense of humor that Americans became familiar with several years later when he appeared in a series of television commercials for the company (oddly enough, many people assumed that the heavily accented "Dr. Z" was a fictitious character). I had cornered Zetsche at the North American International Auto Show and urged him to bring more German businesses to Michigan, to tap our engineering expertise, and to build supplier strength around our manufacturing facilities. He was receptive to the idea, and we agreed we'd discuss it further.

In November 2004, I traveled to Germany, where Zetsche helped us turn talk into action. In Stuttgart, Munich, and Georgsmarienhütte, our team visited small and medium-sized auto suppliers and encouraged them to locate near the Daimler Chrysler mother ship in Auburn Hills. In just five days, we connected with scores of companies and were able to close deals with Behr (paint specialists), pgam Advanced Technologies (makers of high-tech communications systems), and Kipp, Inc. (handles, knobs, and other car parts), bringing research, development, and advanced manufacturing jobs to Michigan. More importantly, we cultivated tens of prospects for future development.

"That seemed almost easy," I said to Genna on the plane ride home. "Let's figure out where we can hook some more."

Genna nodded. "More visits will mean more jobs from more companies. And the more new companies we attract, the more other companies around the world will hear about Michigan. That's exactly the kind of cycle we need."

"It's interesting," I reflected, "how many of these medium-sized businesses are family-owned. They think in terms of generations, not immediate returns."

Genna sipped her water. "Which makes relationships so important. When you're thinking long term, you want to work with people you know and like and trust. And if you've never done business in the U.S., it's got to be wildly daunting. Permits, taxes, infrastructure, hiring—where do you even start?"

"Yep, we've got to make it easy for them to choose Michigan," I said. "Open our arms, embrace them like they're visiting their American relatives." I turned back to my stack of reading materials.

The trip to Germany had convinced me that we could attract international companies, but I knew that it would take some convincing back home. Michigan, like so many places in America, was built by immigrants, yet suspicious of foreigners. Hungarians and Germans, Irish and Italians, Mexican migrants and African Americans a generation or two removed from slavery had all flocked to Michigan, many of them lured in the 1920s and 1930s by Henry Ford's once-munificent $5-a-day salary. Wages rose steadily thanks to the explosion of the auto industry, wartime and postwar production, and the union's ever-vigilant fight to get workers a fair share of the rewards. Soon those immigrant millions were firmly rooted in middle-class life, raising kids who would join their parents in the factories or go off to college in search of even better prospects.

But how soon we Americans forget our historic roots in the rest of the world. Memories of the great wars left some Michiganders feeling uncomfortable about Germans controlling one of our auto companies. And anti-Asian sentiment ran even stronger. Starting in the 1970s, the Japanese had begun making inroads into our proudest industry—cars. It started with cheap imports—Corollas and Civics and Datsuns that attracted frugal Americans when the oil embargo drove gas prices through the roof. Then it was Accords and Camrys that actually beat the Big Three in quality. And finally Lexus and Infiniti ate into our luxury market with world-class design and innovation.

So if there was one thing nearly everyone in Michigan agreed upon—Democrats and Republicans, unionized workers and auto executives—it was that foreign automakers, especially the Japanese, were the enemy. A smart politician wouldn't be caught dead driving a foreign car, even today. The signs at the entrances to the scores of UAW parking lots across the state proclaimed, "No Foreign Cars Allowed," and if some misguided soul did park a foreign ride in the lot, he might return to find his paint job keyed, his tires deflated, or even his windows smashed.

When the economy took a nosedive, as it had in the early 1980s, the anxiety got deeper and the search for scapegoats more intense. One story stands out among the rest.

On the night of June 19, 1982, Vincent Chin attended a bachelor party at a nightclub in Highland Park—a separate city fully contained within Detroit's boundaries. Highland Park was the home of the first Ford factory and longtime home of Chrysler's world headquarters. Inside the club, Chin encountered Ronald Ebens, a Chrysler worker, who took one look at Chin's Asian features and concluded (mistakenly) that he was Japanese. "It's because of you little motherfuckers that we're out of work," Ebens declared. Chin left the club, but the incident didn't end there. Ebens and his stepson, autoworker Michael Nitz, searched the neighborhood for Chin and finally spotted him at a McDonald's restaurant. Nitz grabbed and held Chin while Ebens hit him at least four times with a baseball bat, including blows to the head. As Chin lost consciousness, he whispered to his friend, "It's not fair."

Chin lapsed into a coma from which he never awoke. He died four days later.

The people of Michigan were profoundly ashamed of the Vincent Chin incident. It was an idiotic and inexcusable explosion of frustration that produced a tragedy that would haunt the state. But the underlying tensions hadn't vanished. In the economic war for survival that Michigan was fighting, the state's citizens and businesses remained wary of the growing economic might wielded by Japan and its companies.

But as I flew home from Germany in 2004, charged with leading our side in that battle, I was crystal clear about one thing: Attracting industries from around the globe would be crucial to our economic future. And the single most important arena in that competition would be none other than Japan.

chapter 4

LANDING IN A HURRICANE

DAVID COLE IS THE WHITE-HAIRED GURU OF THE AUTO INDUSTRY. A University of Michigan professor, he founded the Center for Automotive Research (CAR). Engine oil runs in Cole's veins. His father was president of Chevrolet, and he worked in automotive design and marketing before launching CAR, which conducts research and sponsors conferences about technological, economic, labor, and environmental issues related to the industry. Cole knows everyone and understands how all the key players in the auto business think, not only in Detroit but around the world.

Cole was one of the first people with whom I shared my intent to press Japanese carmakers, including Toyota, to invest in Michigan. He strongly endorsed the move. "Given the Big Three's troubles, if you really want to get jobs, you need to go there. Japanese automakers and suppliers are already building cars in the U.S.— mostly in the South, because they want to avoid having to deal with unions. But Michigan has a lot of know-how, so it makes sense for the state to be one of their sites." Cole cautioned, "It'll be a tough sell. The Japanese are nervous about the UAW, and overcoming that won't be easy. And if you succeed, it'll be controversial to some here at home. You know the history—Toyota has been a dirty word to a lot of folks in Detroit."

I knew exactly what Cole was talking about. Within the industry, Toyota was viewed as a competitive juggernaut—the Yankees, the Celtics, and the Montréal Canadiens all rolled into one. It seemed every other cover of *Forbes*, *Fortune*, *Fast Company*, or the *Harvard Business Review* featured some aspect of Toyota's methods and mystique. If Toyota further expanded its presence in Michigan, the heart of our auto industry, the hostility would ratchet up several notches. Not only would Toyota be able to siphon off even more of the American car market; it also would be positioned to poach the best talent from its U.S. rivals.

Wooing Toyota would be both difficult and politically risky. But Cole encouraged me to try and offered his help.

We set about quietly yet aggressively courting Toyota. I kept close track of when Japanese execs were visiting for the Society of Automotive Engineers events or Cole's CAR events and made sure to pay my respects. When Jim Press, then president of Toyota's North American operations, was in Ann Arbor, I met him after a U of M football game. I made regular calls to Dennis Cuneo, executive vice president, who headed Toyota's U.S. government relations and had steered the company's investments in North America. I visited him at Toyota's New York City offices. I joined Toyota and other auto company executives for dinner at the Japanese consul's residence in Michigan. I courted the Toyota suppliers, attended their celebrations, and participated in *kagamiwari* ceremonies—the breaking of the sake barrel. I invited key Toyota executives to the governor's residence for dinner. I made no bones about my interest in their plans for an engine plant, and I pushed them hard to expand their technical center in Ann Arbor. They openly shared their concerns about the UAW, and they also asked me whether it wouldn't be unseemly for them to march into Big Three territory. That concern surprised and impressed me.

Repeatedly, they talked about their respect for the American companies, and they calmly said that they wanted and appreciated strong competitors. "GM's strength makes us compete harder, and we want that," one executive told me. I couldn't help but be struck by their cool, cautious, analytical strategy, yet also by this bigger sense of the game that they shared. The only time they seemed self-righteous was when they expressed their amazement at American auto executive pay schedules. The executives' big bonuses—as well as the way that workers bore the downside costs in bad times—appeared truly incomprehensible to them. "That would never be acceptable in Japan," they said. I told them candidly that I didn't get it either.

I was especially keyed in on George Yamashina, Yas Ichihashi, and Bruce Brownlee of the Toyota Technical Center (TTC). Based in Ann Arbor since 1972, the TTC had grown from a modest start to become the largest Toyota research and development facility outside Japan. Yas and George, two charming men who shared a sparkling sense of humor, both loved Ann Arbor and supported Toyota's desire to expand its presence in North America, build a strong development team in the States, and increase Toyota's sales here. But the company was also being heavily recruited by my fellow governors from southern states where it had manufacturing facilities—Kentucky, Mississippi, and Alabama—as well as by California's newly elected Arnold Schwarzenegger. I told the leaders at Toyota we would do whatever it took to ensure that Michigan would be the site of their future expansion. Bruce Brownlee was a quiet Michigander from a family of missionaries and spoke fluent Japanese; I felt he would help make the case for our state inside the walls of the TTC.

For months, we wooed Toyota. I promised to help get state property for an expanded TTC, which would be the crown jewel of Toyota's investments in the United States. The company planned to employ a thousand engineers there. I took the fight to acquire land on Toyota's behalf through the state legislature and then when challenged, all the way to the Michigan Supreme Court.

In April 2005, we got word that Michigan had won the Toyota expansion. "Fantastic!" I hollered into the phone when Yas Ichihashi gave me the news. I'm pretty sure I heard him smiling, and I imagined him thinking, "Crazy American!" But this was big, a symbolic step that could easily lead to more international investment. It meant that Michigan was capturing international engineering investment and high-paying, talent-attracting, talent-retaining, and talent-developing jobs in the technology, design, and engineering sectors of the auto industry. Unlike the low-skilled manufacturing jobs we'd been losing, these jobs would keep us in the innovation game, an arena in which Michigan, and the country as a whole, could—and needed to—compete.

But the blowback was strong.

I'd been receiving gently anxious phone calls from my friends inside the auto industry. At one of my executive team meetings, I shared the fact that I was getting increasingly negative feedback and probed: "Are you hearing the same things from our friends in the auto industry and the unions?"

Heads nodded. Lynda Rossi, our brilliant, blunt-spoken policy director, summed it up. "Governor, the autos are madder than hell. They can't believe we would be courting the competition. They're asking us to back off."

"No way," I said. "This is about jobs for our people. We said we'd go anywhere and do anything to bring jobs to Michigan. If we're serious, this is when we have to prove it. We love the Big Three—*love* them. But they've been cutting jobs right and left. We can't just sit around and watch that happen."

But others echoed Lynda. Soon after Toyota announced its plans to expand TTC in Ann Arbor, I had a visit from Fred Hoffman, who'd been Chrysler's trusted government relations executive for two decades and had the ear of the new management at Daimler. "Governor, you need to be careful," Fred warned. "The autos are hammering you inside their executive offices. They're asking why you'd alienate your UAW base and the domestic automakers by supporting their biggest competitor."

To me, the decision to woo Toyota was an obvious one. Toyota was going to base its engineering talent somewhere, creating a thousand jobs in the process. It was either going to be in Nagoya, the South, California, or Michigan. Of course I was going to pursue that opportunity on behalf of the people of my state.

Fred understood, but he remained concerned. "Dieter is really ticked," he said. "He thinks Toyota will come and steal our engineering talent and intellectual property. Ford is furious. And don't even get me started on what I'm hearing from GM. They all want you to stop recruiting the enemy."

I thought the world of Fred, his gentleness, candor, and deep knowledge of the industry. He was doing Dieter Zetsche's bidding, but he was also sincerely trying to help. I'd been living this problem, and I had to push back. "Fred, the same day Toyota announced we'd won the Tech Center expansion, there was other news." I paused. Fred raised his eyebrows and spread his hands in a silent question. "It was a joint study from the governors association and the council of state legislatures. And you know what it said? It said that Michigan is *last* in economic momentum. All because of the manufacturing jobs we've been losing."

I wanted to ask, "Is Chrysler on the verge of changing that?" But I bit my tongue. "These are good jobs Toyota is bringing us,

Fred." I said. "Sure, they may steal some talent. But they'll bring talent, too, and that's a good thing for Michigan and an opportunity for you all. It means Michigan will remain the North American center for autos."

Fred shook his head—in disagreement, or perhaps in resignation? He understood what I was doing. That didn't mean he had to like it.

The Detroit Three didn't appreciate our courting of Toyota, but we had to outgrow our traditional fear of things foreign. I seized every opportunity—in radio and television interviews, speeches and town hall meetings—to explain to citizens that we were going to steer right into the winds of global change, pursuing international research and development and making worldwide recruitment a big part of our economic future. We were done being victims. We would compete for jobs and investment in our people.

I was scheduled to visit Japan in July, both to celebrate our agreement with Toyota and to launch a full-court-press effort to woo auto suppliers and other Japanese firms to join them in opening facilities in Michigan. At home, the struggles of our manufacturing sector were worsening. Two weeks before our departure, a story appeared in the papers: "Delphi Announces Steve Miller as new CEO." This was big news in the auto industry and big news for Michigan. Whether it would be good news or bad remained to be seen.

Delphi Corporation's existence as a freestanding company was itself a byproduct of the economic flux we'd been living. One of the survival strategies of the once-monolithic auto giants of Detroit was to divest major corporate divisions. In 1996, for example, GM had spun off its Hughes Defense business, and GM did the same with its Electronic Data Systems subsidiary the following year. Then in 1999, GM spun off its main supplier of auto systems and components, Troy, Michigan–based Delphi, just a year before Ford spun off its leading supplier, Visteon.

The strategy behind these moves made sense: The parent companies got rid of massive legacy costs and simultaneously introduced more competition to the auto parts marketplace. GM and Ford could now choose from multiple suppliers and force the spun-off companies to compete. For their part, the liberated suppliers could be more nimble and compete for work from other automakers. Their newly minted CEOs, fresh from long careers aboard the mother ship, were eager to set off on their own paths, pursuing new business and opening lower-cost facilities in countries around the globe. In the boom days of the early 2000s, it worked. Both parent and offspring companies were profitable, and their respective stock prices rose steadily.

Delphi did not sell directly to consumers, so it was not a household name. It was, however, immense. Boasting nearly 200,000 employees worldwide and operating 166 manufacturing plants, Delphi was a regular presence on the *Fortune* 100 list. In 2005, it ranked sixty-third, in the same neighborhood as giants like Goldman Sachs, Sysco, Pepsi, and American Express.

Size, like past performance, is no guarantee of future results. Just below the surface, Delphi was in the worst shape of any major auto supplier. GM had been executing a strategy of squeezing major costs out of suppliers, shrinking the suppliers' margins to the vanishing point. Now Delphi balked. It was sagging under the weight of aging, inefficient plants and huge legacy costs, especially the pensions and retiree health care plans that GM had negotiated decades earlier when it dominated the global auto market.

It was clear that new CEO Miller would desperately need GM's CEO Rick Wagoner to cut him some slack. Unlike other tier one suppliers (those who sell directly to GM), Miller held a trump card: As part of the spinoff, GM had promised the UAW that should Delphi become insolvent, it would honor Delphi's legacy commitments. That point was now fast approaching.

I asked my legal counsel, Kelly Keenan, to research Steve Miller's background. Miller's career had begun at Ford. Then he'd moved on to Lee Iacocca's Chrysler and several other companies, where he became known as a turnaround guy. Unfortunately, in this case, "turnaround" didn't mean taking a troubled company and making it successful. It meant accelerating the crash, then trying to put the pieces back together after shedding debt, creditors, employees, and the least-productive assets. That's what Miller did at Morrison-Knudsen, Bethlehem Steel, and Federal-Mogul, leading them all into bankruptcy.

"This guy is a professional shark," Keenan said. "Mark my words: His arrival is the first step to Delphi going bankrupt and moving their manufacturing operations offshore."

The message was troubling. The bankruptcy of a firm as big as Delphi could trigger aftershocks through the supplier tiers that would be as jolting as the initial quake at Delphi. I told Genna to watch for Delphi news as we headed off to Asia again.

Our trip to Japan involved a lightning-fast tour of twenty-six companies by the members of our MEDC team, visiting cities from Nagoya to Tokyo to Osaka. With the help of the presidents of our outstanding research universities—the University of Michigan, Michigan State, and Wayne State—I pitched Michigan to attendees at a conference on life sciences in Osaka. I gave another speech to an industry forum attended by seventy more companies, and I met with the Japanese press. The reception we got was warm, curious, occasionally skeptical.

One young reporter approached me after my speech to the press club. "Governor," he said, a shock of straight black hair hanging over his eyes, "do you mean to tell us that Japanese car companies would be welcome in the Michigan of Vincent Chin?"

I was surprised to find that the tragedy of twenty-three years earlier was still arousing anger and suspicion halfway around the world. "That was decades ago," I assured him. "We want jobs. I'm here as the governor of Michigan to convey that we will roll out the welcome mat for Japanese companies. We understand that embracing the competition will make us all stronger." I was flipping the offshoring argument that was so often used to seduce American businesses into building overseas plants: Japanese suppliers, I reasoned, could reach new markets by investing in Michigan. They would be able to sell not only to Toyota and Japanese transplants but also to North American producers.

Our biggest stop was at Toyota's headquarters in Toyota City, near Nagoya, just over an hour by bullet train from Tokyo. The buildings in the vast complex are unassuming—no slick glass towers or architectural showpieces like the Auburn Hills Technical Center that Chrysler opened in 1996. Toyota staff met us outside the main headquarters and led us up to the president's executive meeting room, which was airy, simple, and understated, unlike the grand offices of many American CEOs. (I knew the difference from firsthand experience. The Detroit office of the governor of Michigan was the very office that Alfred Sloan, Roger Smith, and others had occupied before GM had abandoned the building in the late 1990s. Its marble floors, enormous art deco colonnade, spacious hallways, and towering windows had once aptly symbolized GM's status as the richest and most powerful company in the world. Though now redecorated in good-enough-for-government Naugahyde, the space remained cavernous and imposing.)

In Toyota City, our delegation was assigned seats on one side of a large coffee table, with the Toyota team seated across from us. As I'd come to expect in Japan, they were all men in dark suits and ties. Our delegation—Genna Gent, Lynda Rossi, Dave Hollister, Sandy Ring, Ken Masumoto, Jerome Marks, and I—was a classic American mixture: three women, four men, one African American, one Japanese American. We briefly engaged in small talk until President Katsuake Watanabe walked into the room, at which point everyone stood up immediately. We all pulled out our specially printed business cards (English on one side, Japanese on the other) and lined up to greet Watanabe-san, starting with me. I spoke my now well-practiced line, *"Haji may mushtay"* ("Nice to meet you"), took his card in both hands, as I'd grown accustomed to doing, looked at it, bowed, and shook his hand. I loved the gentle ritual greeting. It didn't, however, diminish my itching desire to get to the purpose of the visit.

We took our seats, and I began my earnest pitch. "We are very grateful, Watanabe-san, for the investment you have already made in Michigan. The Toyota Technical Center in Ann Arbor is a wonderful employer of great engineering talent." I smiled at him and waited for the translator to finish relaying my remarks. I told Watanabe how we would like to welcome him to Michigan. "We have many engineers, many lakes, and more golf courses per capita than any state in the country," I said with a lilt, knowing from my detailed briefing book that he enjoyed an afternoon on the links. "I hope we can demonstrate to you how much we appreciate Toyota's presence in Michigan."

I was well aware of the importance of personal connections in the world of Japanese business. The role of Senator Jay Rockefeller in convincing Toyota to build a plant in Buffalo, West Virginia, after the state lost its textile industry owing to globalization, had become legendary. A scion of one of the world's richest business families, Rockefeller had known CEO Akio Toyoda since the 1960s, and he personally appealed to him to use his company's influence to help restore his economically wounded state. Rockefeller showed his commitment by personally tramping through wheat fields with Toyota executives in search of the perfect location. "By the time Toyota decided to make Buffalo its new home," Rockefeller said in 2006 during the plant's tenth anniversary, "I felt like a full-fledged member of that site selection team."

I hoped to take the same approach with Watanabe. "Michigan, I'm sorry to say, has been the place where globalization and competition have had their worst effects," I told him. "Our American auto industry has certainly been impacted by competition from Toyota, as you know. We are also the place where the greatest healing can occur."

He smiled understandingly, I thought, appearing to comprehend the significance of Toyota's potential role in alleviating Michigan's pain. After a pause he said, "I want to express my deep appreciation for all that you did to win the Toyota Technical Center land for our expansion. We are very grateful for this, and I can assure you that Michigan is one of the states we will consider if and when we decide to build an engine plant."

"*Domo arigato gozimus*," I thanked him, exhaling audibly. I caught Genna's eye, encouraged by the hopeful exchange.

Sandy confided later that one of Watanabe's lieutenants had leaned over at that moment and whispered, "Of course, we are concerned about the unions." Sandy had simply nodded in reply.

"Will you also consider encouraging your suppliers to come to Michigan?" I asked.

"I will consider this," Watanabe replied. "I hear that you will be seeing quite a few of them on this trip," he said, flashing me a knowing smile. I hoped my team had caught the subtle gesture. It demonstrated how impressed he was with the aggressive schedule they had laid out for me.

With Watanabe's blessing, Yas Ichihashi, Bruce Brownlee, and George Yamashina had arranged dinners with executives from Denso, Hino, and Tokai Rika, three Toyota suppliers that were part of its *kieretsu*, which functioned like a family of businesses. Establishing a strong relationship with the leaders of Toyota would give us entrée to their many interlocking companies. I assured Watanabe that we were very excited to enjoy Japanese food and hospitality.

The meeting ended with handshakes, photographs, an exchange of gifts, and bowed farewells. I presented Watanabe with a handcrafted glass bowl we commissioned for the occasion from artisans at the Henry Ford Village in Dearborn. And after five days, we were thrilled to announce investment commitments from ten companies—Hitachi Automotive, Sekisui Chemical, Nippon Antenna, Nippon Piston Ring, Advanced Special Tools, Nakagawa Special Steel, Taiko Device Technologies, A&D Inc., DENSO, and Tokai Rika—bringing the promise of $116 million in investment and 630 jobs. Our trip was praised by observers statewide as a resounding success.

But the euphoria quickly wore off. Six hundred thirty jobs were a tiny cushion for what felt like an impending crash landing for Michigan. And when we got back from Japan, our worst fears were confirmed: Delphi bankruptcy preparations were well under way.

From a legal and economic standpoint, bankruptcy serves two purposes. It resolves disputes over contested company resources by empowering a bankruptcy court to decide who is owed what, even voiding obligations to pensioners, investors, and suppliers where necessary. Bankruptcy can also save an entity from utter and complete disintegration, salvaging working parts to permit the organization to recover to the extent possible.

Steve Miller bluntly discussed Delphi's situation with the local and business press, blaming untenable obligations that made it too fat and slow to keep up with foreign competition. He also talked glowingly about the working relationship he'd enjoyed with the United Steelworkers at Bethlehem. But he and the UAW began squaring off almost immediately. Delphi couldn't be competitive paying wages of $26 per hour, he said. And when he demanded that the UAW accept a $10 per hour wage for new workers, the union promptly threatened a strike that could ripple upward and shut down GM manufacturing in a matter of weeks, if not days. The two sides squabbled publicly for three months as the company careened toward insolvency.

On the evening of October 7, I got a call at home from Lynda Rossi. "It's done, Governor. Delphi is going to file for Chapter 11 protection tomorrow."

"Oh, God. Put on your seat belt," I said. "This is gonna be a rough ride."

It was the largest industrial bankruptcy in U.S. history. *Business Week* summarized the strategy:

> Miller filed for Chapter 11 protection only for his U.S. operations, which employ 32,000 UAW and other union workers. He was careful to exclude Delphi's 115,000-worker foreign factories, many of which operate in low-wage countries such as Mexico and China. If Miller gets his way, court filings show, Delphi will end up with a U.S. workforce of perhaps 7,000, leaving the bulk of its production abroad. "The company will only keep U.S. operations that have technological value," says Brian Johnson, an auto analyst at Sanford C. Bernstein & Co. Miller declined comment.

The headline on the story echoed Kelly Keenan's somber prediction: "Go Bankrupt, Then Go Overseas."

If Electrolux was a collapsed three-story office building, then Delphi was the towering inferno. But it seemed that only the American workingmen and -women would get burned. The executives would escape unscathed. The bankruptcy filings described lavish severance packages ("golden parachutes") for twenty-one top executives and a set-aside of almost $90 million for bonuses for senior management. The UAW was clearly going to go ballistic.

I issued a statement: "Delphi's [bankruptcy] decision will undoubtedly have a ripple effect through Michigan's economy—an economy already reeling from outsourcing. I am angry that this action occurs one day after headlines blared that Delphi employees were being asked to accept brutal, draconian pay cuts while upper management is being offered golden parachutes."

I was not in the habit of bad-mouthing Michigan corporate leadership. But the lack of equity in this case was unconscionable, the arrogance revolting.

Miller heightened the tensions and made his own job more difficult through his bellicose public statements. At one press conference in New York, he got carried away and said that paying "$65 an hour for someone mowing the lawn at one of our plants is just not going to cut it anywhere in industrial America for very long." The exaggerated claim (which lumped together salary and benefits, then jacked both figures up far beyond any realistic average) insulted Delphi workers beyond words. At a union rally, Joe Buckley, president of UAW Local 696, fired up the crowd by declaring, "The working men and women of our unions are *not* going to mow your grass for $10 an hour. Maybe you should mow your own grass and let us run the business." Later, the UAW printed up T-shirts bearing the proud title "Miller's Mowers."

The month of the bankruptcy filing, which became known as "Black October," I was exiting a coffee shop in Saginaw when I came face-to-face with a large man in his forties, with a lined face and a tattoo on his neck, wearing a bomber jacket and faded jeans. "Ms. Granholm! I never thought I'd see you here. Wow—!" I took his outstretched hand, as large as a dinner plate, shook it, and smiled.

"Hi," I said. "Just getting some coffee." I started to leave, but something in the man's eyes made me stop.

"How're you doing?" I asked him, searching his face. He looked at the floor. "I work for the brake plant," he said. Saginaw Brake was one of Delphi's factories slated to close. He started to say something else but caught himself.

"I'm sorry," I said. "This is a really hard time for you guys."

He looked at me, his eyes watering. "My God," he said, "this is embarrassing. I don't cry in front of women."

"It's okay," I said. I took his elbow and eased him toward the newspaper boxes in the restaurant's foyer, where we could have a little privacy.

"I don't know anything else," he whispered. A tear escaped and began its roll down his cheek. "I have a wife, a daughter. Now I'll have nothing. *Nothing*." His mouth twisted in the effort to stem the flow. His voice dropped to a rasp. "Please, Governor, can't you stop these motherfuckers from doing this?"

I groaned. "I wish I could. I so wish I could," I said. "No governor can control bankruptcies and the decisions of the automakers. I'm so sorry. It's these damn trade agreements—" I started.

He looked at the floor, mumbled, "Yeah, whatever," and pushed past me, walking through the coffee shop toward the men's room. He never looked back.

I watched him walk away, and then I slowly stepped outside. Jerome Marks, my staff assistant—was waiting for me in the parking lot. A former probation officer, he was a worldly man who had somehow never grown hardened.

"God help us," I said more to myself than to Jerome. "When is this going to stop?"

Jerome seemed to sense my gloom. He shook his head and with his gravelly, southern, but urbanized cadence said, "Governor, you're their hope. We can't give up." It didn't fix the worker's problem, but I was awfully glad to have Jerome on my side, reminding me—as he so often did—about what was most important.

· · · · ·

ON OCTOBER 13, 2005, JUST FIVE DAYS AFTER THE DELPHI bankruptcy filing, I attended the grand opening of Hyundai's North American Research and Development Center near Ann Arbor. We won the investment by assembling an incentive package that was irresistible to the Korean automaker; our MEDC had been working on it for months. I was pleased to think about the positions in engineering, marketing, and sales that the center would create. But the face of the man from Saginaw Brake kept haunting me. "Jobs for engineering graduates don't do anything for him," I thought.

We celebrated Hyundai's investment in Michigan, yet its homeland represented one of our worst trading partners. In 2005, thanks to Korean trade barriers against American imports, U.S. automakers would sell a grand total of 3,811 cars in Korea—while over 730,000 Korean cars were shipped to the United States. Was this a fair reflection of the relative value of our products, or the relative quality of our workmanship? I didn't think so. I wasn't alone.

I recalled how Delphi's CEO Steve Miller had decried our naïve national trade policies while he was running Bethlehem Steel. He'd even donned a union jacket to protest Korea's dumping of steel in the U.S. market. A rare moment when a CEO—driven, of course, by corporate self-interest—recognized what our give-it-all-away trade policy was doing to our country. Now, in the final irony, who should I recognize across the room at the Hyundai ribbon cutting? None other than Steve Miller, chatting with Korean executives, undoubtedly trying to drum up a little business for his restructured Delphi.

I made a beeline for him. His bookish appearance belied the wrecking-ball work he was now doing at Delphi. I asked for a few minutes and led him into a side room.

"Steve," I said, "I know these are impossible times and that you were sent to Delphi to do the tough job of restructuring."

He interrupted me with a chuckle. "You don't know the half of it, Governor."

"Oh, I know a little," I replied. "I've been asking for concessions from my unionized employees, too. Not as deep as the cuts you want, but deep enough to hurt, believe me."

"But I'm also cutting my own salary by 10 percent," I said, leaning forward. "I don't mean to be sticking my nose in your business—but honestly, as governor, your business *is* my business. If I can be candid, the golden parachutes for your execs coupled with the harsh treatment of workers reeks of hypocrisy. With respect, you've got to lead by example."

Miller raised his eyebrows and peered at me through his glasses. I recognized the look. CEOs often go through the motions of listening politely to politicians, but they don't often take what they hear very seriously. They appear to regard politicians as a nuisance to be tolerated, blunderers who meddle unintelligently in the affairs of business without understanding markets or the pressures of the bottom line.

"I can't keep good people if I can't pay them to stay," he explained patiently. "And besides, the severance packages and bonuses are for performance. I need these people to pull us out of the mire. The amount is tiny compared to the overall wage problem in the workforce."

"But it doesn't matter," I said. "Those bonuses are a slap in the face to the workers when you're asking them for 60 percent pay cuts. Symbols matter." I was imploring him to understand. "You've got to demonstrate shared sacrifice. A one-sided approach will be rewarded with strikes, and maybe worse."

Miller sighed. "I get what you're saying. I'll think about it," he said. I couldn't tell if he was just patronizing me or if he really meant it.

A few days later, Miller announced that his executives were taking 10 percent salary cuts; Delphi's president, Rodney O'Neal, would take a 20 percent cut; and he himself would work for $1 a year. But it was tough to put the genie back in the bottle. For days, the headlines had been dominated by stories about the double standard at Delphi—bonuses for executives, wage cuts for workers.

Corporate executives think in terms of numbers. When it comes to compensation, they see a fraction: Their pay is on top, with corporate earnings or even revenues on the bottom. The resulting value is very tiny, meaning that their income is minuscule in the grand scheme of things—not a big deal, they reason. Workers think in numbers, too. But the fraction the workers see is quite different. They see an executive's bonus on top and their pay on the bottom. *That* fraction is top-heavy—an "improper fraction," as we learned in math class. And as we learned in Bible and Sunday school class, such imbalance was also improper from a moral standpoint.

Corporate leaders have a duty to maintain the organization and to honor its ethical and legal obligations to shareholders, contractors, governments, and lenders. But employees remain a critical—if not *the* critical—force in the engine of growth. Alienate the workers through continual demands for one-sided concessions, and it's not just morals but also morale and productivity that deteriorate. Fairness at both ends of the pay scale is not just a legitimate moral end but also an essential element of sound leadership. Morality and morale are deeply interwoven in credible leadership. If leaders destroy the former, they will eventually destroy the latter.

When corporate plans like Delphi's initial executive bonuses come out, or when Capitol Hill and the White House express no outrage at 200-to-1 auto sales imbalances with Korea, we erode worker and citizen trust at a foundational level. In such a context of patent unfairness, how were union leaders and I to inspire Michigan workers to give more and make major changes in their lives? Those workers were assailed in the media (and by southern legislators) for fighting for benefits like pensions and health care. Meanwhile, their corporate "leaders" were simultaneously wiping out jobs and ransacking corporate funds for their personal benefit.

Shortly after the Delphi bankruptcy filing, I called the folks at the Center for Automotive Research (CAR). I asked for a meeting with the center's top researcher. I needed to know the unvarnished truth about what Delphi's bankruptcy would mean for Michigan, and CAR would be better equipped to sketch that future than any place else.

Sean McAlinden was CAR's head of research. He has a reputation for being meticulous and thorough. On November 1, 2005, he entered the conference room where Rick Wiener, Lynda Rossi, Kelly Keenan, Genna Gent, and I were seated. McAlinden was armed with a forty-eight-slide presentation. His expression was drop-dead serious.

He switched on his computer, and the first slide popped up on the screen: "The Delphi Effect."

I couldn't wait. "Tell us the bottom line, Sean. Where is this all headed?"

"Governor, I'm not going to pull any punches. Here's what you're facing in the next twenty-four to forty-eight months," he said. He clicked on the next slide:

MICHIGAN FACES A CATEGORY FIVE
ECONOMIC HURRICANE

"We're going to see 35,000 job cuts at GM, Ford, Delphi in the next twenty-four months alone, and another 10 to 12,000 in the following twenty-four months. That means Michigan will have lost 195,000 jobs since 2000." Another slide showed the list of plants that would close and the communities that would be affected. He paused to let this information sink in.

I looked up at him. "And what's the root cause?"

"It's happening because the Detroit Three have steadily lost market share since 1999. Now they have too many factories building cars with lower and lower demand. They are way over capacity. They simply *have to* restructure. That means closing plants and laying off people, and unfortunately they'll move manufacturing overseas. Michigan just happens to be on the losing end of that equation."

"And their labor costs? Are they statistically as out of whack as Delphi keeps saying?"

"Delphi's costs are higher than their international competitors'. Delphi's employees are averaging $28 an hour. The other suppliers are paying about $20 an hour. On top of that, GM has been squeezing all of their suppliers, demanding price reductions, including from Delphi, until they can't breathe. It's all coming due right now."

McAlinden flashed a slide labeled "The Supplier Table of Pain." It showed all of the industries that would be affected by the Delphi bankruptcy.

"Delphi's bankruptcy is going to start a ripple effect the likes of which we have never seen. They have 2,000 U.S. suppliers. That includes 328 manufacturing facilities in Michigan."

Genna broke in: "Wait. I know they're a tier one supplier to GM. Are you saying that they in turn have 2,000 suppliers of their own?"

"That's right. Their scope is pretty amazing, isn't it?"

Rick said what we all were thinking. "Amazing? No. It's downright brutal. We're watching this country blow up the engines of its own progress."

Lynda's face was dark as she flipped through the handouts. A blanket of gloom had settled over the room.

"So, Sean, in your view, what can the state of Michigan do?" I was hoping that McAlinden's research had revealed some ways out we hadn't yet explored. "Tax relief? Tax credits? *Anything*?"

McAlinden sighed. He was a Michigan resident, too. "Governor, you don't know how much I wish I had an answer for you on that one," he said. "Honestly, state policy will be ineffective for a while. Tax incentives will be meaningless to these declining companies. The best thing you can do is prepare to train displaced workers *now*."

"And otherwise just ride out the storm?" asked Genna.

McAlinden looked from Genna to me. "There is nothing that you or any governor can do to prevent or fix this. These are forces well beyond your control. But you're going to have to deal with it. This is the biggest economic jolt to hit this state in decades. The pain will continue to wash over us, in waves, for the next four years. Michigan will have tens of thousands of unemployed workers to deal with. Sorry to be the bearer of bad news, Governor. But you did ask for honesty." He pressed the button on his remote control one more time. The now-black screen read, "End of slide show, click to exit."

I stood up, offering Sean my hand. "I appreciate your candor. It looks ugly, but we're *gonna* pull through this . . . somehow. Thanks, Sean."

"You can call on us any time," he said, his handshake firm. As I escorted him to the foyer, he smiled kindly. "I'm sure glad I'm not you. I have a tough day at the office once in a while. But no one expects me to fix the unfixable."

chapter 5

BLOWN AWAY YET?

I SUSPECT THAT FOR MANY MAYORS, GOVERNORS, AND PRESIDENTS, the emotional high point of any term in executive office is probably election night. From that euphoric movement, the path generally winds downward, from the sobering honor of inauguration and the short-lived honeymoon that follows, through legislative battles and unforeseen emergencies, and ultimately to the reelection campaign. By mid-2005, I'd been through two and a half crisis-laden years, during which I'd proactively driven only a fraction of the state agenda. I'd spent much of my time resolving inherited dilemmas and fending off disasters driven by national and global forces. But if I wanted another term in which to try to keep some of the promises I'd made to the voters, it was time to begin the battle to win that term.

On June 2, a year and a half before the next gubernatorial election, über-conservative billionaire Republican Dick DeVos

announced he was running to unseat me. DeVos's business credentials were impressive. His father, Richard DeVos (in partnership with boyhood friend Richard Van Andel), had founded
Amway, a successful consumer products company, in Grand
Rapids. Dick, Richard's oldest son, had worked in the company
from the time he was nineteen, holding positions of increasing
challenge and stature, including serving as president of the family's NBA franchise, the Orlando Magic. He had returned to
Grand Rapids to take over as president of the corporate mother
ship in 1993. After ten years at the helm, he had retired from the
business before he was even fifty years old.

Amway employed thousands of Michiganders in west Michigan, and DeVos was credited with taking the company global. It
was a huge success story, and the company's very name—short
for the "American Way"—had a made-for-TV feeling about it.
The story wasn't without controversy. Amway was a multilevel
marketing firm, described by many as little more than a Ponzi
scheme, investigated and fined (though not prosecuted) by the
Federal Trade Commission, and still under investigation by foreign governments. What's more, in the process of going global,
DeVos had restructured Amway's newly created parent company,
Alticor, to eliminate over 1,400 jobs, mostly in Michigan. At the
same time, he'd invested heavily overseas, especially in China.
The shift of resources from the United States to a rising foreign
competitor nation wasn't something the voters of Michigan were
likely to appreciate. DeVos undoubtedly hoped that his tale of
personal triumph would carry the day without raising too many
thorny questions about Amway itself.

Dick DeVos looked the part of a successful mogul—youthful,
tall, tan, athletic. He competed in triathlons for fun; was an accom-
plished sailor who captained his family's eighty-six-foot yacht, the
Windquest; and was reportedly ready to spend tens of millions from
his personal fortune on his campaign, a mind-blowing amount for a

contest in our state. And if this weren't enough, business hero De-Vos had his heroine by his side: Betsy DeVos had chaired the Michigan Republican Party and was sister of Erik Prince, founder of the Blackwater empire, as well as heir to her own family fortune. They supported school voucher campaigns and conservative free-market think tanks across the country. In short, they were Michigan Republican royalty.

DeVos launched the race with a fusillade of attacks on my failure to fix the state's job loss problem. Michigan, he declared, was "last where we should be first," suffering through "a one-state recession." He couched his criticisms in statements like "The governor is a nice person, but the results speak for themselves." As DeVos crisscrossed the state throughout the summer and fall of 2005, his constant reminders of the state's economic woes gnawed at the voters' fragile sense of confidence, cast doubt on the wisdom of our strategy, and pushed my approval ratings slowly downward. We dreaded seventeen months of De-Vos sniping from the sidelines while we labored to turn the state around.

I'd tried to obey the sage advice of Ed McNamara, my first political boss: "Work hard, do the right thing, and the politics will take care of themselves." But the dismal jobs numbers were barely responding. In 2005, Michigan's unemployment rate was 6.7 percent, roughly two points higher than the national rate. Although that number would later seem enviable, in 2005 the figure gave rise to anger and anxiety in Michigan, which DeVos and his advisors were zealous about exploiting.

In early January 2006, the gubernatorial election year, our pollster Mark Mellman convened a conference call to discuss the public's mood as we framed what would be my most politically important State of the State speech. He began with my overall job performance as rated by the voters: now 40 percent positive, 58 percent negative. Only 29 percent of those polled felt the state was "on the right track."

As they heard the numbers, my strategy team members exchanged anxious looks. Dan tried to lighten the mood: "Gee, Mark, I've got a big Catholic family. Can't you include a few more of them in your next poll?" Mark didn't even chuckle in response.

"I can't believe we've sunk this far," I finally confessed.

"With this economy and DeVos's attacks, it could be a lot worse, Governor," Mellman said. He ran through the rest of his data, none of it cheery. As soon as he paused, I asked what everyone must have been wondering. "So, Mark, straight up, with these approval numbers, can I beat DeVos?"

"It's possible to win this race," Mellman replied matter-of-factly.

"Possible?" I half laughed, half sputtered.

"Governor, I'm being honest with you," he said. "You *can* win this race, but it won't be easy. There are a lot of variables, and a lot can happen between now and November."

Genna Gent spoke up. "You've got your ear to the ground, Mark," she said. "We've done a huge amount of policy legwork in preparation for this speech. But what are people feeling out there?"

"They're nervous. They're worried about the economy," said Mellman. "You can see that from the 'wrong track' numbers. Some are unemployed. Others are worried they will be. There's a lot of insecurity out there."

As they continued to talk through themes that might be relevant for the speech, I was stuck on Mellman's blunt response to my question about the coming election. Conventional wisdom held that an incumbent with an approval rating of just 40 percent was in serious trouble. When the meeting concluded, I asked Mellman to stay on the speakerphone for a minute and grabbed Rick Wiener by the sleeve as the others left the room. Wiener looked at me quizzically and pushed his glasses up on his nose. Rick is a fidgeter, someone who must have driven his middle school teachers crazy with his energy. He and I went all the way back to the Dukakis campaign in 1988, and I had fond memories of him at campaign meetings, pacing up and down as he slurped from a can of pop. Now I was the one doing the pacing.

"Mark," I said into the squawk box on the table, "with all our efforts on the economy, nothing is getting through to people. They're angry, angrier than I've ever seen." I paused. "I'm thinking . . . maybe I shouldn't run."

Wiener shook his head back and forth emphatically, but I waved him off and rushed on, all business.

"I need your honest opinion, Mark. I just want someone I believe in to be governor; it doesn't have to be me. I don't *need* to do this. The last thing I want for the state, the party, and for me is to run and lose. If another Democrat has a better chance, I'll get out. Can anyone else win this race?"

After a pause, Mellman responded: "I'd say that's very doubtful. You're the Democratic leader. If you don't run, someone must still run on your legacy. Apart from Carl Levin, you are the only one who can win."

I hadn't been thinking of Levin. He'd done so much for Michigan in the U.S. Senate that it hadn't occurred to me that he might shift to the governor's chair. Yet he was enormously popular. Not only had he never lost an election; he'd also never been seriously threatened. I jumped on Mellman's words.

"How about it? Let's make an inquiry to see if Carl will do it," I urged.

Wiener sputtered, "Governor, with all due respect, that's just crazy. He has a safe seat. He's got seniority. He'd want this job like he'd want a hole in the head. Besides, you have *nothing* to run from, and, mark my words," wagging his finger, "we're going to beat DeVos like a drum."

Mellman, who'd been Carl Levin's pollster since long before he was mine, agreed.

"Governor, you're it," he said.

I still wasn't entirely convinced. Mellman and Wiener had the edge on me in years and experience and had more integrity than anyone in the business. But the skeptic in me also knew I was signing their paychecks. Would they really tell me if they thought I should step aside?

That evening, I brought the issue to my most trusted unpaid advisor. Dan was working at the computer on one of the two side-by-side desks in our bedroom. I took a seat at the other. "Dan," I said without emotion, "we have to make a decision about reelection. You heard how my numbers are tanking, and DeVos has barely started his barrage. We can pull the plug now." With a full head of steam I went on, "This campaign's going to be hell for you, not to mention the kids watching me get beat up for another eleven months. There's still time for someone else to get in and win it. Carl Levin, for example." Dan turned his gaze to me, eyebrows raised.

"With all due respect, Madam Governor," he said with a weary smile, "I think you've lost your mind. First of all, why would Carl want anything to do with this race? He'd be crazy to leave the U.S. Senate to run for governor, especially at a time like this. Everyone's mad about the economy, and Carl can't control global manufacturing trends any more than you can."

Dan stood up and took a step toward me. "Second, and most important, we are *not* running away from this fight—"

"Hey, I'm not afraid of a fight," I said, pointedly interrupting him. "Be clear about that. I just want Democrats to win." He barreled on, ignoring my interruption.

"You have been working your ass off trying to fix this state. Your team is great and totally committed. You know that no one could be doing any more than you have done." Dan usually played the role of sounding board, counselor, friend. This night his competitive juices were flowing. "You and your team have worked too hard to throw in the towel. We are *not* backing down, despite the odds, despite the numbers, and despite all the money DeVos has to throw into the fight."

He pointed at the picture of my parents on the shelf nearby. "And maybe we'll win not despite his money, but because of it. We're regular folks from middle-class stock. And there are more of us than there are of him."

Dan's words stoked my own competitive fires.

That did it. Game on.

My State of the State speech was two weeks away. As always, it would be an important act of governance—an opportunity to declare progress and to educate the legislature, the media, and the citizens about what we planned to accomplish this year, a sort of executive battle plan. We'd been working for months on the policies we'd outline in the speech. As a big believer in management by objectives, I loved using the State of the State speech as a blueprint for the year. Based on the overarching goals presented in the speech each year, we would articulate specific, measurable objectives for every initiative and every department. In my first State of the State, for example, I'd announced twenty-four specific economic, education, health care, and public protection policies we'd pursue; in my second year, I'd announced thirty-four and in my third year, seventeen. We were on track to getting 90 percent of them done. Throughout the year, we would review those objectives on blow-up charts at twice-a-month cabinet meetings, respectfully holding people's feet to the fire when targets hadn't been met and celebrating their achievements when they had. It made me proud to watch my fantastic team checking off boxes, reaching one goal after another, generally falling short only when the legislative votes needed for an initiative failed to materialize.

But in 2006, the address would play a huge role not just in governance but also in politics. It would serve to articulate the core argument we would make for my reelection. I'd look back at the progress we'd made despite the unemployment rate, taking the opportunity to counter DeVos's pronouncements about our ineffectiveness. I'd set expectations, reminding the citizens that Michigan hadn't gotten into this mess overnight and wouldn't get out of it overnight. I'd call for the legislature to pass the rigorous new educational curriculum standards that we'd been working on, I'd talk about how we had created or retained 32,000 jobs through business recruitment and retention efforts, and I'd talk about the trips we'd taken to recruit overseas companies to Michigan.

I was especially hopeful about some of our alternative energy initiatives, and as I worked on the speech draft, I inserted a line to emphasize the point. At a walk-through reading, I punched it out: "In five years, you'll be blown away at the progress we're making in new sectors."

When the team reviewed the text to offer comments and suggestions, Genna said, "I'd lose the 'blown away' line."

"Why?" I asked crisply. I knew it would be controversial, but I wanted to gauge just what others saw as the problem. Before Genna could jump in I said, "With DeVos sounding the alarm bells, people need to know that we're seeing real movement, real progress on our economy. They need to know that I'm bullish on our plans."

"I know you're enthusiastic, Governor," Genna replied, "but I *really* don't think you should say that."

Chuck Wilbur, senior educational advisor and political communications veteran, agreed with Genna. "I'm not sure what that line gets you, and I'd worry it will be taken out of context. They'll say you're out of touch with reality."

"I hear you," I said. Reluctantly, I agreed to cut the line.

But the importance of diversifying the economy remained a key message. GM had underscored it with 25,000 job cuts announced a few months earlier. And on January 23, two days before my speech, another bombshell hit. Ford announced 30,000 more layoffs. It planned to close the Wixom assembly—a sprawling but recently modernized facility between Detroit and Lansing that employed thousands of people, including, at one time, Dan's father, Jack Mulhern.

The news of more job losses in manufacturing meant I had to put even more emphasis on retraining. We had to let people know there was a way out. So I went back and beefed up that section of the speech, pointing out how we were retraining people—19,000 at this point, with plans to retrain 30,000 more in 2006, preparing them for jobs in growing sectors of the economy. I used the speech to push my Department of Labor and Economic Growth to access every possible dime of federal money and deploy it as fast as was practicable. I called a retrained worker—Armenia Smith, who'd returned to school and now had a well-paid job in nursing—and invited her to attend the speech as a living symbol of hope.

Just in case my sense of urgency was not already shooting through the roof, on the day of my speech a front-page story in the *Wall Street Journal* declared, "The question now is whether the cuts at Detroit's giants are the beginning of a new, more competitive era, or just the beginning of the end." The latter prospect was unimaginable; the doomsday language was getting crazy. So before my last run-through, I wrote my line of optimistic promise back into the speech, and I delivered it that night with full conviction from the rostrum in the ornate House chambers: "In five years, you're going to be blown away by the strength and diversity of Michigan's transformed economy."

My supporters met the boldness with a cascading ovation. But as Genna and Chuck had worried, I had handed DeVos a club with which he would beat me during the campaign.

DeVos launched his television ads a few weeks later. His message was elegantly simple: Michigan is a mess, and Dick DeVos is "the change we need."

DeVos had some major campaign advantages. Lacking any political track record, he could introduce himself as a blank screen onto which voters could freely project their hopes for Michigan. Unencumbered by the obligations of a job or any need to raise money, he could travel the state shaking hands while blanketing the airwaves with his ads.

But I'd learned an important lesson about competition from my Scandinavian father: Don't complain—just outwork them. My typical day during campaign season looked like this:

5:00 AM: Get up, get ready, read the newspapers over coffee, e-mail campaign and government teams.

7:30 AM: Attend fund-raising breakfast or make drive-time calls.

8:00 AM to noon: Do governor's work.

Noon: Attend fund-raiser or make fund-raising calls.

1:00 to 3:00 PM: Make fund-raising calls.

3:00 to 6:00 PM: Do governor's work.

6:00 to 8:30 PM: Attend fund-raising receptions.

9:00 to 10:00 PM: See kids.

10:00 to midnight: Do governor's work via online connection.

Like an autoworker in boom times, I was pulling double shifts every day, working the equivalent of two full-time jobs: nine hours spent doing the people's business, six or seven hours trying to earn the right to keep doing it. Fortunately, I loved campaigning, and I was obsessed about governing. I was grateful every day for the work of people like John Burchett, my old friend and new chief of staff. John had agreed to step into the role after Rick Wiener returned to private practice, and he was instrumental in helping me keep the state afloat as the economy spiraled downward.

For efficiency and for legal reasons, we rented a campaign office a half-block from the governor's office so that I could shuttle back and forth without wasting time. (Strict rules forbid campaign activities on state premises, and we followed those rules to the letter.) On Saturday, I'd hustle well into the evening at Democratic events, parades, receptions, and fund-raisers. On Sunday, I was out the door by 7:00 AM for six to eight hours of visiting churches, neighborhood picnics, and similar events, punctuated by phone calls or a quick nap in the car. Sunday evening we had dinner together as a family and took a collective deep breath.

Dan completely took over the challenge of running our household. I still pinch myself about my good fortune in marrying a man who was willing to serve as the primary parent in our family. (When young women ask me, "How did you do it?" I answer, "I married well.") During the campaign, Dan was virtually a single parent. The kids were so understanding of the demands on me and so supportive that I found myself missing them even more.

Complicating things further was the fact that my two full-time jobs were so utterly different from each other. For the campaign, Jill Alper had crafted a detailed, specific, week-by-week strategic plan complete with timelines, key phrases, message blocks, and scheduling. My job was simple and straightforward. It was to communicate one message: It's us against them, the little people against the big money, the public interest against narrow private interests. I had to tap emotions—the emotions of workers who had to fight for every little thing they got and the emotions of the more fortunate people who might be a generation or two removed from such struggle but who cared about fairness and opportunity. I had to paint my opponent with broad strokes: a Bush-backing, voucher-supporting, pro-life-no-exceptions-for-rape-or-incest, drown-government-in-a-bathtub, cut-taxes-for-the-wealthy, billionaire extremist. I put on my white hat and my Wonder Woman cape and set my mind to fighting like hell, no holds barred.

Governance was completely different from campaigning. As governor, I was executive, negotiator, strategist, deal-maker, and realist. That's what a governor does. She can't think in black-and-white, friends-and-enemies, my-way-or-the-high-way fashion. She has to try, somehow, to find common ground on which workable solutions can be built—a vital responsibility that simply becomes more difficult as the gap between campaign rhetoric and reality keeps getting wider. And when people are hurting, she and the thousands of workers at agencies around the state must respond to the fallout.

The gap between campaigning and governance can be a tricky one to straddle, as President Obama has surely discovered. The stark contrasts, vivid narratives, and uplifting emotions on which a campaign is built are a lot more exciting and energizing than the messy, complicated realities of governance. Once a politician takes office, the frustrating pace of progress and the constant need for compromise often leave his or her most enthusiastic supporters feeling disappointed, disillusioned, even alienated. Turning ardent campaigners into citizens actively engaged for the long haul is a delicate challenge, even for a naturally gifted leader like Barack Obama.

In 2006, both campaigning and governance were complicated by the seething anger among working people, which I glimpsed firsthand at campaign rallies throughout Michigan. One was at UAW Local 699 in Saginaw. The Delphi workers there were unemployed or labeled "temporary" as Delphi went through its bankruptcy restructuring and sale. The union hall lacked air-conditioning, so the back doors had been flung open, allowing a faint breeze to alleviate the stifling heat. Workers and their families were packed inside, spilling out onto the grass behind the building, waving disposable cardboard fans printed with American flags.

When I was introduced to speak, I felt their emotions rising and my emotions heightening, too. "We've seen our jobs leave on a fast track to Mexico, on a slow boat to China, and on the Internet to India!" I declared, fist pumping. The hall erupted in loud applause.

"NAFTA and CAFTA [Central America Free Trade Agreement] have given us the Shafta!" I shouted, and the crowd of workers roared in response, as if ready to tear the heads off of those who had made a profit by outsourcing jobs. I waited for them to settle down and for my own angry heart to slow.

"You've heard of 'No Child Left Behind'?" I asked.

"Yeah!" the crowd responded, and boos shook the rafters.

"Well, how about No *Worker* Left Behind?!" Workers in blue jeans and T-shirts thrust fists into the air, whooped and hollered, pumping their Granholm/Cherry campaign signs up and down.

"Do you want to elect a guy who outsourced jobs to China as your next governor?" I yelled.

"No!" thundered the crowd.

"He's an out-sorcerer!" a bearded guy in the front yelled. Those in the crowd around him were laughing and high-fiving.

"He's Lord Voldemort!" shouted a teenager in front. The crowd went wild.

Like any politician, I relished the opportunity to connect with voters and to defend the values we shared. But during those months in the run-up to reelection, I felt like two different people—preaching fire and brimstone on the campaign trail, then executing cool, calm, and objective actions on the job.

Every day I kept working my plan to "go anywhere and do anything" to bring jobs to Michigan. Some days the plan seemed to be showing results. Unfortunately, while our efforts were capturing once-a-week blips on the TV news or page 3B stories in the Michigan papers, DeVos's TV ads were in people's living rooms constantly, piling up the points that measure media impact, reminding people, "We're last in categories where we should be first" and promising he'd fix it. While I was working to keep Georgia Pacific from closing its paper plant in Gaylord, a small northern town that depended on those jobs, and incentivizing Whirlpool to bring Benton Harbor some of the eight hundred jobs from its acquisition of

Maytag, there was DeVos in his designer, next-door-neighbor red sweater nodding empathically as an unemployed working man in a ball cap talked about having to pay $1,000 in health care bills out of his pocket. Six months before the election and DeVos was already up to 700 points per week of advertising, a huge number in a state race and a level I had reached only in the final three *weeks* of my 2002 campaign.

My numbers kept eroding, while DeVos's name recognition and approval numbers were climbing. It was only a matter of time before his upward trend would cross my downward slide. Our campaign budget called for us to get on the air by mid-August, but we were behind in our fund-raising to get there.

"You just have to up your call time, Governor," campaign manager Howard Edelson told me.

But I couldn't subtract more hours from governing. I had already expanded my fund-raising call time to five hours a day, and I was getting only one in five people on the line, leaving messages, trying, retrying, and, when I finally hooked them, battling to land them in the boat.

Howard himself was making calls. So were other friends, my staff (volunteering their time during off-hours from their state duties), and Dan when he could. But to get to $10 or $15 million required big hitters, and those big hitters wanted to hear from and talk to *me*. If they were willing to give, they had campaign advice to dole out. And more and more they pressed me with the same opinion: "You've got to go up with ads, Governor. You can't let DeVos's voice be the only one. He's winning the race and it's only April."

My answer was always the same. "If we go up now, we can't sustain it. We can hit back, but it will be light and short. And then we'll let him see our positions and unload on us even harder. We have to wait."

On the governance side, we kept pushing for meaningful achievements. In April, with much fanfare, I signed rigorous new school curriculum standards into law, and throughout the spring we enjoyed daily successes in recruiting individual companies to set up shop in Michigan. But DeVos's ads kept up the drumbeat of negativity. By May, my polling margin was gone and the momentum had shifted to DeVos.

So I took the beating, absorbing the blows and getting weaker with each passing month. I felt my political life ebbing away. Dan became a quick-draw expert with the remote control to prevent our kids from being overwhelmed by the attack ads on their mother.

Outstanding, high-caliber citizens often shy away from electoral politics because they hate the idea of having to "get on the phone." But in our system, fund-raising is an essential political skill, one that has been made even more demanding by well-intentioned campaign finance laws. In Michigan, $3,400 is the maximum any one person can give to a candidate (and all checks must be personal, not corporate). The only exception to the limit is what a candidate can give to his or her own campaign. That giving is limitless. By the spring of 2006, we figured DeVos had already contributed about $20 million to his race, he had a well plenty deep enough to buy every available ad until the election, and there was no sign that he wouldn't keep tapping it. Just to match the $20 million he'd already given and spent, I would have to attract more than 5,800 individual donations at the maximum amount. Michigan just didn't have that kind of money.

So I went national. In June, I traveled to Philly to meet with a top Democratic fund-raiser who committed to raise $500,000 for me as a favor to my friend Pennsylvania governor Ed Rendell and my finance chair, Gary Torgow. I went from there to Washington, DC, to meet with the leaders of Emily's List, the national organization dedicated to electing pro-choice female Democrats to office. They said they'd try to raise another $500,000. The national AFL-CIO said it would try to do more. To cap off an encouraging week, after several days of playing phone tag with former President Bill Clinton, I finally reached him late one evening while waiting in the Detroit airport for a connecting flight to Traverse City, near the tip of Michigan's mitten. He promised to appear at a rally and two fund-raising events in July. As always, President Clinton was upbeat and optimistic, so our conversation left me feeling buoyed.

Returning home, I had a spring in my step as I moved through the Detroit airport. Then, on a moving sidewalk, I glimpsed a distorted image of myself in a DeVos commercial on a big screen carrying the local CNN feed. In an undisciplined moment, I watched the full ad, cringing. As I sat at the gate, a girl, perhaps twelve years old, had apparently just seen the commercial, too. She pointed at me, cupped her hand over her mouth, and whispered to her mother, "Mom, it's the job killer!"

I smiled and nodded at the girl, then opened my three-ring briefing book and raised it up to study my itinerary, conveniently burying my face from view of other travelers.

The next morning, while stopped at an intersection next to a gas station on my drive to work, I spotted a big banner headline in a rack filled with copies of the *Detroit Free Press*. It read, "DeVos Takes First Lead." The story underneath reported a poll that gave DeVos an eight-point edge.

On that day's conference call at the campaign office, Mellman was, as always, matter-of-fact. He could be a somber traveler when a new campaign was full of hope, but he was the steadiest guide when the bombs were falling all around. For one thing, he said, the group that had conducted the *Free Press* poll was notoriously inaccurate. It had been almost a month since our own pollsters had been in the field, but Mellman doubted the numbers were accurate.

"Mark, that doesn't fix the problem," I said, making my voice as matter-of-fact as his. "The poll numbers may be wrong, but they're in the headlines for voters and potential donors to see." And because Genna, like me, can't stand seeing a problem and not attacking it, she blurted out what most of us were thinking, "Are you *sure* we shouldn't go up on the air? Say, at low levels or for a short period of time? Even if it means we have to go dark in October?"

"Going dark in October would be a huge mistake," Mellman replied. "We've crafted a plan. Stay the course, Governor."

Sensing the team's flagging levels of optimism and energy, Jill tried to reassure us. "Gov, we knew this point was coming. We've got to keep our powder dry. You just had a kickass day raising money. With all our hard work, we can be up on the air in eight weeks. We're gonna be all right."

"Eight weeks, Jill?!" Dan exclaimed. "She may not have a pulse in eight weeks."

Jill responded quickly, "We're back in the field with a poll in, what, two weeks, Mark?"

"We'll have *results* in three weeks," Mark said.

"I'll bet you even then our numbers will be better than what the *Free Press* is saying," Jill said. Her confident tone conveyed her deep electoral experience. "For now, DeVos can define himself and affect how people see you. But he can't inoculate himself against the truth. And people have their own experience of you. He can't totally shape that. Even if he is still ahead by then, that gap will close."

I appreciated the bucking up. "I hope you're right, Jill," I said, wishing we had hard data to back up our hopes.

Jill took one more shot. "Look at it this way, Governor," she said in a lighter tone. "The silver lining is that this poll will wake up our donors! It'll get them motivated."

"Yep. We'll be all right, everyone," I declared, projecting confidence but, knowing from my own experience that the headline would make my calls harder, not easier. I kept that thought to myself. I glanced at the *No Whining* button I had pinned on my bulletin board. *Accept, adjust, advance.*

Meanwhile, Dan and I were passing like ships in the night. He got Cece off to a basketball camp at Olivet College and took Kate, heading into her senior year of high school, to a lacrosse camp at Ohio State. Dan was doing a lot of public speaking on topics like bottom-up leadership, faith and politics, and women in government. He'd pinch-hit for me occasionally at Democratic gatherings and do commencement speeches. He was also finishing edits on his first book, *Everyday Leadership: Getting Results in Business, Politics, and Life*. He'd been elected chair of the Spouses Leadership Committee of the National Governors Association, so, with Jack at camp, he and Cece went down to the govs' summer meeting in Charleston, South Carolina. With the campaign in full swing, there was no way I could break away for that.

The day after the polling confab, Dan got home after 3:00 AM. I was up before 5:00 to do a call-in radio interview with Paul W. Smith, Detroit's biggest morning drive-time host. Smith's radio home, WJR, "The Great Voice of the Great Lakes," had abandoned decades of balanced coverage to steer to the political right, which meant the conversation might be a contentious one, even though Smith and I liked and enjoyed each other. Around 7:30, Dan got up to find me at the bathroom sink, halfway through the interview and growing more irritated by the minute. Dan listened as I responded to Smith's friendly provocations.

"Paul W," I was saying, "it's *not* all about taxes! We've reduced taxes over and over again. If that's all it took, we'd be swimming in jobs." Pause.

"No, that's *not* what I'm saying," I responded. I went back at him, annoyance in my tone, talking in detail about business taxes. When I finished, I gave Smith a curt thank-you, then nearly slammed the phone down. I rarely got that steamed.

"Babe, you open to some feedback?"

I turned my head just a little sideways and with a deceptive air of calm replied, "Sure, tell me what I could have done better."

The usually sensitive Dan completely missed my sarcasm and the cauldron of frustration beneath its lid. He opened fire: "I think you'd get past Paul W to the voters better if you did two things." He started to criticize my irritated tone and my lapse into jargon. My irritation must have sent extra blood to my cheeks, not to mention smoke from my ears, because he stopped suddenly and said, "What? What? What's going on?"

"Dan," I told him, very quietly, "could you just once tell me what you think I should say *before* I go on the air instead of *after?*"

Dan was crestfallen. "I'm so sorry," he said. The hug we shared was well meant, but real closeness seemed impossible. Overstressed, under siege, we were both on edge and hiding behind impregnable emotional barriers—even from each other.

The pressures of that campaign season were as tough on Dan as they were on me. The gender-role reversal we were living through and the stresses it created were happening to families all over Michigan. As manufacturing jobs kept disappearing, along with other "men's jobs" that had moved the economy for decades—truck-driving, toolmaking, and house-building—talented women were in greater demand (though rarely earning enough to make up for their partners' lost wages).

Our circumstances were different, of course. Dan had voluntarily let his business go in order to support my career. He loved the kids and was completely engaged with them. But I knew he hated being out of the action. Like millions of men, he'd been wired from birth to think and strategize and compete, but now he'd been forced to tend to the home, leading quietly and far from the limelight (he would quickly point out, "as women have done for centuries"). As I grappled with Michigan's problems, Dan was quietly suffering in his unaccustomed role, the behind-the-scenes leader in a "woman's world."

· · · · ·

I HEADED OFF TO A FULL DAY AND EVENING IN GRAND RAPIDS, Dan to the campaign office and then to a sports physical with Jack. He called me in the evening. "I'm sneaking in to the ad tests," he told me. He was talking about a secret trial run of our long-awaited ads with focus groups. "I've got my Tigers hat and sunglasses on so I don't get recognized by one of the subjects and blow the whole test. The secrecy cracks me up. Will you make it back for some of it?" he asked.

"I had no idea it was today," I replied. "Take good notes," I told him. "I want to hear everything."

Three hours later, Dan called me with his report. Around sixty paid participants had spent the evening being watched from behind a one-way mirror by Mark Mellman, Joe Slade White (our prize-winning ad producer), Jill Alper, Rick Wiener, Genna Gent, Howard Edelson, Chuck Wilbur, my campaign chair David Baker Lewis, and Dan. They'd seen half a dozen rough cuts of ads we expected to run, four of DeVos's ads that were already running, and a couple of sharply negative ads, samples of the kind we thought DeVos might run against me down the stretch.

"It was fascinating," Dan told me. "The participants had dials to turn up or down during the ads to show how likely they were to vote for or against you or DeVos and how believable they found the ads. So we're watching the graphs moving like EKGs—in real time. And the results were wild. People might love an ad for twelve seconds, then suddenly get turned off by some word or image, and pow! the graph line would plummet. Incredible stuff." Afterward, there was a focus group at which one of Mellman's staff interviewed an assortment of individuals to add flavor and texture to their choices.

"So what's the bottom line?" I asked.

"Bad news and good news," Dan summarized. People simply did not believe the claim from my State of the State speech—one that I had repeated at least 250 times in speeches and radio inter-

views and that was absolutely factual—that we had created or retained over 300,000 jobs. "It's not just that they don't believe it,
Jen," Dan emphasized. "They actually turned their test dials down
to 'makes me less likely to vote for her.'"

"You've got to be kidding me," I said. We were struggling to
make up for an endless stream of job losses, and people didn't even
believe in the modest successes we'd achieved?

"But wait, here's the good news. It turns out DeVos's ads are
quite effective . . . "

"That's the *good* news?" I broke in.

"No, the good news is that they like DeVos's ads about him being a job creator, but then when they hear about DeVos's investments in China and his laying off workers in Grand Rapids, his
numbers fall right off the table. They reacted *much* more negatively
over his outsourcing and layoffs than they did to *anything* they
heard about you. They felt he was a hypocrite. He's been spending
millions building up his job-creation cred, and when voters hear the
truth, they're furious at having been duped."

"And what about our economic plan?" I inquired. We couldn't
just attack—we had to give people a reason to vote *for* me. I said,
"We've been saying I'll 'go anywhere and do anything, we're
diversifying, we have a plan.'"

"That was the wildest part. When we talked about 300,000
jobs, they turned the dials way down, but when the ads talked
about very specific jobs—about so-and-so at Electrolux who got
retrained . . . "

"You mean John Pella?"

"Yes, that's when they turned the dials up. That *moves* them.
Small is big. When a test ad talks about a specific trip to Japan to
bring back specific companies—preferably just handfuls of jobs—
well, that they like, and they believe it strongly."

What's more, Dan explained, Mark found the results utterly
unsurprising. "Mellman says there's just too much experience that

things are real bad for people to believe that they're getting better *fast*. What matters is stories of real people. Stories. Small stories." Dan continued, "I think people believe in you. They believe you're a person of faith, honest, and your scores on 'cares about me' are very strong. We really can win this, Jen."

"And one other thing was amazing," Dan added. "They are just not following this campaign yet. They have only the *vaguest* notion of what's going on."

"What makes you say that?" I asked.

Dan explained that a focus group of fifteen "persuadables" who stayed around to talk had no idea what I'd done on education—the tougher standards I'd imposed, the fights with the legislature I'd won, the early childhood support I'd established. "One kid from Macomb told them you'd slashed money for community colleges. People nodded until an older guy said he thought he remembered some news story about you pushing for 'a promissory scholarship or something like that.'" Dan continued, "It's funny. People started believing the older guy then—not because they remembered the news, but because the young guy was so obviously full of himself and the older fellow had said other things that made sense."

"Wow," I said, shaking my head. "So it means—"

"It means there's no room for subtlety in this, Jen. Keep the story simple, simple, simple. People don't follow details."

My spirits were lifted by Dan's enthusiasm and his advice. Maybe there was hope that we could get through to voters after all.

But things continued to get worse. Manufacturing jobs were still draining out of Michigan—and the country. The unemployment rate edged up for four straight months beginning in April. DeVos's most-played ad used the ill-fated footage from my State of the State address. After reciting dismal statistics on job losses, the gravel-voiced announcer asked sardonically, "Are you blown away yet?"

The DeVos team also cleverly snagged a clip from a Democratic state convention speech I'd given. After listing all the new companies we'd attracted, I'd concluded, "Our plan is working." Excised from its context and surrounded with gloom and doom headlines, it made more great fodder for sarcastic parody.

Running as the incumbent, I'd discovered, was a lot different from running as the challenger. Four years earlier, I'd promised the voters that I'd fix everything that ailed Michigan. I'd believed I could do it, too. Now I had to answer for why it wasn't all fixed. Meanwhile, DeVos was telling people that *he* would be able to fix things quickly, which of course is exactly what the voters wanted to hear. They didn't know how the fixing could get done, nor did they care. They just wanted things fixed—now.

In times of crisis, voters look for a superhero. Sometimes, as with Arnold Schwarzenegger or Jesse Ventura, they'll even elect a fictional superhero to fill the role. Sometimes they place their hope in the "proven business executive" who assures them that methods from the private sector can work magic in government—a Mitt Romney, a Michael Bloomberg, or a Dick DeVos. (The notion that a state or a nation can be run the same as a corporation, though profoundly flawed, has become increasingly popular in Republican circles in recent years, part and parcel of the simplistic "government bad/business good" dichotomy so beloved by the right.)

Four years earlier, I'd fit right into the superhero storyline. I'd filled the role of "smart, tough-talking woman prosecutor"—an action figure straight from an episode of *Law and Order*. But when a crisis is caused by deeply rooted, long-term, structural problems, no superhero cape or magic wand will make everything better. Once elected, the politician is immediately thrown on the defensive, forced to explain why problems persist. And Dick DeVos was demanding those explanations.

We headed into the debates—three chances, beginning on October 2, for me to challenge the falsehoods and misconceptions

I felt were being perpetrated. DeVos wouldn't be able to hide behind his generalizations any longer—but I also knew he'd try to take me down and crush any remaining hope I had for a come-from-behind victory.

The debate preparation sessions, moderated by David Baker Lewis, a thoughtful, high-profile lawyer and my campaign's general chairman, heightened my defensiveness. Playing the role of DeVos, Rick Wiener went for the jugular. He ended every exchange with the words "And, Governor, you didn't get it done." At first, I got angry and bellicose, clenching my teeth and my fists, but gradually, as Rick intended, I became desensitized to the attack. Nevertheless, I couldn't hear the line without experiencing a surge of anger.

Two nights before the first debate, I had a moment of weakness when I allowed DeVos's ads to penetrate my armor. It was after 11:00, and I was having my nightly glass of red wine and a little pity party before I conked out. "I'm doing everything I can to turn this state around and to win a chance to keep trying," I said to Dan. "But it all seems so futile." I probably wasn't looking for a response. But Dan was irrepressible.

"Jen, it's illogical and, frankly, egotistical to think you alone have the power to fix this state," Dan chided me.

"But I'm the governor. It's my job. I'm *supposed* to fix it. If I'd voted for a governor in this kind of situation, I'd expect him to fix it. Who else but me is responsible?"

"There's no one person who can fix this," Dan said. "It's got to be all of us—teachers, entrepreneurs, workers, managers . . . everybody. Our job—*your* job—is to get people to come to grips with that hard fact. This is an 'Ask not' moment, like Kennedy's inauguration—'Ask not what your country can do for you.' Why not take a big risk and challenge people?"

"I know," I said with a sigh. "We need the people to do some of this work. But people want to be rescued. They want hope. They want a savior."

I tried the argument on my debate team the next morning. "Maybe this is an 'Ask not' moment," I said, echoing Dan's words. "I think I should tell people straight up that this administration alone can't fix this problem. No administration can. We need to be candid about the citizens' role. We need a paradigm shift in Michigan. We need everybody to realize that the road from an old economy to a new one is long and hard, and everyone has to be a part of it or it won't happen." I was on a roll. "The old manufacturing jobs aren't coming back. Citizens need to be retrained. *And we're doing that*! They need to send their kids to college. Education will allow us to recruit new, diverse industries, and our higher standards will make a difference. But the big message is that we're all in this boat—so all of our people need to pick up an oar and row." I stopped.

There was a long silence in the room.

Chuck Wilbur cleared his throat. "Hmmm. Governor, I'm just not sure that telling people that you can't fix their problems is a good election strategy."

"And, Governor," cautioned Genna, "just know that if we tell them those things, it will sound harsh and preachy to people who are already hurting. You have to be candid with people. But when they have the choice of hearing DeVos say that he's a businessman with a turnaround plan and he'll take care of things for them or hearing you say that the *citizens* have to do the work, guess who will be the next governor?"

"You have to pace their learning," agreed Jill. "Just wait until after November, or you won't have the opportunity to tell anyone anything."

The impracticality of the "Ask not" message was clear. Yet there was more. A big part of me agreed with those impatient voters. I, too, still wanted to believe that I could single-handedly pull off an economic miracle. My false hopes and those of the voters—reinforced by the analytical arguments of my clear-eyed political advisors—cast the die.

We would stick to our strategy. As Jill had mapped out long ago, I would tout my plan and try to paint the newest would-be hero as the villain. I would go after DeVos in the debates with gusto. I would push him on exporting jobs as CEO of Amway. I would blame him for George Bush's lack of an economic strategy, talking about how he and his wife were Bush's biggest contributors. "So tell us," I would challenge, "do you endorse this national economic policy that's devastating our jobs and our manufacturing businesses? Do you support the unfair trade agreements that have moved our jobs to Mexico, India, and China? Whose side are you on, anyway?" I was no superhero, but I was also firmly convinced that DeVos wasn't either.

When I launched these salvos in our first debate, DeVos looked stunned. For fifteen months, he'd had the freedom to recite soliloquies, to attack me and our down-in-the-dumps state, and to avoid the negative parts of his own record. Now he seemed surprised at my attacks and unprepared to respond. I didn't resist his counterattack charging that things were awful in Michigan, but I shot back with more questions about DeVos: Who and what had made things so bad for working people? Who had a plan to make things better? And what was in the plan?

Politically, our debate strategy worked. One reporter quipped to me that our first face-off should have been dubbed "The Pantsing in East Lansing." The consensus was that I had won the debate.

After our three face-offs, DeVos's momentum was stalled. But intellectually and philosophically, I was disappointed that the real, complex issues facing Michigan were seldom illuminated. DeVos promised tax cuts, but he wouldn't say how he would fund them. That was a tough-choice reality I had to confront every day, assessing, for example, the wisdom of a tax on services versus a broader business tax versus deep and potentially risky cuts to our mushrooming state prison system. It would have been valuable for thought-leaders, journalists, and citizens to ponder such trade-offs and examine how such choices reflect our deeper values and convictions about the roles of government and the kind of society we want to live in. I didn't raise all the hard choices either. Unfortunately, American political campaigns don't reward that sort of thoughtful analysis. If anything, they punish those who attempt it.

Dick DeVos and I both chose not to tell people the things that deep down we both knew to be true: that fixing Michigan was not going to be quick and easy, that our loss of manufacturing jobs was beyond the control of any governor, that we lived in a world that would never again allow high wages for low-skilled work, that business leaders ranked a state or country's welfare well below the good of their shareholders and their executives, and that no governor could shield his or her citizens from this world.

It's not that either DeVos or I wanted to hide the truth from the citizens. We raised and spent almost $100 million to reach out to voters. Yet we did little to challenge people. Instead, we were both guilty of feeding two appetites: the expectations of a citizenry hungry for jobs, yearning for security, and dreaming of a savior; and our own egos.

The debates ended. Two weeks before the election, Mellman began doing small nightly polling samples. And as the fence-sitters and apathetic voters began to pay attention, voters began to climb down on our side of the divide. Since September, we had been hitting the airwaves with the ads that our focus groups had predicted would be effective. Joe Slade White had fashioned one particularly powerful commercial:

Image of a ticker tape parade with confetti. John Phillip Sousa patriotic march plays in background.

Voiceover: "If someone announced tomorrow he was investing $200 million to open factories and create jobs in Michigan, well, he'd be treated like a hero, right?"

Fade in headshot of Dick DeVos in gold picture frame.

Voiceover: "Might even want to run for governor. So when Dick DeVos invested $200 million in creating thousands of jobs, where did he do it?"

Fade to black.

Voiceover: "China."

Image of provincial China. Sound of large gong. Chinese music in background.

Voiceover: "Do you suppose maybe there's a province in China that's looking for a governor?"

The ad drew blood. It offered no subtlety, no nuance, no shades of gray. The rational reasons for a business to invest in China were ignored. Our campaign drew a stark comparison: DeVos had eliminated jobs in Michigan and created them in China, while I had gone to Asia and brought jobs home to Michigan. DeVos was not the solution—he was the problem.

DeVos tried to deflect the barrage we fired at his Amway record. He argued that the Chinese jobs he created weren't caused by or even related to the layoffs he had engineered in Michigan. But the distinction rang hollow. People mistrusted someone who'd benefited from a net loss of good Michigan jobs.

There's an old campaign adage, loosely based on the teachings of Sun Tzu's *Art of War,* that Jill often quoted: "When your foot is on the throat of your enemy, press harder." So we pressed harder, with a second crushing commercial:

Black screen: Image of Dick DeVos in a gilded frame, dollar bills raining down behind picture.

Voiceover: "Dick DeVos and his family have made millions of dollars in political contributions to elect the President and members of Congress. So when Dick DeVos lobbied Congress, what did he ask for?"

Black screen with white script: "Dick DeVos lobbied for unfair trade agreements that outsourced tens of thousands of jobs overseas."

Fade to image of Chinese Amway factory.

Voiceover: "The same Dick DeVos who created thousands of jobs in China."

Black screen with coin dropping, spinning. White script: "Good for Dick DeVos. But how's it working out . . . for you?"

Our ads redirected the anger DeVos had turned toward me right back on him.

On election night, the results were stunning. The governor of the state with the nation's highest unemployment rate, who'd had more than $40 million spent in attack ads against her—more than in any governor's race in the country—came from behind to win the race by fourteen points, receiving more votes than any governor in Michigan history.

The newspaper headlines the next morning blared, "Blown Away!" Mellman's finger was ever on the pulse; his last polls were right in sync with the results. Jill Alper, Joe Slade White, Howard Edelson, and the campaign team won several national "best-managed campaign" awards and widespread acclaim for their brilliant strategy and media. They were ecstatic, and deservedly so.

But in our suite at the hotel on campaign night, despite the scope of our victory, no one was jumping on the bed.

chapter 6

BLOWING UP TAXES, BUDGETS, MIND-SETS . . . AND MATTRESSES

MY NEW TERM IN OFFICE BEGAN WITH A NEW CRISIS—YET
another battle with legislative leaders over the coming year's
budget. Michigan is one of just ten states to employ a full-time
legislature. From the governor's perspective, it's a mixed blessing.
In contentious times or with a divided government, a full-time
legislature often means full-time opposition to anything and
everything the governor might propose. And by 2007, we were
living through contentious times indeed.

For five years, we'd been cutting virtually everything that
moved, but with tax revenues tanking thanks to the collapse of the
auto industry and much of the rest of our manufacturing base, we
had another new hole of $1.7 billion. With the budget deadline
looming, the members of the legislature were crossing their fingers

that someone would save them from the agony of voting for even deeper spending cuts or tax increases. In their heart of hearts, they knew they'd have to do both.

The deepening recession wasn't the only cause of our problems. We'd tightened the handcuffs even further through repeated tax cuts on the popular theory that "smaller government" would stimulate economic growth. It hadn't worked. The agony we were living through in Michigan was just one manifestation of a nationwide ailment—the gradual loss of our ability to communicate rationally about taxes, spending, and the role of government.

Antitax fervor has a long history in this country. As every schoolchild learns (and as today's Tea Partiers are happy to remind us), rebellion against the taxes imposed under the Stamp Act was one of the galvanizing forces that led to the American Revolution—although it's often forgotten that it was the authoritarian and undemocratic process by which those taxes were imposed, rather than the mere fact of taxation, that stirred our forefathers' anger.

A sharp change in political rhetoric as well as public attitudes toward taxation can be traced back to 1980. That was the year Ronald Reagan defeated President Jimmy Carter after a campaign in which Reagan repeatedly promised Americans that he could simultaneously increase defense spending, reduce the burgeoning deficit, *and* cut taxes—a piece of implausible legerdemain that even Reagan's eventual running mate, George H. W. Bush, had derided as "voodoo economics." Nevertheless, Reagan won the election.

Four years later, his opponent Walter Mondale, trailing badly in the polls and exasperated with Reagan's continuing illogic, declared in his Democratic Convention acceptance speech that, without an increase in taxes, America's debt would only grow worse. I remember feeling proud when Mondale forthrightly told America the truth as he saw it: "Mr. Reagan will raise taxes, and so will I. He won't tell you. I just did."

Unfortunately, most of the voters didn't share my reaction. Reagan dealt Mondale the largest electoral college defeat in Democratic Party history. Of course, Reagan *did* sign a massive tax increase into law, largely glossed over in histories as well as American political memories, rolling back about half of his initial, untenable cuts; he also imposed higher taxes on gasoline and raised taxes to stabilize Social Security. Reagan's tax hikes weren't enough to offset an even bigger expansion in military spending. Reagan's policies produced record deficits, tripling the national debt in that time to $2.6 trillion.

Some might assume that the political lesson from those eight years would have been that maybe sometimes we have to pay higher taxes to maintain vital services. Perhaps a new, more informed national conversation would have arisen, focusing on questions like "Should we condemn *all* taxes? Are all taxes really the same? Are there ways to raise revenues while encouraging economic growth and practicing fundamental economic fairness?"

No such dialogue took place. Instead, politicians learned precisely the opposite lesson—that honest discussion of taxes was inevitably fatal to a candidate's chances. In 1988, presidential nominee George H. W. Bush outdid Reagan. Reading lines provided to him by Reagan's speechwriter Peggy Noonan during his speech at the Republican National Convention, Bush mocked his opponent Michael Dukakis, who'd referred to raising taxes as a "third resort" or "last resort." Then Bush made his seemingly unequivocal four-year promise: "Read my lips: No New Taxes."

Of course, we know the reality that followed. In 1990, President Bush said that, owing to rising deficits, he might have to reconsider raising "revenues." (This is the vaguer term that pollsters say produces a milder case of voter revulsion than the dreaded "taxes.") When Bush followed through with a (necessary) tax increase, Republican voters turned on him in fury. Since then, politicians and the political media have insisted ever more doggedly on "no-tax pledges" from candidates, especially on the Republican side, and politicians, including me, continue to replace the word "taxes" with the kinder, gentler "revenues," even as voter anger and cynicism about the whole charade keep growing.

The same game we've seen at the national level has also played out in the states, though each state has its own unique history, drama, and lore that shape all the discussion—and discussion avoidance—around taxes. Today's state-level tax revolution exploded out of California in 1978 with the controversial Proposition 13, which capped property taxes at 1 percent of a home's assessed value and required a two-thirds legislative majority at the state and local level to raise any other tax. These restrictions have crippled the efforts of lawmakers to bring fiscal stability to California and have driven the state to the brink of bankruptcy repeatedly, most recently, as I write these words, in early 2011.

Michigan had its own late-1970s tax rebellion. In 1978, Michigan voters enacted the Headlee Amendment, which tied state tax revenues to state income, so that the government could capture no greater percentage of state income in taxes than it was receiving at that time—roughly 9 percent. Michigan's legislature, unlike California's, was not required to produce a supermajority to raise taxes, but it was constitutionally bound to tax and spend below the Headlee cap.

Almost immediately, a tough recession descended, and the state deficit rose to $685 million in 1983. (Adjusted for inflation, that was about $300 million less than the average $1.7 billion deficit we faced for each of the four years of my first term.) Newly elected governor Jim Blanchard, a Democrat, decided to tackle the beast. Although he'd promised during the campaign that a tax increase would be "a last resort," within three months of his inauguration the situation was so dire he called for a temporary 38 percent hike in the income tax to balance the budget as states are constitutionally required to do. With the crucial support of a single Republican vote, the legislature passed the increase. Suburban voters rebelled, mounting recall efforts against state senators who'd supported the measure, and Senators Phil Mastin and David Serotkin were overwhelmingly ousted—the first time in Michigan history that voters had recalled a senator. In the special election to fill Mastin's and Serotkin's seats, control of the Senate flipped to the Republicans, and there it has remained for the ensuing three decades.

Those recalls are burned deep into Michigan's political consciousness, and the Republicans and the media raised the same specter during my first run for governor in 2002. They reminded voters how Blanchard had broken his "last resort" promise and insisted I would follow suit. I'd avoided at all costs taking a pledge not to increase taxes, but I'd said clearly, frequently, and loudly that we would cut government spending, and when I was thrown into the budget morass in my first month in office, I did just that. We used spending cuts to resolve a $280 million shortfall that year and a $2.8 billion deficit the next. After adopting a cut-laden budget, I was forced to make further midyear cuts in 2004 and then more in the 2005 and 2006 budgets.

The spending cuts during my first four years in office were largely the inevitable consequence of the tax cuts pushed through by my predecessor, John Engler, in the late 1990s. With the state flush with revenues, those cuts sounded reasonable at the time. Lower taxes *of course* meant more money available for private-sector spending and investment. Thus, by lowering taxes, we promoted investment by existing companies, encouraged the formation of new companies, and attracted outside companies to our state. And during Engler's terms in office, the formula seemed to be working. The booming national economy generated higher sales, income, and property taxes in Michigan, as elsewhere, and with consumers flocking to buy SUVs, the Michigan-based auto industry was thriving.

When the boom of the 1990s ended—as booms inevitably

do—the impact of the tax cuts on state budgets suddenly hit home. Without the cushion of an ever-growing economy, lower tax rates now meant less money for state services. And that meant budget cuts, cuts on top of cuts, and then still more cuts.

I had come into office believing that we had some open notches on our spending belt and that we could cinch it tighter. We had done that. I cut government more than any governor in the history of Michigan, and Michigan cut more (in percentage terms) than any other state in the nation. We went from bumping up against the Headlee spending limits to a whopping $6 billion below those limits. By 2007, we had 11,000 fewer state employees than in 2001—our state workforce hadn't been this small since 1972—and workers had given $600 million back in concessions through unpaid furlough days, wage givebacks, and increased benefit contributions. It wasn't fun, but people adjusted.

For my first four years in office, from 2003 through 2006, I remained convinced that the people, as well as the legislators who represented them, were just not ready for new taxes. My team was unified behind this austerity approach. I don't remember a single time during my first term when a staff or cabinet member argued on behalf of a general tax increase. Just the opposite: Through 2007, I had signed into law ninety-nine different kinds of business tax credits, deductions, and tax cuts, as well as seventeen different tax cuts for individuals.* The cumulative effect was that our real tax revenues were at the levels of those in the 1960s.

The austerity produced some positive benefits. Once again, I found myself quoting Kouzes and Posner: "Only challenge produces the opportunity for greatness." The challenges we faced prodded us to devise creative solutions. For example, we developed a prisoner reentry program that shifted resources away from incarcerating nonviolent criminals to preparing and supporting

---

* See the appendix on p. 277 for a complete list of these tax cuts.

them upon release. This program ultimately allowed us to close thirteen prison facilities—more than any other state in the nation, by far—and saved us $250 million per year. At the same time, the crime rate and recidivism actually decreased.

Necessity proved the mother of invention, giving birth to all kinds of savings. Even as we eliminated one-quarter of the state's departments, we sought out opportunities to move services on-line, eventually winning awards from the Center for Digital Government as most digital state in the nation (in 2004, 2005, 2006, 2007, and 2010) and as Best of the Web (2006). The financial pressure we put on local governments, schools, and institutions of higher education also forced them to find new efficiencies, including creative approaches to sharing services and consolidating operations.

But the cuts also took a heavy toll. Classroom sizes increased. College tuition costs soared. Police forces were thinned out. Arts funding was essentially eliminated. Park services and environmental enforcement were strained. Caseworkers for fragile families found themselves saddled with rosters of five to seven hundred clients. Training and travel budgets for state workers basically disappeared. Worker morale, creativity, and excellence all suffered.

"It's amazing how things have changed," Dan said to me at dinner one night. "We Democrats have completely capitulated to the conservative line on financing government. New taxes and revenue increases are off the table. We're playing the game by the rules of the strangle-government crowd. Yet the voters don't seem to think anything has changed."

I nodded in agreement. "I know. I bought into it, too. Here we are cutting through muscle and into the bone. But most voters seem to imagine there's all kinds of fat still left on the carcass. Still, I wouldn't mind if the cuts had produced economic growth. But where is it?"

That was the haunting question. For a decade, Michigan's leaders, Democrats and Republicans alike, had steered by the belief that lower taxes would invariably increase investment, growth, and jobs and eventually generate more tax revenue. Unfortunately, we were learning that this belief *simply wasn't true.* Even as Michigan had greatly reduced its tax burden relative to other states, its economy fell further and further behind. This was no statistical anomaly. The assumption that tax cuts would create jobs had major flaws looming beneath its shiny surface.

To be clear, the cuts *did* create many jobs . . . but not necessarily in America. Michigan's tax cuts, and those championed by President George Bush at the national level, freed up capital for investors and companies. But much of that capital was being invested far from Michigan and away from our country altogether. My morning news clips constantly featured stories like one on May 6 from Monroe, a small town near the Ohio border. The story described how the Michigan Economic Development Corporation was working to attract Chinese investment to Michigan. It noted that hometown La-Z-Boy was now importing nearly all its wooden furniture from China, which was in the process of building massive, state-of-the-art furniture factories.

In our gubernatorial contest, Dick DeVos had argued that the 1,400 jobs he created in China were unrelated to his layoffs in America. But the effect was the same: Freed-up capital was flowing abroad. Rationally, I understood the economic pressures that drove companies to low-cost countries like China, India, and Mexico. What I didn't get was how the doctrinaire free-marketers assumed that every penny in tax cuts would get invested in Michigan. The notion was flawed in theory as well as in practice.

The argument that a state's tax environment in comparison with that of other states would be crucial in determining its economic competitiveness was also true—but only to a point. Since 1975, Michigan had utilized a Single Business Tax (SBT) that was the country's only gross receipts tax—essentially a value-added pay-roll tax that discouraged hiring. A clear disadvantage to Michigan in competition with other states, one would assume. But we'd had the SBT during good and bad times, including the go-go 1990s, when Michigan unemployment hovered around 3 percent, and the tax hadn't discouraged investment in Michigan then.

That tax became campaign fodder in 2006, and it was replaced in June 2007 with the Michigan Business Tax (MBT), which was weighted more toward profits and particularly generous to our troubled manufacturing sector. Although 60 percent of Michigan businesses saw a net tax cut under the MBT, it did not spur an increase in business investment in Michigan, nor did it slow the loss of manufacturing jobs.

The reality unmasked the rhetoric: The loss of jobs in Michigan in the decade from 2000 to 2010 was directly related not to taxes but to globalization, productivity-boosting technological innovations, and the loss of market share by U.S. automakers. According to a survey by the Michigan Senate Fiscal Agency, the corporate and personal income tax burden in Michigan during 1999–2009 fell more than in any other state in the country—from twelfth highest to thirty-ninth in the case of corporate taxes and from sixteenth to thirtieth in the case of state and local taxes—yet people and businesses were still exiting our increasingly inexpensive state.

Some argued that the rush by businesses to invest in bargain-basement operations overseas would at least benefit American consumers by bringing them more affordable products. But those cheap products cost more than their price tags suggested. Michiganders who lost their jobs making refrigerators at Electrolux or auto parts at Delphi got replacement jobs at a fraction of the wages they had been making before. So even though they had access to cheaper goods, their standard of living had fallen precipitously. Thanks to our loss of manufacturing jobs, Michigan led the nation in per capita income decline, plummeting from eighteenth in the nation in 2000 to thirty-seventh by 2008. In other words, a graph depicting our tax burden competitiveness and our per capita income would show them moving in nearly *opposite* directions.

Our politicians who lamented the decline of the middle class were accomplices. The George W. Bush administration was deliberately passive in the face of manufacturing job losses in America. That hands-off strategy, combined with poorly crafted trade agreements that facilitated the offshoring of jobs and increased the availability of cheap foreign products without regard for the consequences on Main Street, contributed to our huge trade deficit and to the hollowing out of the American middle class.

The notion that tax cuts are the magic elixir of business growth also ignores the realities of contemporary business. As one of our college interns remarked one day, "The old tax-cuts-only mind-set is *so* twentieth century." In twenty-first-century knowledge-based economies, tax rates play a minor role in business location decisions. For the kinds of advanced-manufacturing, high-tech businesses we were recruiting, *talent* is what matters. And our local economic development agencies, like Ann Arbor Spark, Detroit's Tech Town, and the West Michigan Business Alliance, have found that quality of life, culture, and the sheer "coolness" factor of host cities are also key to those decisions. Companies need to recruit smart, ambitious executives, scientists, engineers, and innovators—people who want to live in cool cities with exciting things to do and great schools for their kids. And where do talented young employees and the cool cities that attract them come from? From public investments in schools, the arts, universities, and training—the very things we've been cutting for years under the influence of the mantra "Government doesn't create jobs. Only the private sector creates jobs." It's a half-truth we've swallowed whole for much too long.

Business tax rates do make a difference. I know—I had to use them constantly as a competitive tool in the race against other states to attract clusters of businesses and jobs. In July 2006 when Google announced its decision to open a major research facility in Ann Arbor—a city selected from fifty candidates around the nation—a favorable tax plan negotiated with Michigan played a role. But access to the talent coming from the University of Michigan was a far more important factor to Google. Further up the value chain, if Carl and Gloria Page—the father and mother of Google cofounder Larry Page—hadn't taught in the Computer Science Department at Michigan State University, and if young Larry hadn't been schooled at East Lansing High School, it's quite likely we would not have Google creating jobs in Michigan today. Tax-funded investments in great public schools and universities did much more to fuel Google's innovations than did marginally lower corporate tax rates. Public investments play an extraordinary role in generating our most essential form of capital: human capital.

Business leaders know this. At a National Governors Association meeting in 2001, when Carly Fiorina was running Hewlett-Packard (and long before she became a candidate for the U.S. Senate), she told the governors, "Keep your tax incentives and highway interchanges; we will go where the highly skilled people are." CEOs like IBM's Lou Gerstner have warned, "We have a global competition for high-paying, high-return jobs, and America is not investing in the skills to get to that higher level." Today, with continual, angry calls from the Tea Party crowd for more tax cuts and government downsizing, there will be further disinvestment in higher education and other talent-creating resources across America. Why aren't leaders from the business community, who understand the critical importance of investing in America's talent, pushing back? Perhaps it's because multinational companies can meet their need for talent by expanding overseas. So why push against the tide and beg to be taxed at higher rates, especially when conservatives in Congress are practically pushing tax cuts on corporations and the wealthy?

The ones who really suffer are American workers.

Michigan learned from bitter experience the power of public-sector investments being made by America's rivals. Starting in 2004, more cars were built in Ontario, Canada, than in Michigan. But automakers weren't moving to Canada because they liked Canadian taxes and regulations. Canadian-generated tax competitiveness reports showed that Michigan was much more attractive than Ontario and five other American states being benchmarked. They were moving to Canada because health care costs there are borne by the entire country rather than by individual businesses. Examples like this reveal the lie hidden within the half-truth that the only investments that matter are private-sector investments.

In 2007, I decided to stop putting all our chips on the cut-taxes square on the policy game board. My administration adopted a new threefold strategy: We'd identify and implement the most efficient, forward-looking, and competitive taxes; we'd search for the most politically palatable ways to raise revenues for the purpose of investing in talent retention and job creation; and we'd take our case for this new program to the people. I recruited a bipartisan panel of blue-ribbon government and budgetary experts, including former Democratic and Republican governors, my Republican predecessor's first budget director and treasurer, and experts from universities and foundations. I asked them to assess our dire budget situation, with no ideological limitations or preconditions, and deliver recommendations within sixty days. Then we sent our pollster into the field. As the blue-ribbon group assembled, we got our first round of polling results. A memo from Jill Alper summarized the findings. Her first three points read as follows:

1. Voters do not perceive the fiscal crisis.
2. Voters oppose tax increases.
3. Voters reject the view that program cuts or tax increases are required, believing that wise leadership that cuts waste can solve the problem.

Aauuggh! People still thought there was waste to cut. Was it the preceding year of happy talk from Dick DeVos about how he would eliminate the red ink with no pain? Was it my fault for projecting confidence through my optimistic assurances that we could fix the budget? I read on:

4. Voters believe over 1/3 of Michigan's budget is wasted.
5. Almost no one thinks they are paying too little in taxes, with about one half thinking they pay the right amount.
6. Voters oppose raising taxes even if it means devastating budget cuts.

These findings were depressing—and they were about to get worse. I assembled my political team to figure out how to respond to them. Jill warned that a tax increase—if we somehow managed to pass one—would probably lead to a recall campaign against me like the one that had unseated California's Gray Davis in October 2003, less than a year after his election.

"We're between a rock and a hard place," Chuck Wilbur weighed in. "We can't sell a tax increase. But even if we want to, could we sell deeper cuts to education or public protection? We've already got 2,000 fewer police officers on the streets. We're trying to double the number of college grads, but districts are raising class sizes and laying off teachers. People don't want more of that, either."

"Chuck's right, Gov. You can't sell that either," Jill said.

"For Pete's sake," Genna exploded, "where the heck does that leave us? We don't have a single good option!"

I detest fighting over stupid things. But there are times when a righteous battle feels *great*. "We have to bite the bullet and do what we think is right, regardless of the fallout," I replied slowly. "We'll do cuts, reforms, and revenues. After all of the cutting we've done and still have to do, the right thing to do is to rebalance our budget to invest in education." I scanned the faces of my advisors. They looked anxious, frustrated, uncertain. "We may have recall petitions filed against us. There will be protests. We may not win. So be it. It's a fight worth waging."

Tim Hughes, my legislative director and a great warrior on behalf of working people, slapped his notebook. "It's about time. *This* is what I came here for!"

"Holy crap," Genna smiled. "Buckle up, people. We're in for a ride."

Jill nodded. "It's your call, Governor. But I wouldn't be doing my job if I didn't warn you that the risks are huge."

We all knew that. But our prospects weren't completely bleak. The 2006 election had brought one promising development: Democrats had taken back the Michigan House by a 6-seat majority. Andy Dillon was elected Speaker of the House by a slender 1-vote margin. He'd only served a single two-year term, but his inexperience wasn't as big an obstacle as it would have been a generation ago; thanks to term limits, the most experienced representative could have only four years under his or her belt. Hopefully, Dillon could mobilize his caucus effectively despite his narrow victory in the Speaker's race.

Speaker Dillon was a thoughtful Jimmy Stewart type, six-foot-three, lanky, handsome, with slicked-back Michael Douglas hair but for the stray lock that habitually fell across his forehead. He was an enigma: raised in a working-class Irish neighborhood and a proud graduate of Notre Dame, yet super-independent, a former investor in turnaround businesses with a conservative bent. He was full of ideas, loved policy talk, yet he could be hard to pin down. We'd gotten along well in his first term. He was smart and likeable and felt he'd be able to help build the middle road we'd need. As Speaker he seemed eager to take charge and lead.

In the other chamber, Republicans were still in charge. Senator Mike Bishop had won a similarly narrow 11–10 vote for leadership of his Republican caucus. The situation was highly volatile: We faced a major crisis that offered no easy solutions, voters were psychologically primed for revolt, the chambers were divided, and both leaders had but the barest of majorities to lead their caucuses.

To me, Senator Bishop was intellectually soft and ideologically hard—a rigid right-winger. As a new legislator a few years earlier, he held hearings in a ham-handed effort to strip my Attorney General's Office of its powers when I was the lone Democrat among state officials. He lost the battle. At one point during that hearing, he publicly asked me whether I was an attorney—and was then mocked by pundits for asking such a sophomoric question of the state attorney general.

Bishop was young and perpetually tan (no easy feat in Michigan), wore shirts with his initials monogrammed on the cuffs, used more product in his hair than I did, and led a caucus with members who championed more tax cuts and more downsizing. Most had proudly signed no-tax-increase pledges. With Bishop having barely won the contest to lead his raucous caucus, his insecurity made him particularly prickly about taking any action without the unanimous support of his members. This was going to be a difficult negotiation.

The stage was set when our bipartisan commission came back with its recommendations. Michigan needed budget cuts, reforms, and—gasp!—revenue increases. We invited our allies, Speaker Dillon and Senate minority leader Mark Schauer, to a meeting at the governor's residence in December. After Budget Director Bob Emerson and Treasurer Bob Kleine presented the crushing numbers, we shared the commission's preliminary recommendations for cuts, reforms, and revenues. We were in a $1.7 billion dollar hole, and we were prepared to cut hundreds of millions in spending. On the revenue side, we said we were open to either a 1- or 1.5-cent sales tax on services ranging from landscaping and massages to golfing greens fees. Michigan was thirty-seventh in the country in the number of services we taxed, and our proposal (depending on the rate enacted) would raise either $700 million or just over $1 billion.

As we expected, Mark Schauer was encouraging. He passionately believed that we needed revenue for education and for health care for seniors and people with disabilities, and he believed that if we stayed united, we could push the proposal through. We'd assumed Andy Dillon would be more cautious; after all, Democrats held a slim majority in the House, Dillon had been elected Speaker by only a single vote, and the recall sabers were already being rattled. But Dillon surprised us all. "We should go for 2 cents, since we know they'll bargain us back," he reasoned. He also suggested that we go for a gasoline tax, which the road builders and even the Chamber of Commerce had been pushing for. We told him there was no way we could get both, but we agreed to shoot for a 2-cent tax on services. Schauer was on board.

After the others left, Emerson said, "I was shocked Dillon was so aggressive on taxes. It'll be great if he leads on the issue."

"He's being realistic," I said. I was thrilled at the prospect of a united Democratic front. All that stood between us and a solid budget foundation were Senator Bishop and his Republican majority in the Senate. Bishop was sure to be a challenge, but Dillon and I agreed to tackle him two on one.

Kleine produced budget calculations for every possible legislative negotiation and compromise, and Emerson prepared a list of further spending cuts that would yield hundreds of millions more in savings. We knew we couldn't pass any tax increase until we'd made deeper cuts, but the budget proposal was a package, and cuts, reforms, and revenues had to be presented to the legislature all at once.

As we expected, Senator Bishop reacted negatively to our budget proposal, publicly arguing that we needed a "cuts-only" resolution. The media immediately ran to Speaker Dillon, expecting him to provide the partisan contrast with supportive words for our proposal.

Instead, Dillon whiffed.

The same Andy Dillon who the week before had urged us to pursue a more aggressive tax proposal told reporters only that he would "look at" our proposal and that taxes should be a last resort only *after* we had looked at cuts and reforms. What Democrats heard was that their new leader didn't like the governor's tax proposal.

Although Dillon was a friend, I was furious with him. "In one fell swoop, you've killed our plan," I fumed at him in a closed-door meeting in my Capitol office. "We worked together on this. We had to demonstrate unity, that we're a team. Now you've shattered that unity on the toughest vote our legislators will face."

"I just can't get out in front of the caucus on it," Dillon said quietly. "We have to do cuts and reforms first. Then we can talk about the revenues."

"But I had to present a budget that balances, Andy. I have to do it with revenues, and you know that. Your public reluctance will tell the public, the media, and your own caucus that the revenue proposal may not be necessary. So then what? You know damn well you don't have the votes for an all-cuts budget. Are you going to come up with your own revenue proposal?"

"Don't worry," Dillon said. "We'll figure it out."

"You'd *better* figure it out, Andy," I said. "We can't afford to offer them gaps they can drive a wedge through."

Just as I predicted, Democrats in the House got the message that they could separate themselves from the budget proposal, criticize it, and go their own ways. Brokering a deal with legislative leaders is like experimenting in a lab with highly unstable compounds; the tiniest change in conditions can make the whole thing blow up. Dillon's tinkering did just that. Instead of enjoying a two-to-one leadership majority in favor of cuts, reforms, and revenues, we had Bishop against, me in favor, and Dillon floating about in the middle, quixotically seeking some other solution.

Bishop saw the opening and lost no time exploiting it. He began cultivating a friendship with Dillon based on their shared conservative sensibilities and personal similarities. They were about the same age. Bishop, like Dillon, was tall and handsome, the father of young children, and a lawyer; Bishop's dad had served in the legislature, and Dillon's had been a kingmaker, then a judge. Dillon and Bishop were so alike that around Lansing people would come to refer to the two young Turks as "Dillop." I was cast as the unlikely chaperone to the bromance.

I began meetings with the quadrant, which included Dillon and Bishop along with the minority leaders in the House and Senate. Andy began to float various onetime solutions to our fiscal problems, such as borrowing to fill the gap or selling off public assets—something, anything—desperately hoping to avoid a vote on taxes. I remained flexible while Bishop remained inflexible. And so the standoff continued for month after month. Neither Dillon nor Bishop seemed to share my sense of urgency. Bishop could keep promising Republicans and the media that he would block tax increases. Dillon could keep seeking the Archimedean solution. It seemed absurdly obvious to me that both were going to have to support a compromise. Why not get the work done?

I soon realized I had to take the battle beyond Lansing.

I held televised town hall meetings in every corner of the state and every media market. I met with editorial boards and did interviews on morning and evening drive-time radio. I explained how deeply we had already cut the state budget and the risks to education, universities, public safety, and essential investments in our future if we didn't stop the bleeding. I also reminded people everywhere of the things that government provided. "It goes beyond the basics like schools, police, prisons, roads," I would say. "Government ensures that clean water came out of your tap this morning and that the air you breathe is pure and not contaminated by pollutants. Government makes sure that the lights come on when you flip the switch, that you can safely eat the meat you buy at the store, and that emergency medical workers come to your house when you call 911. That park you love? That library your grandchild visits? The university discovering the cure to cancer? Your child's or your grandparent's health care? All provided because there are some things we as a community believe are important enough that we should pool our money for."

The message had the advantage of being true, but I felt like I was dragging people up a steep hill. They'd been told for years that taxes were always bad and that government was the wasteful enemy.

As I was trying to rally people behind my 2007–2008 budget, our revenue projections for the *current* year had further eroded, so by June I was required by law to cut school funding once again, this time by $122 per pupil. Pro rata cuts to schools had been the subject of my first executive order in 2003, and here we were again, without money and with the legislature frozen by fear and unwilling to vote on additional revenues. As Michiganders denounced the cuts, the media drew no distinctions among the various government actors, taking a "pox on all your houses" stance that further fueled the voters' cynicism.

I needed to educate and inspire, and I needed allies. Throughout the spring and summer of 2007, my director of external affairs, JoAnne Huls, orchestrated members of our stakeholder communities to communicate, protest, write letters, and make calls and visits to legislators to help them understand the utter pain that deeper cuts would produce and the urgent need for higher revenues. The stakeholders included people concerned with health care, education, and law enforcement, environmentalists, college students, nurses, and advocates for everyone from the poor, the mentally ill, and seniors to children and the disabled. They staged events, launched letter-writing campaigns, and spoke to the media, begging legislators to do the right thing.

But the opponents of higher taxes were doing all the same things and with just as much passion. During the summer, a ten-foot-tall, sixteen-foot-long pink fiberglass pig on wheels squatted on the street in front of the Capitol. Named "Mr. Perks," it was the mascot of an embryonic Tea Party–like group called the Michigan Taxpayer Alliance. The pig's proprietor, a controversial Macomb County commissioner named Leon Drolet, promised to recall any legislator who voted for a tax increase. He orchestrated demonstrations at the Capitol and in key legislative districts, and he had demonstrators follow me around to my town hall meetings.

By now, polls were registering disgust with everyone in Lansing over the continuing stalemate. Dillon's political advisors were freaking out at the idea of asking new House members to vote for the services tax—the main reason for Dillon's public equivocation. Indeed, Dillon's key strategist was telling House Democrats to *shut the government down* before they voted for taxes and warning them that to vote for taxes *before* a government shutdown would be political poison. The advice was foolish because it dragged out the controversy and fanned the flames of public anger instead of quickly ending the situation. Shutting down the government and then voting for a tax increase would only double Democratic legislators' unpopularity. Sadly, Republicans were getting similar advice from their political advisors. The resulting inaction triggered scathing editorials across the state attacking the "do-nothing legislature" and the failure of leadership in Lansing.

So the legislature remained catatonic, averting its eyes from the painful decisions we all knew were necessary. The state's budget year begins October 1, but budgets had usually been passed by early July when the budget year for schools, universities, and cities begins. We were now in July, and the legislature had refused to even agree on basic budget targets.

Senator Bishop continued to publicly declare that we could resolve the crisis through painful cuts rather than revenues. A stream of prominent Republicans, including Governor Engler and Dick DeVos, addressed Bishop's caucus, reinforcing the message and imploring legislators to hold the line.

But the school cuts and pressure from his own colleagues finally nudged Bishop to at least appoint a negotiating group of senators from his caucus. The members of the caucus announced that they came to the negotiations with the authority to get the deal done. They met in closed-door sessions with my budget team for several weeks and reached an apparent resolution. To eliminate the $1.7 billion shortfall, they agreed to $1.2 billion in new revenues (I had proposed $1.4), along with $500 million in additional cuts. We weren't crazy about this package, but we could live with it. Bishop's negotiators headed to his office, saying they'd be back in a half-hour.

Four hours later they returned, chagrined and apologetic. Bishop wouldn't agree. The only way to get unanimous consent from his caucus, he insisted, would be if the agreement was all cuts. I couldn't believe he set the bar at unanimity from a caucus that included serious right-wingers, many of whom had publicly declared they would not vote for any tax increases. We didn't need 21 votes from Bishop's Republicans in the Senate; we needed only four.

Budget Director Bob Emerson, who had spent seventeen years in the legislature and had served as Democratic leader of the Senate, was ready to blow a gasket. He spoke for all of us when he said, "Why the hell did we spend weeks negotiating with Bishop's emissaries? How can you make a deal with people who won't honor their word?" he raged. "How can you negotiate with people who have no authority? It's a ridiculous farce."

I was genuinely worried that Emerson would walk away from the negotiations. He had tremendous experience and was respected by both sides. We needed him badly. I had no idea how he could keep dealing with people he couldn't trust. I only hoped that—marathon runner that he was—he'd go the distance.

Now August had been wasted. In September, Bishop continued to talk about an all-cuts strategy. We ratcheted up the campaign to force him to show his hand. "Show us your plan," we demanded, and our friends, allies, and constituents echoed that message. "Show us how you can close the budget hole without new revenue. Get specific." Finally, on September 11, Bishop responded to the taunts and pressure by releasing a cuts-only proposal. And all hell broke loose in Lansing. Cries went up from every corner, every lobbyist's office, every school district, university, and hospital. Bishop's plan included cuts to the prison budget that I knew his own caucus would never vote for and wild cuts to cities, schools, and services that the citizens would never support. No wonder Bishop refused to put his plan up for a vote in the Senate—his own members refused to go on the record in favor of such draconian cuts.

Speaker Dillon controlled the House, however, and he seized the initiative to call Bishop's bluff. He put Senator Bishop's all-cuts plan up for a vote. On September 16, the voting board was opened. Red lights lit up quickly as every single Democrat voted against the proposal. And then I laughed out loud. The rest of the board was swiftly filling in with red. For all the Republicans' bluster about insisting on cuts alone, not a single House Republican hit the "aye" button for Bishop's all-cuts proposal.

It was a public relations catastrophe for the Republicans—but no victory for the Democrats, because the logjam had solidified. Democrats couldn't cut any further, and Republicans couldn't tax. By refusing to budge, Dillon and Bishop thought they were protecting their big political ambitions, yet as the deadlock continued, their hold on their leadership posts continued to fray. Bishop would later brag, "I don't mind being called an obstructionist," and said he'd "laid his body across the tracks" to block a tax increase.

My attitude toward both men had moved from frustration to anger to disgust. Yet as the shutdown deadline loomed, we kept looking for scraps of agreement that might point the way toward a compromise. Twelve large flip board sheets were taped on the walls of my Capitol office, listing one hundred reforms we'd proposed to help close the budget gap. Bob Emerson and Lieutenant Governor John Cherry—a respected lawmaker with more experience than all the legislative leaders combined—shuttled back and forth to meetings with Dillon's and Bishop's teams, testing scenario after scenario. I worked directly on Democrats, bringing them into my office for one-on-one meetings to discuss how I could help them deal with the political fallout while doing the right thing for Michigan.

With the deadline less than a week off, I found myself on a double-shift schedule, working in the office from 7:00 AM to 6:00 PM, dashing home to see Dan, Cece, and Jack at dinner (Kate, our oldest, was now a freshman at the University of Michigan), then taking part in conference calls or racing back to the Capitol to do more work until 11:00. Dan was supportive, but I could tell his nerves, and our relationship, were strained. Home life had lost its equilibrium. Ten-year-old Jack was his funny, friendly self, but high school junior Cece, who'd never liked our political life, was feeling quite lost.

One evening during the last week of September, Dan and I were at our battle stations—matching desks in our bedroom.

"I guess I should remind you," Dan ventured. "Kate's turning eighteen on October 1st. I know that's the budget deadline. Should we just expect you won't be with us?"

"I really don't know what's happening in five minutes, let alone in—what is that—five days?"

Gently, Dan said, "I'm just wondering if I should take the kids to Ann Arbor if you're not going to be here." And he added, "I'm not trying to pressure you."

"I'm sorry," I responded. "I'm just totally out of control with these idiots." I didn't need to tell Dan *which* idiots.

"I know. Sorry I asked," Dan said, and walked past me, straight out of the room. I knew he was hurt or mad or both, but I had no energy or ideas for anything other than the impasse at the Capitol. I had no time to feel sorry for anybody else—even for the guy who loved me and was thinking about the feelings of my first-born daughter.

As I leaned across my messy desk to pick up a big budget book, my back clenched up. I felt as if great talons were sunk in around my lower vertebrae. "Aggh!" I blurted out. Dan came back into the room to see me by my desk, stooped over like an old Russian peasant woman.

"What did you do?" he asked

"I'll be fine," I said with a grimace as I hobbled toward our bed. "I gotta get back to the Capitol first thing in the morning. No time for this."

Dan got me ice and ibuprofen, helped me into bed, and propped his laptop on my belly. The state was flat on its back, and now so was I. "You couldn't make this shit up," Dan said. He got Dr. Lisa DiSteffano, the head of manipulative medicine at Michigan State University, on the phone. She promised to be at the Capitol first thing in the morning with her portable table.

Lisa sneaked her gear into my Capitol office and unfolded the table next to my desk. I asked Sherry, my assistant and vigilant gatekeeper, for twenty minutes of privacy, and I gingerly rolled onto the table. Lisa leaned on me, twisted gently, lifted lightly, and pressed. It worked. She seemed to short-circuit the shooting pains in my back, one by one.

"I'm following the budget battle on TV," Lisa said. "I don't suppose I can order you to avoid stressful situations, can I?" I fought the urge to laugh and wreck the good work she'd done as I strapped on the Velcro back brace Dan had lent me and found I could almost stand straight. Then I headed to my conference room to apply my own brand of pressure to some Democratic holdouts.

It was now Thursday, September 27, and the media were conducting a round-the-clock budget watch. Satellite trucks were lined up surrounding the Capitol. Once again, we were making the national news—and again for the wrong reasons. Dillon had ordered House members to be locked in the Capitol until a resolution was reached. He brought in cots for dramatic effect. I loved that. Maybe now we could get some action.

I desperately wanted a deal by the deadline, but despite my admonitions, the Senate passed a thirty-day continuation budget to remove the immediate pressure. I put my foot down. At 7:00 PM on Friday, September 28, I gave a televised speech from my Capitol desk, stating unequivocally that I would not sign a continuation budget and that the legislature had to act before midnight on Sunday, September 30, to prevent a government shutdown.

I lay in bed for four hours, motionless to avoid tweaking my spasming back, and was back in my office early Saturday morning. The place was a mess. Emerson brought in huge bowls of his famous homemade guacamole and tortilla chips to sustain us. JoAnne Huls ordered in deli trays. Garbage and empty pop cans piled up. The large balcony outside my office, fit for a Caesar or an Evita Perón, became our break room, then our room to break people down—a place to persuade reluctant legislators. John Cherry was our shuttle diplomat, prodding, cajoling, carrying written offers between the sides, and smoking like a chimney. I hadn't touched a cigarette for decades, but I resorted to bumming smokes from John as we discussed tactics.

The negotiations continued all day and into the night, becoming caustic, emotional, and volcanic. I vacillated between optimism and despair. I'd given the legislators ten ways to avoid a shutdown, and Andy Dillon had come up with twenty more. (For all his exasperating inconsistency, Dillon's heart was in the right place, and as the clock ran down he came through with the leadership we needed.) There wasn't much more I could do. Months later, I took solace from a quip I heard Lawrence O'Donnell make in a television interview, saying that when he had worked on the U.S. Senate staff, "We found it's impossible to force a grown man to cast a vote he doesn't want to make when you're not allowed to hit him."

By 3:00 AM on September 30, I was reduced to napping on a blow-up mattress wedged between the sink and the door on the black-and-white tile floor of my Capitol office bathroom. I lowered myself onto the squeaky mattress, trying not to split the Velcro on my back brace, and imagined former Governor William Milliken sleeping in the same undignified posture. Twenty-one hours to a new fiscal year, and we still had no budget.

When the day resumed, so did the negotiations. One painful piece at a time, we crafted a compromise proposal that both sides were willing to support. But at ten minutes to midnight, we were still twisting arms for votes. And when midnight struck, as required, I ordered a systematic government shutdown. Our cabinet secretary, Nate Lake, had meticulously outlined the step-by-step, hour-by-hour, department-by-department shutdown process in two enormous white binders. We'd begun by closing the state parks and putting closure signs on government buildings. We now sent notices to 35,000 state employees not to report to work unless notified. Eighty-five percent of our state troopers were told to stay home. Telephone trees to state workers were activated, telling them to watch the news for updates. Bleary-eyed reporters were filing stories about angry campers getting kicked out of the state parks in the middle of the night.

And so the political strategists who had been telling legislators to shut government down before voting for a tax increase had won.

Within an hour, at 1:00 AM, we reached the inevitable compromise with legislative leaders. Now the legislature would be able to prove to the voters that voting for taxes had been the "last resort."

The compromise we'd crafted included a restoration of the income tax to a flat 4.35 percent, a tick below the rate in the 1990s and still among the lowest rates in the country for states that have an income tax. Our 2-cent services tax was shot down; we agreed to maintain the sales tax rate at 6 percent and spread it to a smaller number of discretionary services, such as golfing, baby shoe bronzing, and manicures. The revenue increases were tied to the cuts and reforms in one big, complex package. (Later, at the request of the business community, upset about taxing services, I ended up agreeing to repeal even these in favor of a business tax "surcharge.")

When the compromise was finally put up for a vote in the House, the tally was slow to develop. Our best lobbying efforts had left us uncertain as to which way the final count would go. The electronic voting board was held open as I stopped at the desk of each legislator who had refused to cast a vote. After all the cajoling, pleading, and strong-arming, the 56th green yes vote finally went up on the voting board. The House had gotten the job done.

The bill went over to the Senate. I sat in John Cherry's office with Leslee Fritz, our budget communications whiz, watching the vote on closed-circuit television and pulling reluctant senators off the floor for meetings. Finally, after four attempts, at 4:18 AM, the Senate relented. Four Republicans voted with the majority of Democrats to pass the compromise, revenues and all.

It was over.

After the vote in the Senate, I summoned my exhausted team to my disheveled Capitol office and opened a celebratory bottle of Michigan wine. *

---

*It comes as a surprise to some people, but Michigan does in fact produce some fine wines. Many, I've learned, are made with grapes that are "distressed," with tough skins produced by our long, harsh winters. The sugary juices of the grape ferment better inside the thick skin, making the grape sweeter than if it had been cultivated in a gentler climate. Thus, the white wines from Michigan grapes are award winning not *in spite of* the harsh conditions they've endured but *because of* them. An apt metaphor, I think.

"Thank God our long nightmare is over. We'll never have to do that again," declared Bob Kleine.

Bob Emerson chimed in: "Like Apollo Creed said in *Rocky*, 'Ain't gonna be no rematch.' And, Governor, I guarantee you Mike Bishop would say the same thing that Rocky told Creed: 'Don't want one.'"

As we raised our Styrofoam cups in a toast, the early morning light was just beginning to lift the shadows in the historic office. Even the heavy red wine seemed light.

"This wine is potent—like this team!" I said with a smile.

"And pungent—like this team!" agreed Tim Hughes. We swapped high fives and exhausted laughter.

"Shhh," press guru Liz Boyd warned. "The reporters are still outside the door. We don't want people to think we're celebrating a tax increase."

"Bah!" I said. "This is a victory for Michigan's future! For education, for investing in our state!" Whoops of agreement erupted from the group. A twinkle in her eye, Liz joined in, raising her cup in triumph.

We were slaphappy with our sleeplessness and relief. The government shutdown had lasted just over four hours, but it had seemed like weeks. And not just to us. Citizens were furious over the shutdown. Polls of voter sentiment revealed a level of dissatisfaction none of us had ever seen: The legislature's favorability rating was 18 percent; mine wasn't much better at 32 percent. The outrage was not over the tax increase; it was over Lansing's excruciating slowness to fix the problem, made manifest by the shutdown.

For all our efforts to educate voters before, during, and after the budget crisis, I'm not sure how much the public learned from the ordeal. In a poll we conducted a few months later in preparation for the 2008 State of the State address, we asked voters what we had done on taxes. A quarter said taxes were raised. A quarter said they were the same. Half said they didn't know. While it was all-consuming to those of us inside the Lansing beltway, most of our citizens had paid little attention to the details.

In the aftermath, Leon Drolet, proprietor of the giant pink budget pig, attempted recalls of a number of state legislators, finally focusing exclusively on Andy Dillon. After multiple court skirmishes, the tax rebels were deemed to have gathered enough signatures to put Dillon's recall on the ballot. Sixty-four percent voted against his recall. He, and we, had won some vindication.

But even in that moment of relief in my Capitol office on the morning of October 1, something deep in the foundations of our state—and the nation—was rumbling beneath our feet. We didn't know it yet, but the crisis was far from over.

When I went to collect my personal items from the bathroom later that morning, I found that my air mattress had sprung a leak. There it lay on the tile floor, utterly deflated.

chapter 7
• • • • • • • • •

FREE FALL

"HEY, JENNIFER, HOW ARE YOU DOING?" I WAS IN MY CAR THE morning of January 22, 2007, and the friendly voice on my cell phone belonged to Jeffrey Kindler, CEO of Pfizer, the pharmaceutical company, phoning from New York. Kindler was a fellow Harvard grad who'd held a fund-raiser for me during my reelection campaign.

"I'm doing okay," I said. "I was just reinaugurated—"

"I know! Congratulations!"

"It's one of those 'be careful what you wish for' moments," I continued, with a small laugh. Then I grew serious. "Actually, Michigan's situation right now is astonishing. I'm grappling with the loss of manufacturing jobs because of globalization, a massive budget hole, a really tough downsizing process. But, hey, I'm sure you've faced similar struggles at Pfizer," I said.

There was an awkward pause that lasted just long enough to give me a bad feeling about Kindler's call. "Well, that's why I'm calling," he said. "We're going through a massive downsizing, too. Lots of generics coming online that bump out our main drugs. We have to rationalize our global footprint." Kindler paused again, and I thought I heard him swallowing. "It means that we're gonna have to close our Ann Arbor facility," he continued. "And close some of our operations in Kalamazoo. I'm sorry to be the bearer of bad news."

My mind was racing, trying to assess the body count. How big were those facilities? "Wow, isn't that about 3,000 jobs in Ann Arbor alone?" I said. "That can't be right, can it?"

"Actually, between Ann Arbor and Kalamazoo, it's about 5,000. But we're not going to give out the numbers publicly because we don't want people to panic. I'm so sorry. I know that it's the last thing you need to hear. Michigan has been a great partner for us. But it's beyond your control and beyond my control, frankly."

"Jeff," I heard myself almost panting, "is there anything we can do to keep you here? More tax breaks? Anything?" I was grasping for a lifeline.

"This goes well beyond taxes," he said. "It's about generic drugs coming online. We have to reduce our global footprint. It has nothing to do with Michigan. We're closing facilities around the world. I'm so sorry," Kindler said again.

I hung up the phone and immediately called David Cantor, who headed up Pfizer's enormous labs in Ann Arbor. Cantor had been a close ally of mine, a champion of the entrepreneurial culture spreading through Ann Arbor, a vocal spokesperson for Michigan's move toward life sciences, and a business advocate for my core revitalization strategy. Ann Arbor and Kalamazoo had been key cities in our Life Sciences Corridor initiative, with much of the planned development coming from Pfizer. This news would devastate both communities.

"David, were you part of this decision?" I asked, still trying to comprehend the magnitude of what was happening.

"Governor, I tried to stop it; really I did," Cantor answered, his voice shaking. "But it's all part of Pfizer's global restructuring.

That doesn't make it any easier. I don't know what to tell you, except you can't begin to know how sorry I am."

As I hung up the phone, I looked out the car window. We'd stopped on Liverois Avenue in Detroit, next to a vacant lot. I sat there, lost in thought, watching as fragments of trash blew up against a chain link fence. *My God*, I thought, *when will we catch a break?*

Not yet. Three weeks later, on February 14, Chrysler announced 13,000 more layoffs in the wake of a $1.6 billion loss. Almost half were in Michigan.

Three weeks after that, on Sunday evening, March 4, I got a call at home from Ralph Babb, the chairman of Detroit Renaissance, a corporate leadership group that pushes a message of economic growth and channels philanthropic dollars to Detroit. He was CEO of Comerica, a bank that had been born in Michigan as Manufacturers National Bank and had been headquartered here for 158 years. Babb was a local icon, the first person people called with a community need or a Detroit-based project. He liked to remind me, with a twinkle in his eye, that his mother was a Democrat; I would remind him that my father was a Republican.

But a phone call at home rarely meant good news.

"Governor, I wanted you to hear it from me first. Tomorrow morning, we'll be announcing that Comerica is moving its headquarters from Detroit to Texas."

This time I wasn't just shocked—I was angry. For Comerica to abandon the state, the city, and its own history as our financial anchor seemed unthinkable to me. "Ralph, you have got to be kidding me. When was this decided?"

"The board just decided it, Governor. We kept it confidential until the board voted. I know it's a surprise."

"I'm completely stunned. Can we change direction here? What do you need to have Comerica stay in Michigan? What can we do to keep you here?"

"There's nothing Michigan can do, Governor. I would have reached out to you beforehand if there was a way to solve this. I don't like this either, but this decision is all about where our customers are. The auto industry has been our bread and butter, and it's in free fall. Our analysis shows that our growth markets are in the South. We'll still have a significant office in Detroit; it's just the headquarters that's moving."

"Come on, Ralph. Comerica's name is on the Tigers stadium, for Pete's sake." I heard the frustration and the pleading in my voice. "You're the head of Detroit Renaissance. Comerica is Michigan's main bank. There has to be something we can do to keep you here. Are you *personally* moving to Texas?"

"I will be. Governor, this wasn't an easy decision. But it isn't about the tax climate or anything like that. It's all about where the growth in the country is right now." Ralph sounded somber and sad. He knew this was a gut punch—and delivered by Ralph Babb, Detroit's leading booster, of all people!

The year continued, and so did the body blows. Other venerable corporations in Michigan announced plans to close, reorganize, downsize, merge, or file for bankruptcy. Kimball Electronics announced plans to close a northern Michigan manufacturing plant. "It's all about the low wages in China," CEO Don Sharon told me. "The price pressure we're feeling is enormous. We're going to move all the work offshore—not just from Michigan but from all our plants."

And then we heard about the biggest shakeup yet. Daimler-Chrysler announced a $7.4 billion deal to sell Chrysler to Cerberus, a private equity firm run by Steve Feinberg and chaired by John Snow, a former Bush administration Treasury secretary. Snow was a staunch believer in the theology of laissez-faire, and he had little experience in the automobile business. Cerberus had further enhanced its conservative connections by hiring former Vice President Dan Quayle. That's just great, I thought. The guy who couldn't spell *potato* was chairman of Cerberus's global investments.

Ominously enough, Cerberus was named after the three-headed dog of Greek mythology that guarded the gates of Hades. And when I heard the news about Chrysler, my immediate reaction was *Hades, here we come.* Chrysler employees, dealers, pensioners, and other company stakeholders feared the worst.

Liz Boyd and I met the Cerberus team in July around a glass-topped table in a conference room at Michigan's Lawrence Tech University.

"I want to put your mind to rest," declared a smiling John Snow. "We are American car guys. We're from the Midwest, all of us," he said smoothly, gesturing toward a still-boyish Dan Quayle. Quayle nodded, his eyebrows raised in a perfect, earnest semicircle. The heads of the phalanx of aides lined up behind Snow and Quayle bobbed up and down too, almost in unison.

"When I grew up, my family owned Chryslers," Snow continued. "We believe in manufacturing in America. We're going to make this work. We won't abandon Chrysler. We're in it for the long haul."

"To be candid," I replied, arms folded across my chest, "you guys don't have a reputation that lends much comfort. Private equity firms are known for stripping and flipping companies, and you're the daddy of them all. How do we know that you won't do that here?"

Snow smiled reassuringly. "We're not looking for quick results. We're known for *patient capital*." He leaned back in his chair as if to demonstrate his own unflappable patience.

"Governor," interjected Quayle, leaning forward, elbows on the table, eyebrows still raised, "our hearts bleed red, white, and blue. This is the kind of project that we can all get behind. We want to prove that Chrysler can work in America, and we'll give it everything we've got. We want to save the American auto industry!"

I glanced at Liz; her brow was furrowed. I shut my eyes to keep from rolling them. "Well, for the sake of everyone, I hope you're wildly successful and save thousands of American jobs," I said. "But I'll believe it when I see it."

As we drove back to my office, I said to Liz, "They're not named Cerberus for nothing. My heart wants to believe them. But my head tells me this is a deal with the devil."

In the middle of one night that summer of budget battles and job losses, Dan touched my shoulder to wake me up. "You're huffing and puffing," he told me. "What're you dreaming?"

I sat up in bed. Sweat was dripping from my neck. "It's like I'm climbing a huge wall," I said. "But every time I find a toehold, it crumbles under my feet. I keep trying to climb, but no matter how quickly I move, I can never reach the top."

"Now there's a metaphor," Dan observed.

·   ·   ·   ·   ·

MICHIGAN'S PROBLEMS DIDN'T EXIST IN A VACUUM. BY DECEMBER 2007, a national recession had begun. And against this somber economic backdrop, the 2008 presidential campaign was in full swing. Former Massachusetts governor Mitt Romney and Arizona senator John McCain were vying for the Republican nomination in Michigan. McCain had won Michigan in the 2000 GOP primary, defeating rival George W. Bush by a margin of 50 to 43 percent. Now, eight years later, Romney's message was boastful: "I'll make a commitment: if I'm president, that one-state recession is over." McCain's message was more somber—and more realistic: "Those manufacturing jobs are gone, and they're not coming back." McCain recommended community college retraining as a way for adults to transition to the new world.

But as my advisors had warned me during my own campaign, Michigan was in no mood for a straight-talk express; Michigan wanted a savior. Romney won the state with 39 percent of the vote to McCain's 30 and Huckabee's 16.

Despite Romney's pandering optimism, the reality of manufacturing in America was undeniable. The jobs were gone, and they weren't coming back. And as the election year of 2008 unfolded, the worst recession in memory began to spread across the country, with particular impact on Michigan. As gasoline prices shot up to more than $4 a gallon, people quit driving their gas-guzzling trucks and SUVs, and thousands canceled their plans to buy new ones. With the highest-margin vehicles unmoving on dealers' lots, auto sales figures began a steep slide.

At the same time, a drama of spectacular proportions was playing out in our state's largest city. Detroit mayor Kwame Kilpatrick became embroiled in a riveting sex-and-corruption scandal that absorbed the entire state and came to a head in the summer of 2008.

It had all begun a year before, in August 2007, when the dapper Kilpatrick, dressed in a sharp, dark three-piece suit, a crisp white shirt, and a deep red tie, had taken the stand in a wrongful termination action brought against him and the city by Gary Brown, a Detroit police officer who had been assigned to investigate charges against the mayor. The thirty-seven-year-old mayor was charismatic, six feet, five inches tall, a former football player, married to a beautiful woman, and with three sons all younger than ten. Now that image was cracking. Kilpatrick was accused of having an affair with Christine Beatty, his chief of staff and herself a young mother.

The story was catnip for the media. Kilpatrick denied everything under oath. Beatty also took the witness stand and uttered the same forceful denial.

The denials notwithstanding, after three hours of deliberation, the jury decided that Brown had indeed been wrongfully discharged, and they awarded him a multi-million-dollar verdict. It was a significant embarrassment for Kilpatrick and the city, but it was just the start of the story.

Five months later, at 5:00 in the evening of January 23, 2008, David Hunke, publisher of the *Detroit Free Press*, gave me a courtesy call to prepare me for the bombshell his paper would drop the next day: hundreds of graphic, salacious text messages between Kilpatrick and Beatty, showing they'd committed both adultery and perjury.

When the papers hit the stands, all hell broke loose. People across the state were shocked, horrified—and fascinated. Every detail of the drama grabbed lurid headlines and the rapt attention of millions. The *Free Press*'s blog traffic exploded as the story sucked the oxygen from all other news across the state. The *Free Press* devoted its entire year to exposing and covering the scandal, and the reporters who broke the story ultimately won a Pulitzer Prize. Detroit was thrown into tumult, with politicians, talk show hosts, pundits, bloggers, and community leaders choosing up sides and engaging in increasingly bitter shouting matches. The mayor went into hiding, concocting elaborate ruses with decoy doubles to avoid contact with the media. Detroit's national image, already in tatters, became the butt of jokes by late-night comedians. Finally, in March 2008, Wayne County prosecutor Kym Worthy, a righteous crusader and media magnet, charged the mayor and his chief of staff with perjury and seven other felonies.

By May, after unsuccessfully attempting to oust the mayor on its own, the Detroit City Council made an unprecedented formal request, based on separate provisions in our state constitution and statutes, to have the governor remove the mayor. The political-media circus suddenly shifted ninety miles west from Detroit to Lansing. While the criminal case wound its way through the courts, Kilpatrick's status as mayor was in my lap.

The mayor's mother, Carolyn Cheeks-Kilpatrick, was a prominent member of Congress and chair of the influential Congressional

Black Caucus. She and the mayor rallied their most influential supporters to demand that I wait to hold hearings on removing the mayor until the criminal case had concluded. That might have prolonged the controversy for another nine to twelve months. Even though most in the media favored Kilpatrick's ouster, many Detroiters were angry at the idea that a white governor might decide the fate of the duly elected mayor of a majority African American city. My executive team and I were bombarded with entreaties, advice, and warnings from all sides. As fellow Democrats, the mayor and I had many of the same friends and allies, and they were all dispatched to cajole, warn, and persuade me.

I made my own position clear. We would do what the law required, nothing more and nothing less. We would not be swayed by fear, favors, or political pressure. And during our decision-making process, we would make no public comments so as to avoid fanning the flames on either side. My motto would be "No drama."

I assembled my legal staff, four smart and experienced public lawyers devoted solely to doing the right thing: Steve Liedel, Kelly Keenan, John Wernet, and Suzanne Sonneborn. We analyzed the law and the relevant precedents and methodically crafted a step-by-step process for the mayor's possible removal based upon statutes, the court rules, and the state constitution. Determined to provide no ammunition for a successful appeal, we worked carefully to make the process immune to any legal challenge.

The law required a quasi-judicial proceeding, with the governor acting as judge and jury at a hearing that allowed the mayor to present evidence as to why he should not be removed. The "courtroom" would be a hearing room in Cadillac Plaza, the ornate former GM building now occupied by state offices, and the hearing would be televised and streamed live online. I ordered that the hearing follow a daily schedule from 9:00 to 4:00, including weekends if necessary.

The removal hearing was convened on Tuesday, September 3, 2008. I heard testimony from a number of witnesses and received thousands of pages of documents into evidence. Even after just one day's proceedings, the evidence in favor of removal seemed overwhelming.

The mayor's team members must have read the writing on the wall. After I adjourned for the day, they huddled through the evening and then announced a decision: Before the hearings could resume the next morning, the mayor of Detroit would resign from office and plead guilty to two felonies. City Council president Ken Cockrell, Jr., would become Detroit's interim mayor. It was an unprecedented moment for the city of Detroit and for the state of Michigan.

The crisis in Detroit presented an explosive sideshow—a yearlong distraction from economic news that was almost too much to bear. A psychiatrist might have interpreted it as an extreme case of group pain avoidance: an entire state fixated on a scintillating diversion to avoid the economic heartbreak unfolding around us. While we were consumed with the fate of Kwame Kilpatrick, sales numbers for GM, Ford, and Chrysler continued to plummet, with each company reporting billions in losses. Nationwide unemployment figures began to climb. The housing and credit markets slid from "troubled" toward "imploding." Before September ended, gargantuan investment bank Lehman Brothers collapsed and Wall Street experienced its most devastating week since the crash of 1929.

In the midst of these blows, on September 28, 2008, Barack and Michelle Obama and Joe and Jill Biden visited downtown Detroit to rally tens of thousands of frightened, angry Michiganders. (The national Democratic candidates had wisely avoided choosing sides during the Kilpatrick brouhaha; now that it was finally over, they could safely come to Detroit again.) In one of his first official acts, interim mayor Cockrell introduced the candidates, who addressed the crowd from a platform surrounded by a sea of blue Obama-

Biden signs that stretched across all eight lanes of the blocked-off Woodward Avenue between the Detroit Library and the Detroit Institute of the Arts. I was but one in a crowd of Democratic politicians squeezed into seats behind our standard-bearers.

Speaking in rolled-up shirtsleeves, Obama targeted his remarks to those who had been laid off, those without hope, those who needed to believe.

"We meet here at a time of great uncertainty in Detroit and all across America," he said. "The era of greed and irresponsibility on Wall Street and in Washington has led us to a financial crisis as serious as any we have faced since the Great Depression. We don't just need a plan for bankers and investors. We need a plan for autoworkers!"

I felt the crowd's mood surge. Since 2000, Michigan had lost about 500,000 jobs, most of them in manufacturing. Candidate Obama was saying exactly what we wanted to hear, and the audience was ready to embrace, trust, and follow him.

Out of loyalty, friendship, and deep respect, I'd been a Hillary Clinton supporter during the presidential primaries, and some pundits were predicting that the Obama team would punish Michigan for my choice. We needn't have worried.

After the rally, I was whisked away for a quick flight to Delaware with Senator Biden and his wife. Biden was preparing for his October 2 debate against his Republican rival, a feisty, charismatic, but relatively little-known young governor of Alaska named Sarah Palin, and I'd been tapped to play Palin in practice sessions. Jill Biden offered me her seat next to Joe so we could chat on the plane ride. He was talkative, confiding that he was a "car guy" (his dad had managed the used car division for an auto dealer in Scranton), speaking with energy about saving the middle class, and affirming the importance of manufacturing to America's economic future. I watched his face intently as he spoke, looking for evidence that he truly believed his words. Like millions of voters, I desperately hoped to find reason to believe.

"I know you have it rough in Michigan," Biden finally said. "You need a partner in Washington. I promise you'll have one."

Those were the words I'd been waiting to hear—a commitment to help from the next presidential administration. The manufacturing sector had been left to wither and die during the Bush years, but now I dared to let Biden's promise fill me with hope. I thought of the unemployed guy at the Last Supper at Electrolux who'd asked me, "Who's gonna hire *me*?" If Obama wins, I thought, we might actually be able to help folks like him.

The Obama-Biden debate team took over the Sheraton Hotel in Wilmington. In the hotel ballroom, there was a replica of the debate stage, precise to the inch and to every color used in the decor. JoAnne Huls and I gasped when we walked into the ballroom. "Wow. These guys are pros," she whispered to me. A team of policy researchers, each equipped with a computer, filled the darkened half of the room, sitting in rows perpendicular to the stage. Banks of seats facing the stage had been constructed on elevated platforms for the best viewing. Red carpeting covered the floor of the debate stage platform, and blue drapes hung behind the two cherry wood podiums. "I guess this is what debate practice looks like when you have money," I whispered back, remembering my own humbler sessions in our cramped campaign office in 2006.

With the help of JoAnne, Jill Alper, Nancy Skinner, Genna Gent, Rick Wiener, and Dan, I'd become an expert "Palintologist," studying Sarah Palin's gubernatorial debates and speeches, her positions, verbal mannerisms, and idiosyncrasies.

I knew Palin only casually from our interactions at the National Governors Association. With her glasses and her hair carefully swept up on her head, she seemed to downplay her beauty and could have been cast as a stereotypical schoolmarm or librarian. She was quiet and unassuming, as new governors often are amid the big-bull egos at these meetings; in fact, I don't recall ever hearing her address the group. When she was selected as McCain's running mate, I know I wasn't the only governor to scratch my head and ask, "*Sarah Palin?* She's brand new and as quiet as a church mouse. We don't even know her." I had to scour the Internet to see her in action in Alaska. Her Alaskan gubernatorial campaign debate per-formances and her actions as governor made her seem pragmatic— even moderate.

"The stakes for this debate are just really high," Joe's key aide, Ron Klain, said to me. "If Joe makes mistakes or gaffes, we lose. If he's seen as condescending to a woman, we lose. If he takes the bait when she tries to goad him, we lose. But if the debate is called a draw, we win. So we've got to throw everything at Joe in these next three days. He's got to be prepared to stay on an even keel no matter what happens."

So we ran Senator Biden through the gauntlet. We tested every line of attack and ruse, trying to get under his skin or trip him up, over and over. We worked to keep him from appearing too wonky compared to the folksy Palin and to make sure he didn't become defensive or wordy when responding to a challenge or an attack. Knowing that as a governor, Palin wouldn't have a detailed grasp on international policy, I repeatedly tried to answer in a way that would invite Biden to appear patronizing. He didn't bite.

Palin was in debate camp at the same time as we were, and we were fascinated by the fact that her practice sessions had been moved to Arizona. The McCain camp released pictures of Palin practicing at a wooden podium under some trees. Because most debate prep sessions attempt to replicate the stage, as we had done inside the Delaware hotel, we imagined that she was having some kind of diffi-culty during their rehearsal and they'd had to move the venue to change the dynamic. So during practice I answered questions as a nervous Palin to see how Biden would react. Again he refused to take the bait, remaining gracious and courteous throughout.

On October 1, our last day of prep, I found a minute to call my daughter Kate on her nineteenth birthday. Joe overheard me and gestured for my phone.

"Happy birthday, Kate!" he boomed. "This is Joe Biden. We're at debate camp, and if Sarah Palin's half as prepared as your mom is, I'm in trouble. But we're going to win this election, and Michigan's going to rebound. That's gonna be my birthday gift to you." I could picture Kate's smiling response to Joe's playfulness.

Before passing the phone back to me, Joe switched his tone. "And by the way," he told Kate in avuncular tones, "remember, no guys 'til you're thirty. That's what I used to tell my daughter," he added with a grin. "Happy birthday and thanks for supporting your mom. She's terrific, and she says you are, too."

I retrieved the phone, and Kate echoed my thoughts. "Mom, that was *sweeeet!*" she exclaimed.

Back home the following night, I was on the edge of my chair watching the debate. I had invited my team to a debate-watching party at our house. We were admittedly biased, but we all thought Joe handled it perfectly, Palin winks and all. Although Palin performed well, too, more objective commentators than we were felt Joe strengthened the case for the Obama-Biden ticket.

About an hour after the debate was over, my cell phone rang. It was Joe.

"Gov, I can't tell you how grateful I am for your help on this debate," he said. "Thank God it's over!" He was ebullient.

"You were perfect!" I yelled into the phone, unable to contain my enthusiasm. "I'm not kidding—you handled it exactly as we prepared."

"I think we anticipated every question and every answer," he agreed. "Now it's on to the final push. Thanks again, Gov!"

As I hung up the phone, I thought about the contrast between Joe Biden and Vice President Dick Cheney. By some quirk of fate, I had not once or twice but three times drawn the seat next to

Cheney at the annual White House governors dinner. One year, Governor Mitt Romney took a picture of Cheney and me smiling through a long row of tall white candles that formed part of the decorative centerpiece. Romney laughed when he showed us the snapshot: The way he'd framed the picture, it looked as if Dick Cheney and I were cellmates in prison.

Dick Cheney was perfectly cordial to me, but all I'd ever gotten from him were stories about fly fishing and an occasional "Good luck, Governor, we know you have it tough in Michigan." Now I hoped to have a real partner in the vice president. Lord knew we needed it.

As the 2008 election neared, the tectonic plates beneath Michigan continued to quake. Credit markets were freezing out dealers, suppliers, and consumers, slowing business even further. Many were predicting bankruptcy for giant American corporations where such a thing had once been unthinkable, and many analysts and Wall Street types were saying it was not just inevitable, but desirable.

Michigan was in shock.

The automakers weren't the only industry in free fall. With the U.S. financial markets on the verge of shutdown, several of America's largest banks and Wall Street firms received rapid—and stunningly huge—financial bailouts in September. The automakers saw an opening to request help from Washington. If the banks were "too big to fail," couldn't the same be said about Detroit's Big Three? In a private October 13 meeting, GM CEO Rick Wagoner proposed to Secretary of the Treasury Henry Paulson that GM would merge with Chrysler if the U.S. government financed the marriage with a dowry of $10 billion. Wagoner saw the proposed merger as a source of cost-saving "synergies." Those of us who were focused on Michigan instead saw thousands of people whose jobs would become redundant and get eliminated.

Reporters soon got wind of the merger proposal, and the private meeting became the public subject of newspaper columns, radio talk show hosts, and Internet blogs. Speculation about the consequences of a GM-Chrysler merger fueled widespread anxiety, including in Lansing, where Fred Hoffman, a former director of governmental affairs for Chrysler whom we'd hired after an earlier buyout, orchestrated our state's approach. We created a "Keep Michigan Working" SWAT team of high-profile stakeholders to plan our strategic actions in case of an economic calamity. Even after the merger bubble popped, Fred kept the Keep Michigan Working team engaged to respond to the human fallout of the unfolding automotive restructuring.

One Saturday morning that October, Dan and I were watching Jack's school team play basketball at the Hannah Center in East Lansing. One of the other moms came over and crouched next to my folding chair.

"Jennifer . . . I hope you don't mind me calling you Jennifer—" she began.

"I prefer it," I assured her.

"I got laid off, I lost my health care, and I'm worried," she said. With a glance at Dan, she continued in a nervous whisper, "I'm worried that I have a female problem. Cervical cancer." She nodded at her son, racing down the court in pursuit of a loose ball. "I just can't be sick without insurance. He needs me." I felt my chest tighten.

I pulled a dog-eared business card from my purse. "Here," I said, scrawling a number on it, "this is my office phone. Call me on Monday. Let's see if my office can help."

"I can't tell you what this means to me," she said, her eyes tearing up. She gave me an awkward hug and moved back to her seat.

Dan and I watched the game in silence for a moment. Then Dan quietly remarked, "She is literally one of a million. If the Big Three go belly up, she and lots of others are gonna need health care and much more. How will Michigan pay for that?"

I shook my head.

I remembered a phone call I'd had with Senator Obama to discuss health care policy shortly after the Michigan primary. Under the Bush administration, I'd tried repeatedly to get federal permission to pilot a health care program similar to the one Mitt Romney had created in Massachusetts. Bush Health and Human Services secretary Michael Leavitt at first appeared sympathetic, and we had numerous meetings with HHS staffers to plan our program. I was angry when HHS ultimately rejected our request.

Now I asked Senator Obama whether, if he became president, he would grant Michigan permission to pilot a health care program that would provide access to millions of our citizens. I was struck by his forceful response: He had no intention of doing any more state-level health care pilots. He planned to roll out a national system similar to the one in Massachusetts, and he'd move on it during his first year in office.

I smiled at the woman in the folding chair. For her sake, I hoped Senator Obama would get the opportunity.

Buoyed by his calm, decisive response to the deepening financial and economic crisis, Barack Obama won the presidency. At the Michigan victory party on election night, I was walking from an upstairs room to the ballroom floor and was able to look down through glass windows at the happy crowd. I stopped for a moment and caught my breath as I watched Michigan citizens— autoworkers and preachers, teachers and janitors, plumbers and lawyers, African Americans and Arab Americans, Hispanics and Caucasians, young and old, gay and straight—in a jumbled sea of humanity, hugging and crying as they watched the broadcast of our newly elected president speaking in Grant Park in Chicago, all of us hoping beyond hope that his victory would deliver the change we needed.

Three days after the election, the president-elect convened the first meeting of his team of economic advisors. I was one of them. It was quite a collection of notable individuals around that table, including legendary investor and business philosopher Warren Buffett; Harvard president and former Clinton advisor Larry Summers; former chair of the Federal Reserve Paul Volcker; former Secretary of Commerce William Daley; former chairman of the Securities and Exchange Commission William Donaldson; CEO of Xerox, Ann Mulcahy; Google's Eric Schmidt; Hyatt's Penny Pritzker; Time-Warner's Richard Parsons; former Secretary of the Treasury Bob Rubin; former Representative David Bonior; and former Secretary of Labor Robert Reich. It reminded me a little of my first day at Harvard Law School—I felt like the impostor, the one who'd been invited by mistake.

But everyone knew why I was there. I was the voice of the most troubled state in the nation, home of the most troubled industry in America. At the start of the meeting, President-elect Obama asked me to say a few words about what was happening in Michigan. The automakers' quarterly earnings reports had come out that day, and they were abysmal. General Motors had shocked an already-worried Wall Street by posting a record quarterly loss and warning analysts that it was in danger of completely running out of cash. Ford, supposedly the strongest of the Big Three, announced that it had burned through $6.3 billion in cash and planned to lay off another 2,600 hourly workers.

I sugarcoated nothing. I explained that we were hemorrhaging jobs. No one was buying cars, credit markets were freezing up, and auto companies and the thousands of suppliers that depended upon them were bleeding profusely. I was eager to have our new president feel the pain of our state and our workers, the distress of our families. And I wanted him to know that, although the auto industry desperately needed to restructure and retool itself to build the green cars of the future, it also needed a lifeline to get there. We needed *public* investment in those breakthrough technologies, such as lithium-ion batteries. As candidate Obama had said, this crisis represented a great opportunity, if we were prepared to seize it.

One possibility terrified me, and I was intent on closing it off.

"Bankruptcy," I declared, "is not an option. No customer will buy a car from a bankrupt company."

I noticed that several of the advisors around the table murmured in disagreement. The president-elect did not.

Google's Eric Schmidt spoke up. He offered an idea, already tested in Europe, called "cash for clunkers," in which the government provided cash vouchers to encourage consumers to trade in their old gas guzzlers for new, fuel-efficient cars. Larry Summers shook his head dismissively, but others supported the idea, saying it was critical to stimulate demand for vehicles. Others suggested tax credits, worker retraining assistance, and measures to help automakers survive their ongoing transition. The conversation turned to plans for a federal stimulus package designed to pump money into the economy and, if possible, to reduce the length and severity of the recession.

I left the meeting with a solid sense of hope. President-elect Obama was going to keep his campaign promises, including his vow not to abandon manufacturing.

The meeting also gave me another arrow in our quiver for helping Michigan transition to the new economy. I would do everything I could to influence how the forthcoming stimulus package would be structured so as to support a "rust-to-green" strategy for Michigan.

Ten days later, I landed at Ben Gurion Airport in the Israeli desert. This was the latest stop in my global travels to play offense, wooing industry and jobs for Michigan. The first two days went really well. Accompanied by a delegation that included Gary Torgow, a key leader in Michigan's Jewish community, and Jim Epolito, president of the Michigan Economic Development Corporation, I had private meetings with Israel's Benjamin Netanyahu, Jordan's King Abdullah, and twenty Israeli companies, many in high-tech industries, most of them green. Two made firm commitments to come to Michigan, and many more expressed interest and promised to study the opportunities further.

But I couldn't miss what was happening in DC. On day two of the visit, I made it back to my hotel room in Tel Aviv in time to watch the broadcast of that morning's Senate Banking Committee hearings about a potential rescue package for the auto industry. The CEOs of the Big Three—GM's Rick Wagoner, Chrysler's Robert Nardelli, and Ford's Alan Mulally—somberly filed into the hearing room to make their case for a bridge loan from the taxpayers.

The auto executives took their seats and were quickly brought to their knees.

"It would be insane," Representative Brad Sherman of California declared as the cameras rolled, "if this country stopped designing and building automobiles and trucks." The CEOs nodded. But then Sherman's tone abruptly changed. "It would also be insane," he continued, "if the top executives from the three automakers came here on private jets. I am going to ask the three executives here to raise their hand if they flew here commercial."

Wagoner, Nardelli, and Mulally just sat there, stone-faced. "Oh, my God," I said as I sat, horrified, in front of the screen. I could see where this was headed.

"Let the record show," Sherman said, "no hands went up. Second, I am going to ask you to raise your hand if you are planning to sell your jet in place now and fly back commercial." A long, excruciating pause. "Let the record show no hands went up."

"I don't know," Sherman continued, "how I go back to my constituents and say the auto industry has changed if they own private jets."

My stomach turned. I had to admit that Sherman deserved a Tony for his theatrics. He and his committee members had been blasted for the Wall Street bailout, and he'd found the perfect target to deflect the attacks. The world watched as he fried the auto industry in its own corporate fat.

I reached for my Blackberry. "OMG. Did you watch this?" I typed to Dan.

"The anger is incredible," he texted back.

When any large economic, social, or political system has stopped being viable because the world has changed around it, the system usually retains layers upon layers of denial that insulate it as long as possible from cold reality. Michigan had long exalted its automotive CEOs. We treated them like royalty. They headlined every black-tie charity event, offered words of wisdom on every business or political event, and regularly received glowing media profiles, despite the cold reality of decades of market share decline. And when they talked about how they were restructuring their businesses and revitalizing the lost tradition of quality, we believed them. Sure, when we visited New York or Florida or California, we saw imports dominating the roads, but we believed the domestics were coming back. Now the devastating financial news about the Big Three and the rude treatment received by their CEOs on Capitol Hill were shattering the shields created by those decades of denial.

Within days, in an act many saw as treasonous to the state he'd won through pandering in the primary, Mitt Romney penned an op-ed for the *New York Times* entitled "Let Detroit Go Bankrupt." Auto executives and workers alike were apoplectic. Romney's column was the only topic on the local news shows. My legislative director, Tim Hughes, spoke for many when he declared, "Romney will never, ever win Michigan again. In fact, he'd better not even try to set foot in this state after knifing us in the back like that."

Another blow fell on November 20 when Representative Henry Waxman of California unseated Michigan's beloved John Dingell, the longest sitting member in Congress, from his powerful chairmanship of the Energy and Commerce Committee. Dingell had long championed the perceived interests of the automakers—for example, beating back efforts to increase federal fuel economy standards. It seemed as if Michigan were being stripped of all of its old defenses.

Dan and I were still talking about the Banking Committee hearings when I returned from my trade mission to the Middle East. "We *all* got a huge black eye from those hearings," Dan said on the phone when I landed in DC. "They made the automakers look backwards and out of touch. And Michigan, too. Even though you and I know the companies have come a long way since the seventies."

"The problem is that they *are* still stuck in the past," I said. "At least to some degree. Change is not just a total necessity, but also an incredible opportunity for them. But I don't know if they can see that."

Like schoolboys being given a makeup assignment, the auto executives were told to prepare plans that would justify the loans and return to testify after Thanksgiving. Meanwhile, in an act of perverse symbolism, Chrysler cut 5,000 more salaried workers on the day before Thanksgiving. The people let go were engineers and managers, people with nice lifestyles and mortgages, high-quality employees who had survived many previous rounds of cuts and had never faced hard times like these before. Unemployment was like an epidemic sweeping southeast Michigan. Every block, every family had members who were affected. Foreclosure rates began to skyrocket.

The auto company leaders returned to Congress in December with better plans. This time, the CEOs drove their American-made cars to DC. I phoned Rick Wagoner in his Chevy Malibu somewhere in Pennsylvania.

"Rick," I said. "I don't want to be presumptuous, but I've got a pretty good idea of how politicians think, and I have a couple of suggestions about your testimony. Are you open to some input?"

"Of course," he said with a rueful chuckle, "I need all the help I can get."

"If you can help it, don't be defensive," I urged. "Don't act as if you're afraid of competition or of technological change. Don't let them paint you as Luddites. Say that you're going to claim the future, that the American auto industry is going to lead the nation to energy independence, that America can't reach its goals *without* the American auto industry." I could hear my own voice straining; I was standing at my desk, gesticulating to my empty office. I *so* wanted Rick to hit it out of the park, for the good of his company, his workers, and our whole state.

"Tell them you're going to take the lead and leap the industry forward," I continued. "You're going to be the accelerator, not the brakes! Don't read from a script—look them in the eye! Be passionate about your great product! The American auto industry, leading the nation to a clean energy future!"

I stopped talking. I'd shot my bolt. There was an awkward silence. Finally, Rick spoke. "Well, thank you for that coaching," he said. He sounded sincere, I thought.

Or maybe he was just being polite.

When they arrived in Washington, the CEOs turned in their plans and asked Congress for $34 billion in low-interest loans to tide their companies over. But Congress was not in a receptive mood. Taxpayers, who counted themselves lucky if they could afford to fly commercial, were making little distinction between Wall Street CEOs and auto CEOs—they were all fat cats in the eyes of the average voter. Many in Congress understood that middle-class autoworkers would lose much more than CEOs if the car companies collapsed, but in the atmosphere of the time even that point was lost on most Americans. Polls tilted decisively against any more government bailouts, even in the form of loans.

Economic ministers from at least five nations, including Canada, Germany, and France, contacted the Bush administration to warn that a collapse of GM and Chrysler would set off the same kind of global calamity in manufacturing that the downfall of

Lehman Brothers had triggered in financial markets. They found it hard to believe that the United States might countenance such a disaster.

But policy was being set by President Bush—the same man who, just two years earlier, had seemed to disdain any federal role in ensuring the future of one of our country's most far-reaching industries. "I can't make your automakers profitable," Bush had told me during a tour of the United Solar Ovonics facility in Auburn Hills. In January 2006, Bush had been quoted as saying that the automakers simply needed to make "a product that's relevant." Both remarks implied that the Detroit Three fully deserved their economic troubles—and if millions of workers and their families suffered along with the executives, well, that was just too bad.

So now, in the devastation of late 2008, the unimaginable notion that the federal government might stand idly by as the American auto industry crashed and burned seemed all too frighteningly plausible.

The auto industry's turmoil was now rolling across Michigan like a tidal wave. October was the first month of our fiscal year, yet State Treasurer Bob Kleine warned me that we were already facing a $600 million shortfall. Some on his team projected that a GM bankruptcy could cause state revenues to drop another 40 percent. With voice cracking, the normally tough, expletive-spitting budget director, Bob Emerson, told a reporter, "You'd have people without health care, you'd have hospitals closing, pharmacies closing. How that would ripple out and impact the state budget is incomprehensible. Please, dear God, don't let this happen." The companies filed dramatic restructuring plans with more plant closings and thousands of layoffs. Even if they survived, the impact on people and communities in Michigan would be deep and long lasting.

As the CEOs pleaded their case for federal loans, I called other governors and members of Congress, wrote op-eds for national publications, and made the rounds on cable and network news shows in their support. I pointed out that allowing financial institutions to walk away with billions and no accountability for the damage they'd caused our economy through malfeasance and, in some cases, fraud, while refusing to help auto companies that were guilty of nothing more than failing to anticipate a series of unprecedented economic shifts, would represent an illogical and unfair double standard. We sent a blizzard of policy papers, e-mails, and letters to all the key decision-makers. Our biggest fear was about timing. If Congress didn't step up now, the auto industry might not be able to last until President-elect Obama was inaugurated on January 20.

On December 2, the November sales numbers were released. They were shocking. GM sales had plummeted 41.3 percent; the company needed $18 billion in loans, $4 billion just to survive the rest of the year. Chrysler reported a 47 percent sales drop; it was seeking a $7 billion bridge loan to stay afloat. Ford reported a 31 percent drop; it, too, was hoping for government aid.

The next day, at a meeting of governors in Philadelphia convened by the president-elect, I sat next to Governor Janet Napolitano, who would soon be secretary of homeland security.

"How's it going?" she asked.

"Candidly, we're drowning. If Congress doesn't give loans to the auto industry, I can't tell you what it will be like. Janet," I asked on a whim, "how many WARN Act notices do you think you've received in Arizona?" The federal WARN Act requires a company to notify a governor when it intends to do a "mass layoff," defined as fifty or more workers. She looked at me curiously.

"I don't know, maybe a handful since I've been governor," she said. "Why? How many have you received?"

"Fifty-five in the past thirty days," I answered.

My friend Governor Jim Doyle of Wisconsin had been listening. "Every time I think of how bad we have it in Wisconsin," he commented, "I look at you and am grateful that I'm not the governor of Michigan."

"Glad that my mere presence uplifts you guys," I replied.

There was hardly even time for humor. Everything in Michigan seemed to be failing at once, like the bodily systems of a patient approaching death. Calls to the unemployment insurance system, now up to 800,000 in a single day, were completely overwhelming our phone network and staff. Cities and school districts couldn't make payroll or debt payments; some were having to shut down. I had to put the Detroit Public School District into emergency financial management, the equivalent of receivership. Other institutions, including the Pontiac School District, the Inkster School District, and the city of Highland Park, soon followed suit. Other municipalities, including Detroit, were put on a crisis watch list.

All eyes were looking to DC for help. Surely, the members of the Senate would soon act. They had to realize that the jobs of one in ten Americans were related in some way to the auto industry, that the loss of the auto industry would damage not just tens of thousands of auto suppliers and thousands of car dealers but the steel industry, the glass industry, the rubber industry, the plastics industry, the trucking industry, the electronics industry, and the advertising industry. They had to understand that abandoning the drive to modernize our auto industry would cripple the manufacturing capabilities needed for national defense and the technology breakthroughs required to achieve freedom from foreign oil. All of this was obvious, wasn't it?

No, it wasn't. On December 11, the Senate voted down the request for auto industry bridge loans.

The news plunged the entire state of Michigan into despair.

I was furious. "Their no vote is an astounding blow," I told a radio interviewer. "They've chosen to ignore the livelihoods of 3 million American families, and in the process have chosen to drive the American manufacturing industry—and perhaps the American economy—into the ground. They're choosing foreign competitors over American industry and American workers! A nation without a strong manufacturing sector is a nation without a viable defense sector. This is a shameful day, a day we will not forget."

I was especially angry at the Republican senators who'd cast the crucial votes; many of them were clearly serving the interests of foreign car companies located in their states. Others wanted to crush the influence of the UAW. The double standard meant billions in bailouts for Wall Street and a back of the hand to Main Street. "These guys are such assholes," the normally polite Kelly Keenan proclaimed in disgust at the morning meeting. "Republican governors from Alabama and South Carolina give hundreds of millions of dollars to lure BMW and Mercedes, and now senators like Alabama's Shelby are blowing hot air about how terrible it is to use taxpayer money to help the auto industry? Effing hypocrites."

Our only remaining hope lay with President George Bush himself.

I called the president's office and was politely transferred to the White House department charged with liaison to governors. At my wit's end, I issued a public statement: "I implore President Bush not to let the American economy slide from recession into depression as he leaves office. Mr. President: American workers are depending on you. Save these jobs."

The next day, on December 12, the Bush administration indicated it would "consider options" to help the U.S. auto companies. Bush was said to be weighing the possibility of bypassing Congress and issuing loan guarantees on his own authority. I could scarcely believe my ears: The same president whose eight years of failure to create an industrial policy for the United States had frustrated countless Americans and earned him eight years of harsh criticism from me and many of my fellow governors was considering throwing the auto industry a lifeline. I issued a new statement unlike any I'd ever made: "I want to thank President

Bush for standing up for American jobs, for American manufacturing, for our country's future. I want to thank the President for doing what members of his own party in the United States Senate refused to do: save jobs. Mr. President: Thank you for coming to the rescue of millions of jobs."

But it seemed I'd issued the statement too quickly. Days went by with no announcement that the president was moving from "considering" a loan to actually granting one. Chrysler then announced it would be shutting all thirty of its manufacturing facilities for one month, from December 19 to January 19, to preserve cash. General Motors announced it was pulling back on its plans for the plug-in Volt—a painful blow to America's bid for competitiveness in the international quest for alternative fuel technology dominance. Every single day of Washington inaction was killing us.

Finally, at 9:00 in the morning on Friday, December 19, 2008, the Bush administration granted $17.4 billion in bridge loans to Chrysler and GM (Ford had withdrawn its request). In one of his last acts in office, George W. Bush may have saved U.S. manufacturing. We took a long, deep breath.

Detroit and the state of Michigan had survived the crash of 2008—but just barely. As the last days of the Bush era whimpered to a close, we were clinging to economic life and to the hope that a new administration would bring a change in our fortunes. Even the Detroit Lions football franchise reflected our state's desperation. It finished the 2008 season 0–16, the worst record in the history of the NFL.

The new year couldn't begin soon enough.

Campaigning for governor with the family and Dan's wonderful mom, Mary Mulhern (far right), at the Michigan Democratic Convention in 2002. PHOTO COURTESY OF ED RICHTER

Dan was a great advisor while celebrating my first gubernatorial win on November 6, 2002, but his greatest gift was holding Jack, and holding Kate, Cece, and me together as a family. PHOTO COURTESY OF THE DETROIT FREE PRESS

With Budget Director Mary Lannoye, presenting the first, all-cuts budget of my administration to the legislature in 2003. PHOTO COURTESY OF GOVERNOR GRANHOLM AND DAN MULHERN

The massive electrical brownout in the summer of 2003 sent me to the Emergency Operations Center to manage a statewide response. PHOTO COURTESY OF GOVERNOR GRANHOLM AND DAN MULHERN

On the steps of Reverend Atterberry's Brotherhood of All Nations Church of God in Christ in Benton Harbor, where we took a hands-on approach in response to a police shooting that led to widespread violence—one of the three major crises that dominated my first year in office. The community came together to work on short- and long-term strategies. PHOTO COURTESY OF THE *HERALD PALLADIUM*

In Greenville, a small community that had lost a major refrigerator factory, celebrating with Dr. Subhendu Guha the commitment of United Solar Ovonics to build two plants to employ the displaced workers there. PHOTO COURTESY OF GOVERNOR GRANHOLM AND DAN MULHERN

Debating Dick DeVos in the gubernatorial race in 2006. PHOTO COURTESY OF THE ASSOCIATED PRESS

On January 1, 2007, at noon, we braved the cold for my second inauguration. Dan's mom and our children, Jack, Cece, and Kate, joined us on the frozen steps of the Capitol. PHOTO COURTESY OF ANDREW L. MCFARLANE

Lieutenant Governor John Cherry, Speaker Andy Dillon, and I on the balcony of my Capitol office during the budget meltdown of 2007. PHOTO COURTESY OF PATRICK MCCARTY

In September of 2008, I held hearings to remove Detroit Mayor Kwame Kilpatrick from office amidst his texting, sex, and perjury scandal. The hearings led to the mayor's resignation. PHOTO COURTESY OF *THE DETROIT NEWS* ARCHIVES

On the porch of the governor's residence on Mackinac Island overlooking the straits of Mackinac, with former governor William Milliken. PHOTO COURTESY OF GOVERNOR GRANHOLM AND DAN MULHERN

After six years of a hands-off administration in D.C., I worked hard for Change. Al Gore endorses Barack Obama at Detroit's Joe Louis Arena in 2008. PHOTO COURTESY OF *THE DETROIT NEWS* ARCHIVES

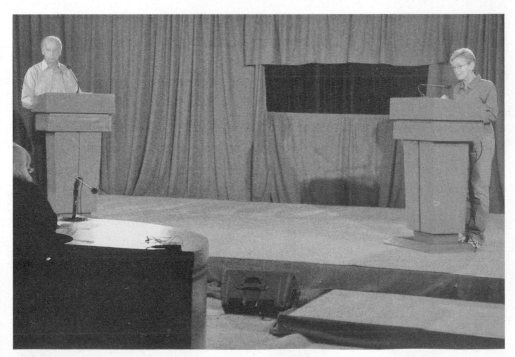

In debate prep with vice presidential candidate Joe Biden, I did my best Sarah Palin. PHOTO COURTESY OF THE OBAMA/BIDEN 2008 CAMPAIGN

At President-elect Obama's first economic transition team meeting in Chicago, with Joe Biden, Paul Volker, and others. PHOTO COURTESY OF THE ASSOCIATED PRESS

In the Rose Garden, governors Deval Patrick, Arnold Schwarzenegger, and I congratulate President Obama on aggressive new national automotive emissions standards. PHOTO COURTESY OF THE ASSOCIATED PRESS

Auto recovery "czar" Ed Montgomery and I tour GM's Flint Engine South plant. PHOTO COURTESY OF THE DETROIT NEWS ARCHIVES

With CEO Alan Mullaly and Bill Ford, Jr., celebrating Ford's commitment to build their small and electric vehicles at the Michigan Assembly Plant in Dearborn. PHOTO COURTESY OF *THE DETROIT NEWS* ARCHIVES

Beaming for good reason: Vice President Biden announced that Michigan would receive 12 Recovery Act grants for batteries for the electric vehicle—more than half of all of the battery grants in the country. This announcement led to 17 battery companies coming to Michigan, pledging to create 63,000 jobs by 2020. OFFICIAL WHITE HOUSE PHOTOGRAPH BY DAVID LIENEMANN

Dan surprised me by flying out my parents, Vic and Shirley, for my final State of the State speech in 2010. PHOTO COURTESY OF *THE DETROIT FREE PRESS*

King Carl XVI Gustav of Sweden honored me with the Order of the Polar Star for promoting clean energy. Sweden, where my father's father was born, offered a great model for embracing clean energy and the good jobs it brings. PHOTO COURTESY OF HENRIK GARLÖV, SWEDISH ROYAL COURT

• • • • • • • •

chapter 8

THE UNTHINKABLE

ON JANUARY 20, 2009, UNDER COLD BUT SUNNY DC SKIES, DAN and I watched Barack Obama take the oath of office at the U.S. Capitol. A new day was dawning for Michigan.

"The cavalry is coming," I said to Dan, watching my cold breath float into the air. I felt lighter, more hopeful than I had in years. Surely it would be an entirely different world for Michigan with a partner in the White House.

At the inaugural balls that evening, I did my own kind of dancing, making a beeline to those who needed to learn the urgency of Michigan's plight. In particular, I sought out Larry Summers and Timothy Geithner, the new president's chief economic advisors. At a formal dinner held by philanthropist Eli Broad in honor of Hillary Clinton, I made my way around the tables in my shimmery blue ball gown over to the tuxedoed Summers, who was trying to eat his meal.

"Larry, I'm so sorry to bother you today of all days," I said, "but I'm not sure when else to convey to you the urgency of the moment for people in Michigan. We're getting 800,000 calls per day to our unemployment insurance system."

He wiped his mouth with his napkin and digested this fact. "Did you say 800,000?" he asked, looking up at me intently.

"I did, sir. We are in crisis." He shook his head sympathetically and brushed some crumbs from his lapel. "I know we'll be in touch when you get settled," I said. "But our situation is urgent."

I moved around the table to Secretary of Education Designate Arne Duncan. "I know you have a lot to think about," I told him. "But I'm sure you realize that Detroit has the worst school system in the country. Now it's in receivership. We need all kinds of help—with school reforms, finances, even recruiting a new superintendent."

I was delighted with Duncan's empathetic response: "I lose sleep at night when I think about Detroit," he said. Welcome to the club, I thought. He assured me that the economic stimulus bill that the new administration was developing would definitely include significant funding to encourage and support education reforms. In response, I promised Michigan would help in any way it could—by running pilot programs, by serving as the poster child for national reform.

I moved to my friend Secretary of State Hillary Clinton and gave her a warm congratulatory hug. This inaugural dinner was in her honor, but she turned to me immediately, her face serious. "Jennifer, how is Michigan doing?" she asked.

"Truthfully, it's terrible," I said. "We're in free fall."

"This administration will help," she said, squeezing my hand. "Reinforcements have arrived."

Dan was waiting for me at our table. "Take it easy on these folks," he laughed. "They've worked hard. It's a big celebration. Don't be the turd in the inaugural punchbowl." Dan was thinking about the human side of the equation, but I had no time for niceties. Our situation was too desperate.

On February 17, Rick Wagoner called me with the outlines of the final plan that GM would file with the Obama administration in hopes of avoiding bankruptcy. The company had reached an agreement with the UAW on more flexible work rules. It would close five more plants and eliminate a number of once-admired auto brands. "We're going to try to sell off Hummer," he continued. "If we can't, we'll liquidate it. We'll try to get Sweden to take Saab back. And by 2012, we plan to shut down Saturn. Pontiac will be gone, too."

Wagoner was pleased with his tough, aggressive plan. "The administration has to be happy with this deal," Wagoner declared. "Bankruptcy is not in the cards." I was hopeful, but hardly pleased. The hand Wagoner was preparing to play included the loss of thousands more jobs.

Chrysler weighed in later in the day with its own bankruptcy-avoidance restructuring plan. Daimler, Cerberus, and a potential merger with GM were the past; Fiat was the new hope. In combination, the plans forecast cuts of 50,000 jobs, the lion's share of them in Michigan. The bloodletting was far from over.

I had a new job: to serve as the state's chief PR booster for a couple of horribly painful plans. I went on news shows to proclaim that the restructuring plans for GM and Chrysler would at least prevent bankruptcy, the worst possible outcome for the carmakers and our state. "After their home, a car is the second-biggest purchase most people ever make," I said. "Who's going to buy one from a bankrupt company?"

The plans faced opposition, much of it political posturing masquerading as principle. The Sunday after the restructuring plans were submitted, I was pitted against Governor Mark Sanford of South Carolina and Governor Tim Pawlenty of Minnesota on a Fox News program. Sanford was disdainful of the auto companies' proposals. He said the furniture and textiles industries had been "decimated," but it "didn't take a series of bailouts" to fix their problems. He didn't mention that textiles and furniture manufacturing had all but disappeared from the South. He and Pawlenty dismissed the degree of "restructuring" that was in the auto companies' plans.

"You probably haven't read those plans," I asserted, furious at Sanford's demagoguery. His silence was deafening; clearly he had not.

Governor Pawlenty tried to defend Sanford, but I interrupted him. "Governor Pawlenty, have *you* read the report that the carmakers have just submitted? I bet you haven't." Pawlenty admitted he hadn't read the plans either. He argued that the automakers should have gone into bankruptcy six months sooner. "They should do it now," he concluded.

I responded by strongly reasserting the importance of the auto industry to the American economy. I hoped the audience realized that *one* of us knew what she was talking about.

After the show, I received a text message from Debbie Dingell, vice president for government relations at GM and wife of Congressman John Dingell: "You tore them up!"

But the bankruptcy talk was making me nervous. I called Rick Wagoner's office again and spoke with his right-hand man, Fritz Henderson. "Fritz, tell it to me straight," I pleaded. "I'm out here defending you publicly, sticking my neck out for you. I'll be angry if I find out you guys were planning bankruptcy all along."

"We have no plans for bankruptcy," Henderson said. "I assure you. Bankruptcy would be the worst thing possible." His formal, as-if-rehearsed tone wasn't completely reassuring. But I decided to accept him at his word. *Okay*, I thought, *I'll keep at it.*

At least the new atmosphere in Washington gave us some reasons for hope. I'd gotten to know Barack Obama when he came to campaign for me in 2006, and my appreciation for his intelligence and judgment had grown in the years since then. I loved his ability, reminiscent of that of Robert F. Kennedy, to move people's hearts by calling them to a higher purpose. He also intuitively understood Michigan's deep pain, and his national agenda for jobs, clean energy, education, and working people mirrored my agenda for Michigan. "His policies sound exactly like ours, and in your speeches, you use the same language," Genna Gent told me on more than one occasion. "It's uncanny how in sync we are."

Obama's staff selections were great for us. Ron Klain, the vice president's chief of staff, was a classmate of mine from law school. Gene Sperling, deputy treasury secretary, was a Michigan native and friend. Vice President Joe Biden and I had forged a strong bond, beginning with that plane ride following our Detroit rally back in September. Secretary of Health and Human Services Kathleen Sebelius, Secretary of the Department of Homeland Security Janet Napolitano, Secretary of Commerce Gary Locke, and Secretary of Agriculture Tom Vilsack were all former governors and allies with whom I had served. Secretary of the Interior Ken Salazar and I had both been state attorneys general (as had Locke and Napolitano). Cecilia Munoz, the White House liaison to governors, was from Michigan. With all of these friends in the administration, I knew Michigan would get a sympathetic ear.

With the national economy quickly following Michigan's into free fall, I found allies around the country as well. Some of my fellow governors became like brothers and sisters, able to commiserate with the challenges I faced. I'd forged strong friendships with several Democratic governors, particularly Deval Patrick from Massachusetts, Jon Corzine from New Jersey, Jim Doyle from Wisconsin, Ted Strickland from Ohio, Bev Perdue from North Carolina, Bill Ritter from Colorado, Ed Rendell from Pennsylvania, and Chris Gregoire from Washington. Our conversations generated and spread ideas, and we amplified each other's voices, as when the White House sought our input in shaping the stimulus package. We all pushed for programs that would help the hardest-hit states, including unemployment insurance extensions, investments in keeping or creating new jobs, and future-focused investments in a green economy.

The package came together quickly. By February 17, the American Recovery and Reinvestment Act (ARRA) was ready for the president's signature. Republican and Democratic governors alike rejoiced at funds that preserved health care, unemployment benefits, and education. In Michigan, ARRA enabled us to make strategic investments to reshape Michigan's economic landscape: broadband, energy efficiency, high-speed rail, alternative energy, advanced batteries, race-to-the-top education reforms. ARRA funds let us advance our rust-to-green diversification efforts at a time when our own legislature refused to make such investments.

The new activism from Washington gave me, and millions of other Americans, the first reason we'd had in several years to be truly hopeful. But at the same time, tough negotiations were going on between the carmakers and the Obama economic team. I was in constant contact with the administration, e-mails flying— like this one to Jason Furman, deputy director of the National Economic Council:

> Friday, February 27, 2009. 3:49 P.M.
> From: Granholm, Jennifer
> To: Furman, Jason
>
> Jason—
> I am going to send you the specifics for Michigan, but in addition to the OEMs, the supplier base is crumbling. Total meltdown. As you know, there are 5,000 auto suppliers in the country. They are laying people off and closing shop at a breathtaking rate. I'm deeply worried about the cascading effect. They need liquidity. Can the government help to guarantee receivables? Can we have special debtor-in-possession financing available for

them? Or can we ensure debt support to suppliers in some way? . . . Thank you for putting this crisis on your radar screen as well, along with the many other fires you are trying to put out. Sending more data shortly.

Others in the administration were on the receiving end of my missives, each laden with desperate statistics and arguments that seemed to me irrefutable:

SATURDAY, FEBRUARY 28, 2009. 10:39 A.M.
FROM: GRANHOLM, JENNIFER
TO: BLOOM, RON; RATTNER, STEVEN

. . . In Michigan, we are experiencing a snowballing of supplier failures, and I am writing to urge you to continue to act on behalf of the entire U.S. auto industry. . . . In addition to the OEMs, the suppliers are now in rapid meltdown.

I know you are aware of the scope of the crisis, but let me bring it to a fine point. The nation's 5,000 suppliers are closing up and laying off employees at a breathtaking rate. In Michigan, I received 213 notices of mass layoffs in the past four months alone, with 163 of them from auto suppliers and manufacturing companies. Of the 28,953 jobs affected just on these notices, 24,097 were from auto suppliers, manufacturers or auto related firms—83% of the total. The notices have begun to accelerate at an alarming rate.

The "perfect storm" of depressed auto sales, reduced OEM capacity, and the credit crisis all spell disaster for these firms—and I am told a million more jobs are at risk.

WEDNESDAY, MARCH 4, 2009. 11:00 P.M.
FROM: GRANHOLM, JENNIFER
TO: BLOOM, RON; RATTNER, STEVEN; DILLON, ANDY

. . . Thank you for your intensity on this critical issue. Our
unemployment numbers come out tomorrow—embargoed
until 1:00, but I believe it will be over 11.5%. At that level, I
know you comprehend the fierce urgency of the moment.

We simply must create demand for vehicles. You may
have seen that German auto sales are up 21.5%—the best
February in 10 years. The reason? A new "cash for
clunkers" program where the government pays 2500 euro
($3150) to those who turn in cars nine years or older.
Similar programs are in place in France, Italy and Spain,
and now Ford of Europe is calling on the British government to adopt the incentive. I know a version of this was
rejected in the Recovery Act. I wonder if there is a different path to achieve similar results?

Thank you again for your time and the meeting. Thank
you for assuring us that help is on the way.

THURSDAY, MARCH 5, 2009. 7:28 A.M.
FROM: GRANHOLM, JENNIFER
TO: SPERLING, GENE

Gene,
Thanks for being at the meeting on Tuesday—it was a
great relief, frankly, to see you there. Our unemployment numbers come out today, and they will be bad.
The official number is 11.6%.

Despite my best efforts, within a few weeks I found myself waiting for the phone call I'd hoped never to receive.

March 29, 2009, was a cold Sunday evening. I was seated in my usual spot amid piles of paper at the desk in my bedroom in the governor's residence, in front of the computer, reading stories online. I had written down a list of things to say, placing it carefully in view. After an agonizing, anxious wait, the phone finally rang, and Kathy, the security officer, said, "Governor, I'm transferring the White House."

"Hello? Mr. President?" I asked nervously. Getting a call from the president of the United States always makes your heart pound—even if you know what he's going to say. And especially if you suspect he's about to rock your world.

"No, please hold while I get the president," a woman said. I hastily typed an e-mail message to my executive team: "Can we get a conf call # for our team ready? I'm on hold w WH now."

Then the familiar voice: "Jennifer, this is Barack Obama."

"Hello, Mr. President," I said. "I've been reading the stories. I'm guessing you have some news for me."

"I do." The president was somber. He told me that the business plans he'd received from Chrysler and GM were "unacceptable." The next day, he'd be announcing that he was giving Chrysler thirty days and GM sixty days to revise them. Otherwise, the administration would put them into bankruptcy. And he added that Rick Wagoner, GM's CEO, was "stepping down."

I stared at the paper with my scrawled list of talking points. My mouth was suddenly dry. But I managed to get the words out in a desperate rush.

"Please, Mr. President. I hear what you are saying, but I hope you will keep these companies out of bankruptcy. Consumers won't buy cars from a bankrupt company," I asserted, repeating my now-familiar argument. I knew I couldn't change the president's mind about leveling the *threat* of bankruptcy, so I was praying I could keep him open-minded on the ultimate conclusion.

I continued: "And the words you use in your speech tomorrow are important. . . . " I paused, hoping I could adequately express the anguish my state was feeling, wanting to push the pain through the phone into his heart. "This is all very deep. It goes to the core of our identity in this state." I knew I was explaining things that he undoubtedly already knew, but they were things I had to say.

"People here take enormous pride in manufacturing the American automobile, and when they perceive an attack on the industry, they feel it's an attack on them.

"I know that you'll show that you understand how the workers feel and that you're not giving up on the American auto industry. And that you understand that this auto crisis is our own version of a hurricane and that we need a response from the federal government more robust and more sensitive than the response to Hurricane Katrina."

The president was compassionate and understanding. "I will communicate that my administration is supporting the auto industry," he told me. "Believe me, I get it. I understand that this is very difficult." He said he would appoint someone as the head of auto community recovery who shared his supportive attitude and would dedicate himself to making the transition work. But—and here was the tough love—the president made it clear that if the shared sacrifices necessary for a fix were not achieved, a "quick-rinse" bankruptcy would be the only other option. (This is a bankruptcy process rendered faster than normal through prior negotiations among government representatives, creditors, and other stakeholders. Because of its speed and the supporting role of government, there was hope that a quick-rinse bankruptcy wouldn't scare away potential auto buyers as a traditional bankruptcy might.)

"Thank you for the personal call, sir," I said, and hung up. I took a deep breath.

Chrysler had thirty days. GM had sixty. They had to fix themselves or face bankruptcy.

It was 8:20 PM. I sent an e-mail to my team: "Please call in now, everyone."

It was going to be a rough sixty days.

The morning following his call to me, President Obama made his auto speech. True to his word, he stood up for American auto manufacturing: "We cannot, we must not, and we will not let our auto industry simply vanish," he said. But the president's message was no-nonsense. He named Dr. Ed Montgomery, an economist and former Clinton administration official, as the director of recovery for auto communities.

Within days, the pundits, the auto execs, and the auto beat reporters were all speaking as though bankruptcy for Chrysler were now a given. The only way that suitor Fiat would agree to a management deal would be if Chrysler weren't a liability, which meant significant concessions and a fresh start. The focus over the next month was on getting the hedge funds to agree to concessions that would speed Chrysler through a quick-rinse bankruptcy.

As the clock ticked down toward the Chrysler deadline, rumors circulated about Fiat's willingness to partner with Chrysler and whether bankruptcy or liquidation would ensue. Tension was everywhere. We had daily communications with the companies involved and with officials from the Obama administration:

WEDNESDAY, APRIL 15, 2009. 3:18 P.M.
FROM: GRANHOLM, JENNIFER
TO: BLOOM, RON; RATTNER, STEVEN

Steve and Ron:
I am getting very concerned as we approach the Chrysler deadline at the end of the month and I keep hearing about loose ends and loose cannons in the process. Today, I was annoyed to read [Fiat CEO] Sergio Marchionne's comments about "walking" if he doesn't get further labor concessions. My question, to be blunt, is: is there a Plan B? If he does walk, and the Administration has said Chrysler is only viable with a partner, what then

is the strategy? As you know, my strong position—and I think the President's—is that liquidation is not an option; I'm sure you have been thinking this through. And, if you are marching toward liquidation on April 30, please advise us asap so we can be prepared for all the dominos that will fall, and there will be many.

In addition to this matter, there are several other issues I would like to discuss, including the status of the banks and bondholders. Can we arrange an update call in the next two days?

The president's auto restructuring and finance team—Steve Rattner, Ron Bloom, and Brian Deese—put me to work calling on the lawyers who represented groups of hedge funds and banks that owned Chrysler debt, trying to persuade them to share in the sacrifice that was necessary to give Chrysler a future. Rattner was hoping to craft a bankruptcy deal that would minimize the drain on Chrysler's leadership, organization, and, especially, reputation and goodwill among businesses and car buyers. A few holdout creditors could wreck that deal. I argued for workers, for Michigan, and for America, and I reminded the lawyers that if Chrysler went into Chapter 11, their clients might collect just pennies on the dollar.

The response from the investors' lawyers was always the same. "We appreciate your call, Governor," they would say. "We want to help. But we have a duty to our clients, who will be losers in this matter no matter how it ends." I publicly called out the recalcitrant investment firms—Parella Weinberg Partners, Stairway Capital, and Oppenheimer Funds—describing them, quite accurately, as greedy Wall Street fat cats who were prepared to destroy the lives of workers and crush the state of Michigan for the sake of higher profits.

They would end up hearing from a much larger voice than mine.

On the evening of April 29, the Obama auto team called me to confirm that the president would announce the following day that Chrysler would be put into bankruptcy. After the call, Gene Sperling reached out to me via e-mail:

WEDNESDAY, APRIL 29, 2009. 11:06 P.M.
FROM: SPERLING, GENE
TO: GRANHOLM, JENNIFER

I know the news was not exactly what you were hoping to hear—but I promise you, this was an all-out and successful effort by the part of the Obama team who were most dedicated to saving Chrysler. I really mean that. It was touch and go and there were people on the team who were worried it costs too much etc—but it was pro-Chrysler folks who prevailed and I don't think any more could have been done. The effort on the financing at the end—including by Tim G was heroic.

So good luck tomorrow and feel free to call anytime, but all in all, I think the story is that Chrysler was saved.

THURSDAY, APRIL 30, 2009. 12:32 A.M.
FROM: GRANHOLM, JENNIFER
TO: SPERLING, GENE

Gene—
Thanks for your message. Yes, it's unspeakably disappointing that bankruptcy is inevitable. Despite all of the incredible work that has gone into this deal, you know the media: what will be reported tomorrow is that

Chrysler has filed for bankruptcy. And that means that
people will be less inclined to buy Chrysler cars unless
something dramatic happens to create demand. People
here will be listening very closely to the President's
speech on this tomorrow. Because of the ravaging we
are taking (e.g., American Axle's announcement today
[Detroit plant to idle, five hundred more layoffs], just
another in the daily barrage) he will have to message this
in a remarkable way. It's a tough messaging balance,
given the American people's disdain for the auto industry. He'll have to communicate that Chrysler is a great
company making great cars with a great future, a green
future, expressing full support for workers, pensioners,
families and communities—his tough love turns it
around. Positive, firm, complimentary and empathetic.
I'd throw in some righteous anger at the hedge funds.
If anyone can do it, he can.

Gene, there is another looming issue here on the GM side. I
told Deese and Rattner and Bloom that once the Chrysler
crisis is over we really need to work on the GM plan—lots
of anger here. . . . We really need to strategize to avert a
major problem. I'll try to catch you in the afternoon after
the Chrysler announcement.

Thanks for reaching out, and for all your help and concern.
And for your love for your home state.

Sure enough, less than twelve hours later, at 11:50 AM on April
30, President Obama called me again—a courtesy call, given that I
already had the news. "Today I'm announcing that Chrysler is going into bankruptcy," he told me. "I intend to express my gratitude
for the workers and for the concessions they are making. The

banks have been willing to work with us. So far, everyone is prepared to take a haircut except for the hedge funds." He called them "greedy"—and he was right.

The fallout over the next month and a half would be uncertain, but the president expressed his confidence to me that Chrysler would be stronger and more profitable after it emerged from bankruptcy—and that the restructuring would save 30,000 jobs. He also indicated that the administration was working on getting Congress to pass the cash for clunkers plan that Eric Schmidt had proposed to help generate demand for cars.

I gathered my team in my office. "The president just called," I reported. "The bad news is that Chrysler is definitely going into bankruptcy. The good news is that the president has given us his assurance that Chrysler will survive and thrive." I told them that Chrysler should be in and out of bankruptcy in thirty days. We'd still have to work with the administration to get the hedge funds to compromise. But the Fiat merger meant that jobs would stick around—in fact, Fiat was proposing to actually bring in 5,000 new jobs.

I tried to sound optimistic. My hardworking team needed and deserved a boost. Inside, I was deeply worried.

"I'm still glad I took the buyout," Fred said with a smile. Unlike many other former Chrysler employees, Fred had landed on his feet.

"So are we, Fred," I put my arm around his shoulder. "So are we."

With Chrysler's bankruptcy filing a fait accompli, all eyes now turned to GM. For decades, General Motors had been the largest auto company in the world—outselling the rest for eighty-two years, right through 2007—and by far our state's largest employer. Everyone in Michigan knew the old adage "As GM goes, so goes Michigan." To Michigan citizens, it was inconceivable that both of these enormous, storied auto companies could go into bankruptcy.

It felt as if our state's identity and history would go into bankruptcy, too. Every political leader in Michigan was doing whatever she or he could to convince the Obama administration that we couldn't sustain such a blow. But we knew that the ultimate decision was out of our hands. I was praying that we could keep the Michigan GM plants open.

Meanwhile, the president's executive team was working on a parallel strategy: laying the foundation for a new, green auto industry. In the past, the carmakers had fiercely resisted any efforts to raise the corporate average fuel economy (CAFE) standards, arguing that the technology was too expensive and would put people out of work. Michigan's representatives in Congress had backed the automakers on this point. In fact, fuel economy standards were one of several auto-related issues on which members of both political parties as well as representatives of both labor and management were in agreement within our state. Many in the delegation also joined in railing against toothless trade policies that exported jobs, and they agreed that rising health care costs were killing our competitiveness (though they differed on the best solutions).

The auto industry's dogged resistance to increasing fuel economy standards was one of the reasons it had been viewed so harshly by much of the country. Now the president, who had promised in his campaign to push for improved auto fuel economy, had the leverage to accomplish a quick win on this front.

On May 19, 2009, President Obama emerged from the White House into a spectacularly sunny Rose Garden. Standing next to him were the CEOs of all of the major car companies, domestic and foreign; Ron Gettlefinger, the head of the United Auto Workers; and the president's green team, including environmental czar Carol Browner and Environmental Protection Agency (EPA) administrator Lisa Jackson. The president announced that his team had reached agreement on the most aggressive, uniform auto fuel efficiency standards ever set. The new rules mandated that by 2016 automakers' passenger vehicle fleets had to achieve a combined average fuel-economy standard of 35.5 miles per gallon—39 mpg for cars and 30 mpg for light trucks and SUVs. That represented a 40 percent improvement over current standards.

Representative John Dingell, California governor Arnold Schwarzenegger, Massachusetts governor Deval Patrick, and I sat together in the first row. Schwarzenegger, a sincere environmentalist, was pleased with the tough new standards. Dingell was pleased that the return to a single nationwide standard would keep California or other states from creating their own idiosyncratic rules. The CEOs of the car companies looked pleased, too, perhaps about having secured a commitment to their survival from the White House. I thought to myself, what a difference it makes to have a hands-on administration.

Long-term prospects: promising. Immediate crisis: scarier than ever.

The national recession and credit freeze, on top of the auto implosion, had been sending aftershock upon aftershock across our state. In the six months since Obama's election, I had received 316 more WARN Act notices from companies announcing mass layoffs. We'd lost 72 percent of our automotive jobs since 2000, and record numbers of families were moving out of Michigan in search of work. In a state of less than 10 million people, 700,000 citizens were collecting jobless benefits. The unemployment rate now hovered over 14 percent, almost five points above the national average; unofficial estimates in Detroit pegged the rate at 50 percent. Lines at Department of Human Services offices snaked around buildings, populated with many middle-class folks, anxious and angry, who had never before dreamed of seeking public assistance. There were reports of human service workers being assaulted by desperate people, and violence broke out at a housing assistance event at Cobo Center in Detroit among a crowd of 50,000 frustrated help-seekers.

I got home from the Rose Garden CAFE ceremony to learn from Dan that our friend John, a brilliant Harvard-educated advertising executive with six kids—four in college—had been laid off from his auto industry job. His home was already in foreclosure. Another couple, dear friends of ours, were underwater and, with their marriage in tatters, had decided to split up and abandon their 3,500-square-foot Detroit Tudor. Dan and I spent the evening sitting at our side-by-side desks staring numbly at our computer screens.

This night and every other during this time, I was out of gas by 10:00 PM. I felt as if I were leading a dwindling band of survivors on a desperate trek across the desert. Downcast by Dan's news of our friends, I wandered off online into the badlands of the blogs, where I found the usual vicious attacks on my leadership skills, political judgment, IQ, and appearance. Feeling numb, I continued to stare at the screen until Dan came over, gently pulled me up, and walked me the eight feet to bed. I couldn't sleep.

At our 8:00 AM daily meeting the next morning, Nate Lake reported on progress with our unemployment processing; we'd had to hire hundreds more unemployment workers to deal with the peak million-calls-per-day that we'd been receiving. Lord knows, my team was practiced in resolving crises. "The Constituent Services team is doing an amazing job fielding difficult calls," Nate said. "It would be great if you could just take a minute, Governor, and thank them for their work. It would mean a ton to them."

I had a half-hour available, so I went down to the floor below to thank the beleaguered team answering the phones. I touched shoulders and offered thanks in between calls. Then, in the spirit of teamwork, I sat at an empty cubicle and picked up a ringing phone.

"Governor Granholm's office, how can I help you?" I mimicked those around me.

"That stupid governor!" the caller burst out, not realizing who had answered the phone. "She needs to quit talking to Obama and *order* those plants to stay open!"

"She doesn't have the power to do that, ma'am," I began, as politely as possible.

"Well, if she don't have the power, then what good is she anyway?" The woman slammed the phone in my ear.

The fellow at the next desk grinned over at me and gave me a thumbs up. "Goes with the territory," he mouthed. I was overwhelmed with admiration for this Constituent Services team. They were wading through a daily morass of anger and fear, keeping their cool and calmly, skillfully educating citizens on how the process worked and where they could get help.

We were also responding to the statewide distress in more systemic ways. We passed foreclosure moratorium legislation. We coordinated with human services agencies across the state to reach those most in need. Shepherded by policy director Regina Bell, our information technology office created a "Helping Hands" outreach program and a statewide partnership that allowed people to file for benefits like food assistance, unemployment, and Medicaid online rather than at a local office. We held cabinet-level town halls across the state to let people know about the Recovery Act, the assistance available, and how they could get help. I did public service announcements and radio addresses and spoke to as many groups as possible. And during GM's sixty days in bankruptcy limbo, we worked feverishly to try to give people hope, despite the drumbeat of negative news about the auto industry and the economy in general.

Our team began showing human signs of stress. In the middle of my State of the State address that year, communications director Liz Boyd fainted from sheer exhaustion on the floor of the House. Poor Liz was mortified, but I was only surprised that we hadn't *all* cracked under the strain. At that same address, a normally unflappable staffer loaded the wrong version of my speech into the teleprompter—every speaker's nightmare. When I mounted the podium and realized what had happened, there was no turning back—I had to wing it and use my notes instead.

I kept trying to make time for what time-management guru Steven Covey calls quadrant III activities: not urgent but important. Those are the kinds of vital long-term projects that inevitably get neglected in times of crisis, leading to even deeper problems in the months and years to come. I kept telling our team that we had to continue to play offense—to seek daily, small wins. We were relentless about recruiting green companies and posting their job offerings on our Web site. We ramped up training activities under the No Worker Left Behind program at an unprecedented rate. Every few days, we'd announce a new battery company or film studio or research operation setting up shop in Michigan. The state Economic Development Corporation was working so hard recruiting companies that it ran out of authorized tax credits.

The effort was there. The small wins were accumulating. But when would the overall curve finally bend upward? How soon would the unemployment rate respond to all our work?

. . . . .

IT WAS 8:00 ON SUNDAY NIGHT, MAY 31, 2009. DAN AND I WERE at home at our usual battle stations. I'd been told to expect the call.

The president's first words were lighthearted. "Jennifer, we've got to stop meeting like this," he teased.

He continued, serious now, "I'm calling to let you know that General Motors will file for bankruptcy in the morning."

I'd known it was coming. But I made one final attempt to change reality, talking quickly about the potential impact of bankruptcy on our auto suppliers and an economy already in meltdown.

President Obama understood. But his response was candid.

"The worst is not over," he said. "This will be hard. My administration will stand behind the industry, and we will do everything we can to help you get through this. But it will take time. I need your help in telling people that the government is not going to run General Motors, but that we are going to do what it takes to keep this industry alive."

I told him we'd do all we could, and added quietly, "I sure hope you guys know what you're doing." It was clear that this was no easier for President Obama than it was for me. "We appreciate your efforts to save the American automotive industry, Mr. President."

I hung the phone up and turned to Dan.

"It's over," I said. "General Motors is going into bankruptcy, too. Fourteen more plants to close, seven in Michigan. Twenty-one thousand more jobs lost."

I let out a long sigh, closed my eyes, and put my head in my hands. Behind my closed eyes, I saw the face of the Delphi worker at the Saginaw coffee shop. "When is this ever going to end?"

· · · · ·

I DON'T KNOW WHETHER IT WAS A MINUTE LATER, OR TWO, OR ten when Dan said, "Jen, it's Kathy. She says Gene Sperling from the White House wants to know if you're available. You want the call, don't you?" As Kathy put the call through, I had enough time to exhale heavily and remind myself, "Accept, adjust, advance."

Gene explained that he'd been in the Oval Office when the president had called. "Are you okay?" he asked me.

"I'm okay, Gene, but I can't tell you how worried I am for this state. You know how sweeping this damage will be." Gene, a Detroit area native, would understand.

"You'll make it work. And we'll help. Jennifer, when the president hung up, he shook his head and said to us, 'She has the toughest job in the country.' And he's right." I laughed out loud at the irony. Imagine it—the president of the United States, beset with gargantuan challenges including wars and recession, would think *my* job was hard.

"Gene, that's something, coming from him," I said, dismissing the hyperbole. "But I'm glad you guys are going to help because Michigan sure needs some TLC right now."

I thanked Gene for the personal call. Then, scarcely aware of what I was doing, I washed my face, changed into my sweats, fell into bed, and pulled the covers up over my head.

Not even Dan could fully appreciate how I was feeling. I had slammed into a wall after six-plus years of constant forward movement. Now the destination was sealed off. The president had uttered the unthinkable. The largest bankruptcy in U.S. history was about to happen in Michigan.

At 5:00 AM, I rose to take on the day. I turned on MSNBC, and my thoughts snapped to the factory workers hearing from Joe Scarborough or Ann Curry or their local morning newsperson the same news I'd heard the night before from President Obama. I was determined to project confidence for those workers hearing the news.

At our regular 8:00 AM meeting, the big topics were stimulus funds, energy companies, and No Worker Left Behind. I started a new push that had been forming in my mind around No Worker Left Behind. I told my team that we had to take full advantage of every drop of DC empathy and max out on every possible penny of federal stimulus money.

Through the subsequent days, I continued pushing the Obama administration, meeting with its team members in DC, pressing for assistance, and insisting that they not turn their attention from us via e-mails like this one:

FRIDAY: JUNE 05, 2009. 11:00 A.M.
FROM: GRANHOLM, JENNIFER
TO: SPERLING, GENE

Gene, thanks for taking the time to meet with me. I'm so very grateful you are part of the team. I just wanted to give you a flavor of what I am seeing here in the trenches. It's not even 11:00 a.m. and already this morning I have received three notices of mass layoffs of auto supplier employees. I will be seeing more fill my inbox this afternoon. These past few weeks have seen scores of such notices coming to me, with many, many more predicted. It is a deluge. These suppliers need help immediately. . . . I hope you can express that we are on a burning platform.

We were already in triage mode, pushing hard to channel government assistance toward those who needed it most. Now we had to redouble those efforts. With my team, I remained focused and encouraging, trying to keep everyone on task.

But I was completely faking the confidence I was projecting.

I think there were only two people who weren't fooled by my relentless focus on the positive. One was Dan, and—though I was determined not to acknowledge the heaviness I felt—the other was me.

Dan was the one safe person to whom—or *on* whom—I could unload my frustrations and worries. As he had throughout our twenty-three years together, Dan gently probed, pushing me to go in and explore the hurt inside. My coping mechanism was to "deflect," as Dan would call it, turning his inquiries back to issues of Michigan, strategy, politics, and leadership.

After one low-energy Friday fish-and-chips date-night dinner at Claddagh, our favorite Irish pub, we started to really talk in the safety of our Ford Flex on the drive home without our security detail. After listening to me vent about how some *Detroit News* blogger had made it sound like I'd personally laid off the latest tidal wave of workers, Dan finally blurted, "You're in an impossible loop. You know that no matter how hard you work, you're not going to succeed by traditional measures. You want to be perfect. You're not. At some point, you have to accept it."

We went silent for rest of the ride home.

Later, in front of our twin computer screens, I tried to reconnect. "I'm sorry," I said. "I just have to get through this. I really don't mean to be such a load."

"This may sound harsh," Dan said quietly, "but if you're a load, it's because you won't let anyone help. The load is your damn ego. You're identified with it, with this image of yourself, and it's not helping you, us, or, frankly, your beloved Michigan." I steeled myself for what I could feel was coming.

Dan softened momentarily. "You are being called to something more right now, Jen. To somewhere you've never been. This is your crucible. So many factory workers are lost, and this state feels lost, so you're lost, too. But you're human, just like they are. And it's time to just admit it to yourself."

I started to tell Dan that this wasn't all about me, that it was precisely those workers who needed me not to give in to despair. But he was on a roll.

"Maybe it's *okay* for you to be lost, Jen. Maybe it's okay for you to be human. Read the Bible. Moses had his days of frustration with the Israelites and even anger and despair with God."

I broke in: "I'm not Moses. Don't be ridiculous."

"Of course you're not, Jen. But my point is, you're not God. So let it go. Let go of the ego."

His words finally pierced my hard, self-pitying armor. It was my ego that was sucking me down. My ego that had always been rewarded and fueled by success. My ego that blocked my ability to accept the reality: It would take longer than I had to fix the state.

"I'll try," was all I could manage to say. And "Thanks for caring so much," from as deep a part of me as I could reach at that moment.

· · · · ·

IN THE WEEKS THAT FOLLOWED, I FELT BOLSTERED BY THE FACT that the Obama administration was strongly behind us. My team and I talked almost daily with Summers, Geithner, Montgomery, Sperling, and others on the president's core team. They were intent on using stimulus funds to help American firms—including the cash-starved auto suppliers—finally begin competing with Asia for the green economy. The carmakers themselves remained on the long-term disabled list, but we could see they would be back on the field, smaller but stronger. Much as I had dreaded the bankruptcies, there was no question that the "cleansing" that the automakers were going through—including radical cost contractions and huge concessions from the UAW—would revive their competitiveness.

In a Detroit speech to business leaders about the economy, I tempered my enthusiasm with a sober tone. During the question period, a woman asked, "As you reflect on your terms in office, what do you most regret?"

I paused. I knew what a business audience would want to hear: that I regretted allowing the government to shut down, not cutting business taxes more, or perhaps not reducing government spending even further.

But I was honest. "I most regret that there are things I cannot fix. I regret my powerlessness over the global economy, the bankruptcies, the loss of jobs. I regret that citizens are still hurting. That I'm governor during the transition from one type of economy to another. And the hardest thing for me personally," I said, speaking directly to my questioner, "is that our recovery won't happen fully until after I'm gone. I won't be in office to see the full fruits of our labors."

She nodded, a solemn yet sympathetic look in her dark eyes. I was glad that my security detail was signaling that my car was waiting. Suddenly I wanted to be gone.

chapter 9

GREEN SHOOTS

The people of St. Johns made bearings, bushings, and washers for the auto industry. Until 2006, that is, when auto supplier Federal Mogul decided to close its factory. A rural community twenty miles north of Lansing, St. Johns is home to 2,000 families. Federal Mogul eliminated 435 jobs—one job loss for every five families. The company sent the work mostly to Puebla in Mexico and Shanghai in China. Like so many towns, St. Johns had mounted a valiant effort to remain competitive. Just a year earlier, it had given Federal Mogul $5 million in tax abatements; the state had kicked in $65 million, and the UAW had provided $11 million in concessions. All this wasn't enough. The St. Johns plant was just one of twenty-five facilities Federal Mogul had vacated in a global restructuring that eliminated 4,500 American jobs.

Glenn Voisin's was one of them.

Glenn is in his forties, a handsome guy with salt-and-pepper hair. His wife, Terrilynn, works at St. Joseph Catholic School, a wonderful, mission-oriented job for a back-up earner. In the wake of the plant closing, they grappled with two lousy choices: have Glenn take a job, any job, assuming he could even find one (understanding he would never replace his Federal Mogul salary) or get Glenn back to school to upgrade his skills. But how could they live for the two years he'd need to get retrained? What about college for their three daughters? How could they pay their bills today without sacrificing the investments they needed to make for tomorrow?

Terrilynn said, "We'll find a way."

Glenn had unemployment compensation and federal Trade Adjustment Assistance support coming in. Traditional unemployment forces laid-off workers to report their job searches weekly and take just about anything that comes their way. But through our groundbreaking retraining program, No Worker Left Behind, Michigan had received permission from the feds to allow workers like Glenn to pursue full-time schooling without having their unemployment terminated. So through No Worker Left Behind, Glenn spent two years earning his associate's degree in alternative energy at Lansing Community College. Through study and determination, he remade himself and gave himself a new chance.

By 2008, a market for Glenn's new skills was emerging.

That year, I signed a new state law that encouraged energy efficiency and the development of renewables. Under the old energy regime, the more electricity or natural gas an energy company sold, the more money it made. We had changed that incentive structure in 2008 through something called "decoupling"—breaking the link between the amount of energy used and the profits utilities were afforded. Under new Public Service Commission guidelines, the big utilities had an incentive to sell *less* energy. If they were able to make homes and businesses more efficient, they'd receive credits that would enhance their profit margins. Consumers would spend less, fossil fuel use would fall, and companies would prosper. Glenn Voisin was able to take advantage of the state's new demand for energy efficiency. He got a job at CLEAResult, a private company incorporated in 2009 after the passage of Michigan's energy bill. It had contracts with major utilities to perform energy efficiency audits in people's homes and businesses. By 2010, it employed over sixty people; Glen was one of them, grateful to be working at a growing company that paid him wages and benefits on par with what he had made at the Federal Mogul plant.

"I used to be one of you," the new Glenn said to the adult students at Lansing Community College when he was invited back for a visit. Their faces reminded him of the people he used to make bearings and bushings with. "I lost my manufacturing job. I didn't know what I was going to do. And now I have a new lease on life. If I can do it, you can, too."

Glenn had crossed over to the New Michigan. By the time I left office, we'd enrolled 151,000 workers in No Worker Left Behind. Michigan had four times as many adults being retrained as the national average. Between 2000 and 2010, community college enrollment increased by 50 percent.

But for every Glenn Voisin, there were many who hadn't made the transition. Those confronted with going back to school and mastering a new set of skills faced the prospect of long periods of unemployment or underemployment. The daunting midlife difficulties faced by working families heightened our imperative: We must get *kids* to go to college, starting with these workers' children. I remain flabbergasted at how difficult it was to get this message through.

Dan and I caught a glimpse of this one day in west Michigan. We asked a local realtor how the schools were doing.

"Truthfully, the district's scores aren't very good," she admitted. Then she hastened to explain the reason: "Many of the kids just don't plan on going to college."

My mind boggled at her matter-of-fact tone.

"After all we've been through," I sputtered, "how can they not see that their future is tied to higher education—that it's not the old Michigan anymore?"

"It's the parents," she said quickly. "Believe it or not, they still don't get it. They still hope the old jobs are coming back."

I closed my eyes in disbelief. The theme of John Kotter's famous *Harvard Business Review* article on change, so often quoted by Dan, came back into my head: You've got to overcommunicate the vision by a factor of ten. From day one of my administration, I'd talked about the importance of education at every opportunity—in interviews, campaign speeches, town hall meetings, press conferences, citizens' forums, business gatherings, and every single time I met with a parents, students, or teachers group. I wasn't alone, as business leaders and editorial writers, among others, were amplifying the same message. Yet the people I'd been trying so hard to reach hadn't absorbed the message.

Changing Michigan's self-image would require a lot more work—like the work Glenn Voisin had undertaken to remake himself.

· · · · ·

As I neared the end of my second term as governor, I found that I, too, had some remaking to do.

I'd come into office with a clear, ambitious, optimistic agenda, focused on education, job creation, and community revitalization. Now, with just a short while remaining as governor, by the goals I'd set for myself and Michigan, I'd fallen short. I'd hardly be feted as one of Michigan's most admired governors: far from it. Too many people

were suffering too much economic hurt for that. I'd worked cease-
lessly to lessen their pain, but it had all happened on my watch.
Many Michiganders resented me for not stopping the economic free
fall, and I felt frustrated that I'd been unable to prevent it.

It took a toll on me, one that those who knew me best couldn't
help noticing.

"Walk with your head up, Jen," Dan said as we strolled east
down sunny Market Street on Mackinac Island. Tourists in bright
shorts and T-shirts toted bags of souvenirs while horse carriages
clopped by, their bright white-and-yellow-striped canopies snap-
ping in the breeze. I was wearing my usual disguise—a Tigers cap
and sunglasses, my head bent down to watch only the sidewalk and
the sandaled heels of the people in front of me.

"You shouldn't keep your head down," Dan repeated. "It's
weird."

"I just don't want to be recognized," I said in a low voice, hoping he'd lower his. The heels in front of us turned into Richard
Wolfgang's art gallery, where luscious watercolors matched the island's lushness. I tilted my head up as we headed toward Fort Hill
and turned the corner to climb to the governor's summer residence
on the bluff.

"Are you afraid?" Dan asked.

"Afraid? Hmm, that's an interesting question." I squinted out
at the blue waters of the straits. I knew Sergeant Vic Latimore was
somewhere behind us. Threats and hate mail from angry citizens
had increased substantially, but my disguise wasn't motivated by
physical fear. I was hiding from something else.

"It's really more *avoidance*," I said. "I'm avoiding knowing
that anyone I meet is probably out of work, in financial crisis, or
just plain angry with me. I'm avoiding the realization that many of
the people we pass on the street blame me for Michigan's crisis."

Dan paused for a moment and then let loose. "Jen, that's
ridiculous. It's your ego, dancing with a roomful of hurt and angry

people. You're letting some unspecified 'them' shape your mind, heart, and actions. You're letting them take the joy for you—for us—out of this beautiful place." He quietly added, "I resent that."

"Sorry," I said, thoroughly hating that I sounded pitiful.

Dan sensed he wasn't getting the results he intended, and he tried again. "Jen, you did not cause Michigan's problems. You are working your ass off to fix them. No one could fix them alone—not Abe Lincoln, George Patton, Bill Gates, and Mother Teresa all rolled into one. So you won't be able to succeed in the way you want. So you won't end up being beloved. So what? Let go, Hon." He gently pulled me to a stop and removed my sunglasses, searching for my eyes. "Let it go."

When we got to the cottage, I changed into running clothes and put on my iPod. I pressed the menu to listen to an audiobook, *The Power of Now* by the inspirational writer Eckhart Tolle. Dan had suggested I give Tolle a try. He's not the kind of writer I would normally have been drawn to. History, economics, and biographies are more my style. But I decided I might benefit from a new perspective.

I sprinted out of the cottage and ran across the road, down the carriage path, and into the forest. The sun was dancing through the forest canopy a good hundred feet overhead, dappling the trail. In his German accent, Tolle was talking about the difference between a person's real self and the "egoic mind," which can never be truly content. He went on: "The most common ego identifications have to do with possessions, the work you do, social status and recognition, knowledge and education, physical appearance, special abilities, relationships, personal and family history, belief systems, and often also political, nationalistic, racial, religious, and other collective identifications. None of this is you."

I ran hard as I listened. Ran from the anger of others. Ran from my own egoism and disappointment. Ran to get strong again. I lost track of Tolle's train of thought as my mind drifted to the challenges my family had been wrestling with, not just this past year but also for the decade prior.

There was no doubt in my mind that the person most challenged by my ten years in public life was Dan. My career had forced an identity crisis on him. He joked that growing up he'd wanted to be a few things, but "First Gentleman" had somehow never made the list. He'd been raised to be an assertive, competitive, high-achieving male, but here he was stuck in this peculiar, traditionally female role. He was like a big old Ford F-250 truck in a context that cried for a Toyota Prius or a Chevy Volt. His issues were deeply personal, yet they were inextricably interwoven in the context of my being governor.

He tried—as many *women* do every day—to manage it all, to be a great spouse, parent, and professional. He had intended to fully share that stretch of the road *with* me. But in long spells or just excruciating moments, it became clear how impossible that now was. He was too busy flying solo in the parent plane to touch down for long in my world. And when he was there, his opinion was always a second opinion: interesting, helpful, but minor relative to mine. He supported me intellectually and emotionally at every turn. Yet there was a slow-burning resentment in him: my preoccupation with all things Michigan had made him feel that he'd given up both the wife and the life he'd expected.

Dan had plowed himself into his writing, his speaking, and his chairmanship of the community service organization Mentor Michigan, and he'd run two marathons. But he remained restless, uncomfortable with the role forced on him as "the governor's husband."

He worked it spiritually, always coming back to St. Augustine's line "My soul is restless, and only in God will my soul be at rest." Yet even there he was affected by my public role—a fiercely dedicated lifetime Catholic, he found himself persona non grata with a Catholic bureaucracy fixated on my pro-choice position.

And I grew ambivalent about attending church after our bishop met with us privately to tell me that, as a pro-choice politician, I was not worthy to receive communion.

Perhaps the greatest gift for me was that in an odd way, Dan's internal struggle illuminated my own. I didn't need to fix every problem and be loved by voters to have merit and worth, just as Dan didn't need to be the governor to have merit and worth.

Dan's own ego challenges led him to turn outward. He became the primary voice in the governors' spouses group for healthy marriages and happy children. He wrote empathetic and searching letters to the other first spouses as they all watched the slow procession of public humiliations that struck their friends—Silda Wall Spitzer, Deena McGreevy, Jenny Sanford—and others less publicly humiliated. He invited his governor-spouse colleagues to a retreat focused entirely on the contribution that they could make to the public—not through engaging in public initiatives but through helping their spouses to stay humanly alive and connected. He organized a retreat for incoming Michigan legislators and their spouses, hoping to help them avoid some of the pitfalls of life in a capital city. Dan was steering into the wind, sometimes soaring on updrafts, sometimes tossed wildly in the swirl.

And so in his early fifties, there was breakthrough and then there was acceptance. Dan walked down a new path uniquely his. He discovered over time that the role of first spouse, which seemed a permanent second prize, was actually the most gratifying one in a life of many careers with many different uniforms. When our daughters entered college and he realized what fine people they had become, he was overwhelmed with a sense that he had done the most important work he would ever do—work that in its own domain was every bit as important as mine. He had and still has a strong desire to publish, speak, broadcast, and attain recognition for such work. But no one can ever take away the blessing of his identity as father and husband.

I came to the end of Leslie Trail and turned right onto the North Bicycle Path. Tiring, my mind slid back into Eckhart Tolle's track. He was summarizing how to achieve peace: through *acceptance* of, rather than resistance to, the things we cannot change.

Dan had accepted and embraced his situation. I knew, deeply, that I had to, and could, accept the reality that being governor at this time would never result in a satisfied public. People would continue to be angry at me. I would not be able to carry Michigan on my back to the victory circle. I would not be in office to pop the champagne cork as we crossed the finish line. I had to be okay with that. And I was.

I thought of the prayer that Fred Hoffman had given to me after a speech the year before. It had been written by Michigan's beloved Bishop Ken Untener. I tried to recite the key lines to myself as I pounded the trail:

> It helps now and then to step back and take the long view.
> We plant seeds that one day will grow. We water seeds already planted, knowing that they hold future promise.
> We lay foundations that will need further development.
> We are prophets of a future not our own.

With those words in my head, I emerged from the forest path into the bright sunlight spilling into the clearing next to Fort Mackinac. I felt lighter than I had in months. I ventured a smile at the tourists disembarking from the carriage in front of the Fort, and the tour guide quickly grabbed his microphone and said, "There goes the governor!" I waved as I passed them, my head up.

I arrived back at the cottage and took the steps to the kitchen door two at a time. The Mackinac faucet gushed clear cold water and I headed to the porch to cool down. I dragged one of the high-backed white wicker rocking chairs into the shade, put my heels on the rung, gulped my water, and watched the blue straits of Mackinac—ever different, ever the same, ever spectacular.

My laptop was sleeping on the wicker table next to me. After a few minutes, I logged in and saw that I had left my Facebook page up. A young blogger had posted a comment: "keep on workin dont look back."

I smiled to myself, adding, *and keep your head up*. I e-mailed Sherry to schedule an executive office conference call. We had work to do.

····· · ·

BACK IN THE OFFICE, A HASTY E-MAIL FROM JOANNE HULS popped up on my screen: "Veep's office on phone w/ battery decision—can u come down?"

I ran down the long hallway, my heart thumping, my own cautious brain chanting in my head, "Don't get your hopes up. Don't get your hopes up. If we don't do well, it's not the end of the world."

Vice President Joe Biden's office was calling with a heads-up about grants to be awarded under the American Recovery and Reinvestment Act—the Obama stimulus bill. We'd put our all into this effort. We'd worked with scores of Michigan companies on applications for grants to research, design, and build advanced, high-efficiency batteries for the electric vehicles of the future. We'd persuaded the state legislature to pass irresistible incentive packages to match the federal funds. If we didn't win at least a few of these projects, it would be a devastating blow to Michigan's efforts to diversify into clean energy while remaining the epicenter of the auto industry.

As I burst into Jo's office, she and Leslee Fritz from our Economic Recovery Office were on the phone with Evan Ryan, a Biden aide. Jo put her on the speakerphone. "Evan, it's Jennifer

Granholm—I just walked in," I said, catching my breath. "What's the news?"

Evan began to describe the grants awarded to Michigan. JoAnne took furious notes on a coffee-stained yellow pad as she spoke. "KD Advanced Battery Group—$161 million, factory to be built in Midland, Michigan. Johnson Controls—$299.2 million, factory to be built in Holland, Michigan. A123 Systems to get $249.1 million—factories to be built in Romulus and Brownstown. Compact Power, also known as LG Chem—$151.4 million for battery cells for the GM Volt, facilities to be built in Holland, Pontiac, and St. Clair. General Motors and Ford—two awards each for four different projects. Chrysler's getting one. Magna E-Car Systems of America is getting $40 million for a plant in Holly. Eaton in partnership with the Coast Air Quality Management District is getting $45.4 million for a plant in Galesburg. Hmm, I think that's all."

I stood over Jo's shoulder and squinted at her scrawled notes, my heart still pounding. "Evan, if I count this correctly, Michigan got twelve awards?"

A pause while Evan completed her own count. "Right," she said. "I have that Michigan got twelve awards worth $1.35 billion dollars."

Leslee's eyebrows raised. "We got *all* of our big ones—" she whispered.

"Remind me, Evan," I said into the speakerphone, "how much was awarded overall?"

"$2.4 billion," Evan replied.

"Wait. This means Michigan—one state—got more than half of all of the battery projects in the U.S.?" I'd hardly dared to say it out loud, for fear of pointing out our oversized share.

"Yes. Michigan had great submissions, Governor. Congratulations!" she exclaimed. "Remember, this news is embargoed until August 5th, when the vice president comes to Detroit to make the announcement."

When Jo hung up, we stared at each other a moment. I broke the silence by pumping my fists into the air. "Yes!" I yelled.

"Woo hoo!" exploded Jo, giving me a high five.

"I'm counting one more time—seems too good to be true," said Leslee as she recrunched the numbers. After a moment, Leslee looked up and shook her head in disbelief, grinning.

"Holy crap," she said. "This is a game changer!"

· · · · ·

IT TOOK SOME MONTHS—A PERIOD OF INCUBATION AND fermentation—before the battery investments started to do their work. Then, suddenly, new jobs began to appear.

On May 24, 2010, I headed to Ypsilanti, home to Eastern Michigan University and the Ford Rawsonville assembly plant. Opened in 1956, the plant in its heyday mushroomed to 1.5 million square feet, equivalent to about twenty-five football fields, and provided work for 6,000 people. By 2009, it was largely empty, employing about 780 people and slated for closure.

Then Ford received the grant to assemble its electric vehicle batteries in America. Now one section of the Rawsonville plant had been set aside for a new purpose. Ford was going to hire hundreds of workers over the next few years to work on plans and systems for integrating the new battery into Ford vehicles.

A riser jutted out from a backdrop dotted with blue Ford ovals and UAW logos, a row of chairs sandwiching a wooden podium. I sat with Mark Fields, Ford's president of the Americas; Bob King, soon to be president of the UAW; Congressman John Dingell; and local UAW leaders. Fields spoke first, thanking everyone for partnering to bring jobs back to America. Bob King, looking two decades younger than his sixty-five years and wearing plain black-framed glasses straight out of a 1964 high school yearbook photo, spoke with passion, congratulating the autoworkers on their obsession with manufacturing quality products in America. Then the powerful John Dingell, "Dean of the House," moved almost regally to the podium, his six-foot-three-inch frame ever-so-slightly bent over the cane that supported him. His comments were upbeat and feisty, peppered with digs at the "rascals" and "scalawags" who'd opposed aid to the auto industry.

I'd been to scores of groundbreakings and ribbon cuttings. It's part of a politician's job description. This one was different because the underlying reality was earthshaking. Ford was defying the prevailing economic laws by bringing manufacturing work and jobs back *to* Michigan *from* Mexico and Japan. With this project, Ford was reversing the outbound tide.

Organized labor, too, was making a paradigm shift. The "new UAW," as Bob King calls it, had played a significant role in making it possible for Ford to choose Michigan while still being globally competitive. The new contract was more flexible, imposed fewer work rules, and supported team manufacturing rather than rigidly defined job assignments; it was less expensive, with starting wages at $15 an hour; and, most importantly, it reflected the UAW's new obsession with product quality. The battery lines would require sophisticated robotics skill, programming ability for guiding the computer controls that have revolutionized the manufacturing process, and a relentless commitment to process improvement and teamwork. The UAW was committed to ensuring that its members would have the advanced manufacturing skills needed to make Ford cars the best in the world.

Finally, there was the unique financial package that had made Rawsonville possible. Every level of government had stepped up to the plate. The upfront government investment came from three sources: Department of Energy battery grants; state battery tax credits, which I had asked the legislature to pass in anticipation of the federal support; and local property tax abatements. In order to access all of the government assistance, the company had to locate the battery assembly in the United States, in Michigan, and, specifically, in Ypsilanti, using American workers. Government pressure in support of American manufacturing was a crucial counterweight to the systemic pressure multinational companies like Ford, Dow, or General Electric feel from shareholders to operate anywhere in the world that costs can be minimized and profits maximized. If American workers are to compete with the Chinese, they need the American government on their side.

Figuring this out had been the biggest challenge of my administration—and it remains one of the biggest challenges our nation faces. How do we manufacture products competitively in America when other countries are so inexpensive? It was a joyous relief to glimpse at least part of the answer in Rawsonville. As we left the plant, Fred Hoffman said as much. "Gov," he began, "I believe we've begun to crack the code on how to create advanced manufacturing jobs in America."

"We're cracking the code," I repeated, half to myself. It seemed almost too good to be true.

The following sunny Saturday, I described the Rawsonville event to Dan, and he asked the most revealing question. "With Electrolux, you had the same ingredients: UAW concessions, state incentives, and tax breaks. Yet Electrolux went to Mexico. What was the difference here?"

"The feds," I said without hesitation. "The federal government decided that there is a critical national need to manufacture electric vehicle batteries in America rather than relying on foreign makers. And the feds were willing to give financial help to companies in exchange for a commitment to build the batteries here."

We were back on Mackinac, watching the kites flying above the shore below, their bright hues vivid against the azure waters of the Straits of Mackinac sparkling in the afternoon sun. "Look!" I said, pointing. We saw one striped kite break from its string and float for a long distance in the breeze, gently passing over the stone break-water and drifting out toward the horizon.

Dan wanted to tease out the larger meaning of what we'd learned. "So if the feds had thrown in, could you have saved Electrolux? Could you have induced them to stay?" he asked. "And if that's our strategy for keeping manufacturing, how do we avoid competing with China, which has a lot more cash and no rabid right-wingers terrified of state intervention? Seems like a risky path," Dan said, his tone heating up. "How do we afford it? And how do we choose? Why autos and not refrigerators or textiles or shrimp, all of which are pretty darned important—especially to the southern states?"

"Those industries are important to local economies for sure, but autos are the manufacturing backbone of America, the nervous system for all kinds of invention. Auto technologies are essential to defense preparedness. And they're gonna lead us to energy independence. So we have a critical *national* need for auto manufacturing."

Dan was skeptical. "You really think so?"

"I'm telling you, what's happening is huge. Auto batteries are teaching us tons about energy generation and storage. By 2030, 70 percent of the cars on the road will be electric, all of them with these advanced lithium-ion batteries. And where are the batteries going to be made? Here!" I pointed across the straits to the Lower Peninsula of Michigan.

Dan adopted a look of mock horror. "And you're comfortable expecting government to pick the winners and losers?" These were the words of condemnation frequently employed by right-wing advocates of laissez-faire, like the economists at Michigan's Mackinac Center, based in Midland.

"Of course! Businesses do it all the time—they invest to capitalize on their strengths and their needs. They choose based upon their company's strategic direction. What's the problem with the U.S. government being smart and strategic, too? We definitely have to pick *industries*, like autos, that are central to our national manufacturing, energy, and defense infrastructure. Hell, yes."

The sun was at its peak. I squinted and hooded my eyes with my hand as I gazed at the gently rippling blue water. A sailboat was gliding past the red-and-white lighthouse on the tip of Round Island, just across the straits. The remaining kites, five to a string, were straining at their tethers in the stiff late-spring breeze.

Dan sipped from his cup of tea. "So you pancake local incentives on top of federal ones. Plus you streamline the regulatory process. Plus you reform education and training to give workers advanced skills. Plus you take an aggressive role in fighting unfair trade. Seems like a lot. Maybe too much government for Americans to tolerate."

I snorted. "Come on! What can possibly be more important than creating jobs here in America? What matters more to real people? We either invest in job creation or allow other countries to take the jobs. It's as simple as that."

"Hey, I'm just asking the questions," Dan protested with a smile. "I'm with you."

I sighed. "I don't really get it," I said. "Why do Americans say they hate an active government, then get mad when government does nothing while their jobs disappear?"

· · · · ·

MILLIONS OF AMERICAN FAMILIES HAVE HAD SIMILAR DEBATES about government and the economy. After eight years helping to lead a desperately struggling Michigan, I knew where I stood: convinced of the need for active, strategic economic planning, led by government. Three weeks later, on Friday morning, June 25, 2010, another move took shape in my campaign to make it work.

I was at the Rock Financial Showplace in Novi, sharing the big roundtable with VIPs from thirty companies as we waited for the Great Lakes Renewable Energy Association's Energy Fair to begin. My economic development team had invited these CEOs to help strategize ways to sustain our state's momentum around renewable energy. I envisioned this as a torch-passing session, empowering business leaders to lead the charge even after a new governor took office.

Beginning in 2005, the fair had been held in Manistee, a cool little vacation town on Lake Michigan, and had showcased the work of a handful of green activists. This year, mushrooming interest and hundreds of attendees had forced the fair to move to the expansive Rock Financial Showplace in suburban Detroit. A few of the companies represented at the table were storied Michigan businesses that had diversified into energy, including Dow Chemical, GM, Chrysler, and Ford. Most of the others were newly minted firms or outside companies we'd lured to our state.

Heat Transfer International was a biomass company that had emerged from a Michigan farm that converted animal waste such as turkey feces to power. ("Poop-to-power"—the concept delighted our middle school son, Jack.) Toda America and Techno Semi Chem were battery supply firms I'd recruited from Japan. Mastech was a former auto supply firm in northern Michigan now making small wind turbines called "Windspires" under the banner of Mariah Power. Evergreen Solar had moved from Massachusetts to make solar panels in Michigan. LUMA Resources was a traditional Michigan roofing company now installing solar roofs. Grid Logic had received a grant to manufacture connectors for the smart grid, and URV from Sweden had come to Michigan to manufacture castings and hubs for large wind turbines. The list went on and on. Over the next decade, these clean energy firms and others were projected to employ almost 90,000 people in Michigan. I'd studied them, called them, visited most of them.

Now I called the meeting to order. As group members turned toward me, I caught the eye of Doug Parks, vice president for the Michigan Economic Development Corporation. Doug is a former military man, a three-time cancer survivor, and an intense advocate for the new clean energy sector. I called Doug our "secret weapon": His Republican leanings had made him an effective liaison with our Republican-led Senate, and his persuasiveness had led to the creation of the powerful, targeted clean energy incentives now in place in our state. I gave him a thumbs up. He smiled and nodded, understanding what this roomful of new companies meant—and what it had taken to get them here.

"Welcome to you all, clean energy revolutionaries, our friends," I began. "You're here because you have all partnered in some way with state government to ensure you would grow clean energy jobs in Michigan—to create an entirely new sector of our economy. I know that you understand the significance of your decision for the beautiful state that we call home. We're grateful for your choice to grow here, and we're bullish on your future. You are exhibit A that our energy strategy is starting to work."

After some introductions, I turned the meeting over to Doug.

"Some people say that government should just lower taxes for everyone and let the chips fall where they may," Doug said. "That's one economic development strategy. But as you know, we have recently been trying something else, which is to strategically invest in growing sectors such as energy. It's a targeted rifle shot. In some cases, we've co-invested in you with the federal Department of Energy. In other cases, your support comes from just us. We have placed our bets. And I think you can tell by looking around this room that our strategy is starting to pay off."

Charlie Pryde from Ford brushed back a shock of silvery hair from his forehead as he raised his hand. "Four years ago, we came in and asked for help on the battery side, Governor," he said. "You listened, and you led. We think that a public-private partnership on clean energy for Michigan is absolutely critical, and by the looks of this room full of companies, it's working!" Heads around the table nodded.

Roger Cope from MAG Industrial Automation Systems, a wind sector machine builder, chimed in, "You challenged us, and we did it!"

Ann-Marie Sastry spoke up. CEO of advanced battery company Sakti 3, Dr. Sastry is a petite fireball, a brilliant engineering professor and entrepreneur from the University of Michigan. "We can't succeed without the partnership of government, at least at the beginning of commercializing breakthrough technology," she said. "I simply could not do this by myself, and anyone with an advanced technology firm is kidding themselves if they think they don't need a financial partnership with government to start.

"I've been recruited by other states and other countries," she added. "But I'm staying here because of Michigan's commitment to this sector. We've moved from defensiveness to leadership, from uncertainty to certainty, leading and helping each other."

"Now we have to make sure the legislature understands that this strategy is the right one," boomed Jeff Metts, president of Dowding Industries, which was doing revolutionary work in machining wind turbines.

I caught the eye of Skip Pruss, the state's chief energy officer. For years Skip had been prodding and encouraging us at cabinet meetings and strategy sessions, part prophet, part walking encyclopedia of the new green economy. Now he was grinning from ear to ear. "Looks like this whole group is taking up the cause," I whispered to Skip. "You can be very proud of your work here."

The atmosphere in the room was ebullient, infectiously so. But as I scanned the faces of the CEOs, there was one reaction that disturbed me. It was the furrowed brow of Dr. Subhenda Guha, leader of United Solar Ovonics (Uni-Solar), one of our earliest clean energy companies. I glanced in his direction and raised my eyebrows, as if to say, "Aren't you going to speak?" He just shrugged his shoulders, a glum expression on his face.

I immediately knew what that meant. Uni-Solar had been waiting for a Department of Energy (DOE) loan guarantee it needed to finance the next phase of its technology expansion. Guha's gloom told me that his emotional roller-coaster was on another downslope.

As the meeting adjourned, I made a beeline to Dr. Guha. "I take it you still haven't heard from DOE?"

"No, Governor," he replied. "I don't know how long we can hold out." I was struck, as always, by Dr. Guha's old-fashioned, gracious manner.

"Let me see what I can find out. I'll get back to you."

"Thank you, Governor," he said. I shook his hand, committing myself one more time to do what I could for this brilliant engineer-entrepreneur.

In 2006, we had convinced Uni-Solar to locate in Greenville after the departure of Electrolux. The company had opened two solar manufacturing plants in the town, hiring many former Electrolux workers who had been retrained by Montcalm Community College—a symbolic yet substantive move that had brought hope to that devastated community.

Then in September 2009, Uni-Solar had applied to the U.S. Department of Energy for a loan guarantee under a program championed by Senators Stabenow and Levin for the purpose of promoting clean energy manufacturing. The company needed funds to bring to market a new product it had invented—a flexible photovoltaic film built with nanotechnology, thinner than a strand of human hair. Uni-Solar hoped to quadruple its manufacturing in the United States and add 2,600 jobs in Michigan. But now nine months had passed with no answer from DOE. I could see why Dr. Guha was concerned.

As soon as I got to my car, I sent a Blackberry note to our DC office. Joe Dooley got back to me quickly. "The feds are taking forever to make these decisions, Gov. They are hearing complaints from businesses all over the country."

I also followed up with Mark Morelli, the CEO of Energy Conversion Devices, parent company of Uni-Solar. "Governor, Uni-Solar is facing critical decisions about our future. India and China are offering us irresistible packages. If we don't hear about the federal loan guarantees soon, we'll have to move. But we don't want to leave the United States. We have a proud Michigan heritage and an excellent manufacturing and technical base here. And NREL just confirmed that our high-frequency technology breaks the record in terms of energy conversion rates," he added. That meant that the National Renewable Energy Laboratory in Colorado had found that Uni-Solar's technology was much more efficient than others at converting sun to energy. "Plus we've halved the cost of the technology in the past three-quarters. But the well is running dry. India has already gone on TV announcing our partnership. The federal government needs to act if we're going to keep the jobs here."

Twelve years in government, and I still had frequent moments of frustration with how slow it worked. "If the feds act, will it level the playing field for you?" I asked. "Will you be able to stay in Greenville and be competitive?"

"It won't level the playing field, but it'll keep us in the game. We'll be able to innovate to carry us the rest of the way. But China's flooding the market and providing incentives. We won't be able to compete unless our government gets in the game."

I'd heard enough. I called Joe Dooley back: "Get me on the phone with whoever is responsible at the Department of Energy."

Joe's contact told me that the process was moving as fast as it could. I was frustrated. "If you guys don't grant these loan guarantees, all of the work we've done to keep United Solar in Michigan will be for naught. Can you please speed it up?"

"We're trying, Governor."

"I'm afraid that's not going to be good enough," I said. "If we don't act soon, it will be too late and the jobs will be gone."

As I write these words, nineteen months after Uni-Solar's loan application, there's still no approval from the federal government. Dr. Guha's company is clinging to Michigan, but by a thread. In May 2011, Uni-Solar could wait no more. It announced that it was laying off 300 people in Michigan and opening a new plant in Ontario, where government policy supports a solar market. If our government doesn't figure out how to compete with other countries, we will all be the losers.

· · · · ·

MY LAST YEAR IN OFFICE, 2010, BROUGHT OTHER CHALLENGES to communities still struggling from a decade of job losses. Early in the year, I had to appoint an emergency financial manager for still-fragile Benton Harbor. Despite our program of assistance to Benton Harbor's human and physical infrastructure, since 2005 the city's expenditures had exceeded its sharply dropping revenues by $8 million, and it had accumulated liabilities of $5 million. Benton Harbor had failed to make appropriate contributions to the retirement plans of its public employees. Now the city was fiscally insolvent, another victim of the hollowing out of manufacturing jobs owing to globalization and the consequent disappearance of tax revenues in industrial towns.

Whirlpool had been a stellar corporate citizen in Benton Harbor; in fact, it had just announced plans to invest $85 million in a beautiful new headquarters building downtown. But the company had also closed down an older manufacturing facility in the city, costing another 216 jobs. The people without college degrees who'd once worked on the line making appliances were unlikely to find jobs at the new company headquarters.

Benton Harbor illustrates the generational disconnect Michigan and much of America is grappling with: The time it takes to educate a human being for a new career is much longer than the time it takes to move a manufacturing job overseas. That's why the time required to revive struggling cities like Benton Harbor must be measured in years, not weeks or months.

· · · · ·

WHILE BENTON HARBOR STRUGGLED, ANOTHER CITY ON THE shore of Lake Michigan was celebrating. July 15, 2010, was a hot, humid day in Holland, Michigan. But inside a white tent erected for a groundbreaking ceremony, the atmosphere was deliciously air-conditioned. Bowls of fruit and water bottles were laid out for the dignitaries; the restroom featured cherry wood, gold-plated faucets, and faux marble counters; chandeliers hung from the ceiling.

Chandeliers in a tent! The last time I'd seen such a thing was at President Barack Obama's first state dinner. I remembered grabbing then-presidential spokesman Robert Gibbs and exhorting him to use specific, individual stories about jobs created by the administration's efforts to educate and encourage the American people, much as I'd done during our gubernatorial reelection campaign.

Now the storyteller-in-chief was coming to Holland to celebrate one such success.

Two clusters of helicopters flew overhead, including multiple decoys so that a sniper couldn't know which helicopter was carrying the president. We knew he'd landed when the Secret Service and his aides began scurrying and talking into their wrists, making the final arrangements for the president's appearance.

President Obama entered the tent quietly, extended his hand and that broad smile to the young mayor of Holland, Kurt Dykstra. Youthful and lanky, the two men looked as if they could have faced each other at small forward or shooting guard. The president appeared upbeat, despite carrying the world on his shoulders, with his approval ratings dragging behind.

The event was a great opportunity for him to take a well-earned bow. The headline the day before had read, "Korea Invests $12.5b In Lithium-Ion Battery Sector." Now we were here with Bon Moo Koo and Peter Kim, the chairman and the vice chairman, respectively, of the giant Korean company LG, which had won the contracts to supply lithium-ion batteries for electric vehicles made by GM and Ford. Obama administration policy had us on track to increase the U.S. share in production of lithium-ion auto batteries for the electric vehicle from 2 percent to 40 percent—and most of the work would be done in Michigan. LG Chem was bringing its battery expertise to Michigan, partnering with local company Compact Power and hiring hundreds of Michigan workers. And LG was just one of eighteen battery companies or suppliers that had announced plans to come to Michigan, with projections for 63,000 jobs over the next decade.

Outside the tent, the president shook the hands of dozens of construction workers, baking in their hard hats, who'd be building the facility over the next twelve months. Then we were ushered back inside to examine a General Motors Volt and a Ford all-electric Focus, cars that would be energized by the batteries from this plant.

Like President Obama, Mayor Dykstra had two young daughters. "Imagine," I told him, "someday you'll be able to tell your daughters and your grandchildren that you were present with the president of the United States at the start of something really important. These new electric cars are the dawn of a new era."

Mayor Dykstra smiled and nodded, running his hand through his short blond hair. "It's a huge moment for Michigan," he agreed.

I thought back to a recent visit to the GM Tech Center in Warren. Mickey Bly, the head of the battery lab, had led me and a knot of reporters through a display of batteries for electric cars, arranged in evolutionary sequence from the earliest to the latest. The battery for EV-1, the electric car put on hold back in the 1990s, was a massive rectangular box some six feet tall that cost about $35,000 to produce. By contrast, the battery for the first run of the Volt was perhaps a third of the weight and size, and it cost about $15,000 to make. Further down the line, into the future, were models in development that were smaller and cheaper still.

"Battery development is following Moore's Law," I observed, referring to the famous dictum of Gordon Moore, cofounder of Intel, describing how computing technology efficiency, speed, and cost would improve rapidly over time. Moore's Law explains why today's computer is markedly cheaper, smaller, faster, and more powerful than the computer bought in 1980 or 1990. Similar efficiencies will happen with the electric vehicle battery, until there's no need for tax credits or upfront incentives to spur consumer demand.

Just two weeks after coming to Holland, President Obama was back in Michigan to celebrate another success story: Automobile factories in Detroit and Hamtramck had added new shifts. For the first time since 2000, employment in the auto industry had grown year over year; in all, 55,000 new jobs had been created.

The president addressed a cheering crowd of workers in Hamtramck, many fresh from their morning shift. "I placed faith in you and all of America's autoworkers, and you've vindicated that belief," he said. "So today, this industry is growing stronger. It's creating new jobs. We are moving forward. I want you to remember, though, that if some folks had their way, none of this would be happening. There were leaders of the 'just-say-no' crowd in Washington who didn't think it was a good idea. There was one who called it 'the worst investment you could possibly make' [Nebraska Republican senator Mike Johanns, who'd fought the loans]. I wish they were standing here today. I wish they could see what I'm seeing in this plant and talk to the workers here who have pride in building a world-class vehicle."

I was ecstatic for him. And for us.

The president had stopped a terrifying downturn in a massive and important American industrial sector. But for his actions, I don't know where we would have been. Yet even in *Michigan*, of all places, many people didn't seem to understand how the president's fortitude had not only saved thousands of jobs but had also helped us reclaim a competitive role for the future.

· · · · ·

IN JUNE 2009, CHRYSLER EMERGED FROM BANKRUPTCY. A MONTH later, GM did the same. By July 2010, Michigan was leading the nation in job creation. Michigan added 27,800 jobs in July; the next highest state total was 17,000 jobs in Massachusetts. Manufacturing jobs alone had increased in our state by 20,000. It was the first year-over-year job growth Michigan had experienced since 2000, a decade before.

Yet at the same time, parts of the state continued to suffer the fallout from globalization's impact on manufacturing. In Ontonagon County, the Smurfit Stone paper mill had recently closed owing to price undercutting from China; all of the employees had been laid off, and there was no replacement work. The county unemployment rate was 17.4 percent.

The summer of 2010 was a time of mixed emotions. All of us in Michigan had been thirsting for good news for so long that when it arrived, we couldn't quite bring ourselves to believe it. Suddenly, there were new businesses opening, new jobs being created, talk of "green shoots." Our unemployment rate was ticking down, from 14.1 percent in September 2009 to 12.2 percent in August 2010. By December, it would be down to 11.1 percent, a drop six times as steep as the nation's. Yes, the rate was still far too high, but it was moving steadily in the right direction. Yes, the perennial question still loomed: How could we compete in America against low-cost manufacturers abroad? But after seven years of doom and gloom, this story, indicating that U.S. job creation was being led by Michigan, was finally thawing our cold-frozen hope.

And to the amazement of observers around America and across the world, GM itself was turning into a center of that newfound hope.

In April 2010, GM had surprised nearly everyone when it repaid $8.9 billion worth of government loans five years *ahead* of schedule. The ultraconservative *Wall Street Journal*, which had fought the notion of government support for the auto industry with all its considerable influence, admitted, "A year after predictions that the industry and its suppliers could face a drastic decline, the situation has clearly stabilized." As *U.S. News & World Report* then commented, "One year ago, that's a statement few of us would have thought we'd ever see in the *Wall Street Journal*."

GM had emerged from bankruptcy, completely reorganized and in its strongest financial position in years. In the first three quarters of 2010, it earned over $4 billion and was poised for its first annual profit since 2004. Then on November 17, GM conducted the largest IPO of stock in the history of American business. When the dust settled, pundits and business commentators agreed that the IPO had been successful beyond anyone's dreams. GM had sold hundreds of millions of shares of common and preferred stock, raised $23 billion in cash, and reduced the share of government ownership in the company from 61 percent to 26 percent. GM executives, led by their new CEO, Dan Akerson, were justifiably beaming.

The afternoon of the IPO, I sent the following e-mail message to the key members of President Obama's auto industry team:

THURSDAY, NOVEMBER 18, 2010. 11:50 A.M.
FROM: GRANHOLM, JENNIFER
TO: BLOOM, RON; DEESE, BRIAN; KLAIN, RON;
SPERLING, GENE

Gentlemen:

Just a note to say thank you, on behalf of 10 million citizens in Michigan, for saving the American auto industry. I hope you take a minute today to smell the roses as GM's IPO launches. I know you know that the Obama Administration's intervention was essential, critical in saving us from an economic apocalypse. While our unemployment rate is still far from "normal," I am pleased to report that our unemployment rate continues to inch down from a high of almost 15%, and is now at 12.8%—the first time since March of 2009 that it has been below 13%. Progress is good!

With deep, deep gratitude from the heart of a wounded-but-recovering Michigan,
Jennifer Granholm

Ron Bloom's response was heartfelt: "You are very welcome. It was truly one of the great privileges of my life to be a part of this."

GM capped its comeback year with the triumphant launch of the all-electric Chevy Volt. I attended the ceremony on November 30, with just a month remaining in my tenure as governor. The event was held at the Detroit Hamtramck GM plant, known informally as the "Poletown Plant." Fully contained within the boundaries of Detroit, Hamtramck had once been a Polish enclave. Over the years, the area around the plant had become more ethnically diversified, with immigrants from Pakistan and Yemen as well as African Americans moving in. Now, the factory was about to take on new historical significance as the home of the launch of the nation's first commercially produced electric vehicle.

Arriving at the plant, we met with dignitaries like the colorful former GM vice chairman Bob Lutz, who had once called global warming "a crock of shit" but now considered the ecofriendly Volt the best GM project he had ever worked on, bar none. Former head of product development John Lauckner was also present. Lutz and Lauckner had been dubbed "the inspiration and the perspiration" behind the Volt.

Most of the plant was dark, focusing everyone's attention on a stage aglow in klieg lights. Huge screens flashed video of the Volt being assembled and driven. A table beside the podium showed off the awards the Volt had already racked up, including *Motor Trend*'s Car of the Year (the first electric car so designated), *Automobile Magazine*'s 2011 Car of the Year, and *Green Car Journal*'s Green Car of the Year (again, the first electric car to win the award). A few key people were introduced to the excited crowd of about seven hundred—factory workers, other GM employees, suppliers, dignitaries. Then, after a dramatic pause, a gray Volt shot up a ramp onto the stage, horn honking. It was a classic bit of auto industry theater, a sure sign that Detroit was ready to find its swagger once more. Dan Akerson emerged, flashing V signs with upraised arms. The crowd went wild. It felt like a pep rally bursting with euphoria, fueled by years of pent-up frustration and anxiety.

As I left the ceremony later, reporter Mary Conway of Channel 7 asked, "Now that you're leaving office, is a moment like this bittersweet?"

"Nope," I replied. "It's only sweet."

· · · · ·

BEFORE I ENDED MY TIME AS GOVERNOR, I WANTED TO GO BACK to Greenville—the town where we'd lost Electrolux and its 2,700 jobs; the town where it had become clear that Michigan's challenges were structural, not cyclical; and the town where Uni-Solar was still struggling to survive its long wait for federal funds. Montcalm County had seen its 3.2 percent unemployment rate (April 2000) soar to over 19 percent during the crisis. Now it was at 15.2 percent—improving but still stratospheric.

City Manager George Bosanic was waiting for us when we pulled up. Through everything Greenville had experienced, George had been the constant, positive voice of progress. He greeted me with a bear hug.

"Welcome back, Governor!" he exclaimed. "We've come a long way!" George's eyes were dancing. He was happy to show off Greenville's progress.

We met with about thirty city leaders and businesses in city hall, where George explained part of their new strategy. "Greenville will be the first Michigan city where the government buildings go entirely off the grid," he declared. Rooftop solar panels made by Greenville residents at the Uni-Solar plants had already sprouted at the school, the airport, and the municipal offices, and more were planned.

"Our official name is Greenville," George said, "but we hope to be known as GreenERville, and someday GreenESTville. Eventually, we want to become somewhat of a global attraction where people can see and hear about every aspect of solar energy."

"We're already Michigan's first solar city and solar school district," added Pete Haines, the school district superintendent. The businesspeople and community leaders in the room were justifiably proud of how they'd reimagined Greenville for the twenty-first century.

The group led me outside to a fire truck with a large cherry picker. At the group's insistence, I climbed inside the basket, and the fire chief slowly cranked the wheel to hoist me up above the buildings.

It was a crisp fall day, the sun brilliant and the trees bright orange and red. A slight breeze through the glowing leaves made the valley look like a fiery wave. As the firefighters cranked me higher and higher, I looked out at the countryside exploding with color. I was a million miles away, I thought, from the Greenville I'd visited in a bleak, gray winter seven years earlier.

Eventually, the cherry picker hovered over the city hall rooftop, where I could watch the sun heat the panels doing their energy-creating work. I lingered there for several minutes watching the activity below—the people gathered near the fire truck, the tops of the local businesses and homes, and, in the distance, the solar panel plants. There was a still a giant void where the Electrolux factory had been torn down. I knew Huckleberry's bar and grill was out there, probably still hosting locals who'd be railing against unfair trade regulations while they downed a beer or two. I knew that a Wal-Mart had opened up in town a couple of years earlier and hired many of those Electrolux workers at a fraction of their old wages. I thought of the thousands of conversations that had taken place under Greenville roofs over the past few years, and the uncertainty, anger, fear, despair, and hope they'd expressed as the human impact of the changes to our economy had reverberated.

I smiled as I saw George and Pete waving to me below—the city leaders who never gave up, who continued to remake themselves and their community during the long, harsh economic winter, determined not to allow the Electrolux loss to define the city's future.

I was struck with an overwhelming sense of pride to be governor of this resilient state and its people. I took one last look at the landscape exploding with color, gave the fire chief a thumbs up, and the cherry picker gave a small lurch and began its descent to earth.

"Whew! It's beautiful up there," I said as I climbed out of the basket.

"Inspiring, isn't it?" George smiled.

"In more ways than one," I agreed.

George directed me to the school building. A large-screen monitor inside the high school's entrance showed in real time how much energy the solar installation on the building's roof was generating. Superintendent Pete guided me to a science class, where clusters of enthusiastic students from high-schoolers down to elementary grade kids made presentations explaining how solar panels convert sunlight into energy. Before I left, I did what I always do when I meet student groups: I made them all raise their right hands and pledge, with the governor as a witness, that they would go to college.

As we left the building, Pete summed it up perfectly: "As you can see, Governor, this has less to do with the generation of power than with the power of a generation."

Having endured the harshest, most distressing of seasons, I thought to myself, Greenville was going to be all right.

And so were we all. Michigan had been knocked down, hard and repeatedly. But now we all were rising from our knees—me included—brushing off the dust, and standing tall on a new foundation.

chapter 10

CRACKING THE CODE:
KEYS TO CREATING AMERICAN
JOBS IN A GLOBAL ECONOMY

THE GLOBAL ECONOMIC HURRICANE MAY HAVE HIT MICHIGAN first and hardest, but it's coming to a community near you. We tried lots of things to shelter ourselves from the storm, including—early on—denial. But we abandoned that passive stance and adopted a proactive strategy. We experienced some failures and a growing number of successes. In the process, we learned a lot about what works and what doesn't.

As Dan's running buddy Charlie Ross says, "Change is good. You go first."

We did. And in this chapter, we'll outline what we discovered— eight strategies that are working in Michigan and will work for the United States as we strive to reinvent our economy to be competitive in the twenty-first century.

1. Government Must Get in the Game

In 2011, as this book is being published, the terms of the debate over government spending have shifted far to the right. All now agree that government must shrink. Republicans and Democrats are arguing about the relative scope and pace of the shrinkage, but shrink it must.

But shrinking government is not an end in itself. As federal, state, and local workers have heard a hundred times, they must "do more with less." Doing more is a crucial part of the equation. America's middle and working classes are more in need of a disciplined, assertive, and strategic government role than at any point since Franklin Delano Roosevelt used targeted, innovative government programs to lead us out of the Great Depression.

In the first six years of this new century, Michigan tried the standard laissez-faire prescription for growth: Cut taxes and cut government. Yet contrary to conventional theory, despite these cuts we lagged further and further behind the rest of the nation in job creation. So, as you have read, we began to ratchet up direct activity by government. We made strategic choices. We invested in companies and in crucial industries, with the goals of diversifying our state's economy, adjusting to the demands of the global marketplace, and developing technologies that the world increasingly needs. And we began to get results. In 2010, our unemployment rate dropped six times faster than the nation's. By late 2010, manufacturing job losses had bottomed out and, for the first time in a decade, Michigan had begun to create private-sector jobs. The Detroit Metropolitan area was the 7th fastest-growing regional economy in the country, after having been 147th out of 150 before the recession. In February 2011, the Gallup organization listed the states with the most improved job climate from 2009 to 2010: Michigan was number one.

I don't claim that our administration did this on our own. Nor am I claiming any final "victory" over economic distress. And as my successor is learning daily, Michigan's challenges aren't over. Diversifying an entire state economy requires a long-term commitment to structural change. But the growth we've enjoyed has been driven largely by federal and state policies that consciously and actively intervened in the market.

Frustrated that the pace of growth was still too slow, many voters in Michigan and around the United States called for change on Tuesday, November 2, 2010. Some interpreted the midterm election results as reflecting voters' veneration of small government and the old doctrine of laissez-faire. I wish those calling for a retreat to that failed policy prescription could have come with me on November 3, when I visited South Korea.

My trip to Korea was yet another mission of economic pump-priming. JoAnne Huls, Fred Hoffman, and Eric Schreffler from the MEDC went with me to pursue more battery companies for the electric vehicle ecosystem we were developing in Michigan—the final investment trip of my governorship.

At the LG plant at the massive Pyeongtaek Digital Park in South Korea, we saw 8,000 workers assembling a dizzying array of fun products, from fifty-five-inch-diagonal, one-inch-thick, 3D plasma screen televisions to next-generation video cell phones. In the test lab, machines whirred, flipping hundreds of cell phones open and shut to gauge the durability of their cases. In the vast quality assurance labs, I saw maybe three workers; all the testing was done by robots. Phone assembly, too, was done by sophisticated robots. No human hands touched the circuit boards or the interior of the phones.

At our dinner that night, LG Chem vice chairman and CEO Peter Kim was a delightful and charming host. I asked him, "Now that machines do so much of the work, labor must be a relatively small part of the cost of production. Why, then, is so much manufacturing work still going to China?"

Kim explained that in China the government subsidizes production and construction, making investment very inexpensive.

And the Chinese government is very determined, he said. "When they want to get something done, they just say so, and it happens," he snapped his fingers.

"But why employ so many Chinese people to work in factories if machines can now do the work?"

"People there are less expensive than robots," Kim said. "And, of course, the Chinese government wants its people employed."

"Do you see any way to keep manufacturing jobs in America?" I asked.

He raised his eyebrows. "I can't see it, unless it's very specialized, like with the batteries for the electric car."

Fred Hoffman asked, "Is there any way to bring electronics manufacturing back to America?"

"I can't see it," said Kim again, shaking his head. He asked whether we had seen the stories about Foxconn Electronics in Shenzhen Province. It's a vast corporation that manufactures millions of iPhones for Apple, Inspiron laptops for Dell, and many other electronic devices, using workers gathered from rural provinces throughout China. "They sleep eight workers to a dorm room," Kim remarked. "The workers are so many—a quarter of a million in one location in Foxconn City! And I'm sure you've read that there have been lots of suicides."

Sure enough, the next day I woke to the story of yet another worker suicide at Foxconn. The company announced it was installing nets outside the workers' dormitories to catch those who might try to kill themselves by leaping from high windows.

This is what America is up against. China is not our enemy; China is simply our largest and most intense economic competitor. The Chinese government stands at the ready to help first world corporations to "deleverage" (today's newest, vaguest financial euphemism for what used to be called "offshoring" and "outsourcing"). And Chinese leaders will do whatever it takes to keep their people employed.

In his memoir, George W. Bush recalls hosting Chinese president Hu Jintao on his first visit to America in April 2006. Bush told the Chinese leader that the thing that kept him up at night was fear of another terrorist attack on the United States. Bush then asked Hu, "What keeps you up at night?"

Hu's response: Creating 25 million new jobs a year for his people was the challenge that kept him up at night.

China is focused on creating jobs, and when China is focused, China gets what it wants.

By contrast, our stubborn fealty to laissez-faire doctrine has left the United States helpless to combat the continuing departure of manufacturing jobs from our shores. Between 2001 and 2010, 42,000 factories were closed in America. One-third of all manufacturing jobs in the United States have disappeared. At the same time, manufacturing in other countries is on the upswing. No wonder—businesses can shift their production overseas and get twice the workforce at half the price.

Jack Welch, former CEO of GE, summed up the business philosophy behind such shifts in these words: "Ideally you'd have every plant you own on a barge to move with currencies and changes in the economy." That might work well for GE—but woe to workers and communities.

The central error behind the conservative dogma that tax cuts automatically lead to economic growth is the assumption that we operate in a closed economic system. In reality, both the Michigan and U.S. economies are very small parts of a much larger global system. So when we cut corporate tax rates in a single state, like Michigan, many corporations will be just as likely, if not more likely to invest the savings in foreign workers, foreign companies, or foreign financial instruments, as to invest in America. And when Michigan consumers get a tax break, they may or may not "buy American"—if they have the option. Try to find a cell phone, a television, or even a shirt made in America.

The numbers bear this out. Recent Commerce Department data show that in the decade between 2001 and 2011, domestic employment by U.S. companies declined by 2.9 million workers, but in the same period, overseas employment at U.S. companies *grew* by 729,000, to 11.9 million. A large part of the reason jobs have not returned as the recession has ended is that from the companies' standpoint, the jobs never disappeared in the first place; they simply moved. The stories are legion. When Delphi filed for bankruptcy in 2005 as Kelly Keenan had predicted, it had 50,000 U.S. employees; today it has just 5,000, and 91 percent of its 100,000 hourly workers are in low-wage countries. In 2008, Sony announced that it would close its last U.S. LCD television factory and move it to Mexico. In 2009, Dell closed its computer factory in North Carolina and moved the jobs to other factories outside the United States. Between 2003 and 2008, as Michigan was leading the United States into the Great Recession, U.S. companies *more than doubled* their employment rolls in China.

And, high-skill jobs, too, are moving at an alarming rate. Of the ten U.S. companies that spend the most on research and development, eight of them have R&D facilities in China or India. According to the Chinese Ministry of Commerce, in 1999 there were only 30 international R&D facilities located in China. By 2008, that number had grown fortyfold to 1,200.

There are business reasons for these moves, such as the need to access growing markets abroad. Some profits are repatriated, and some jobs, especially white-collar jobs, remain in the U.S. But the net decline in U.S. jobs is huge and growing.

The statistics make it clear that government is not the problem with the American economy and tax cuts aren't the key to future growth. A handful of business leaders are showing the intellectual integrity to bring this to light. When legendary investor Warren Buffett was asked about "trickle-down capitalism," he replied, "The rich are always going to say that, you know. 'Just give us more money, and we'll go out and spend more, and then it will all trickle down to the rest of you.' But that has not worked the last ten years, and I hope the American public is catching on."

I'm aligned with leaders of both parties who want to simplify the federal corporate tax system and reduce the rate. But tax cuts aren't enough. It's time to overcome our fear of a more active government and to recognize—and deploy—the power of well-designed competitive economic policy.

2. Cut Government Where We Can to Invest Where We Must

America today is simultaneously overindebted and underinvested. So we must perform intelligent triage on the national level, just as we did in Michigan, by cutting what we can in order to fund what we must.

Let's start with the need to cut. Today, our national debt is 62 percent of our gross domestic product (GDP). The Congressional Budget Office has projected that by 2020 our debt will reach 90 percent of GDP. At current rates, within fifteen years, tax revenues will be sufficient only to fund entitlements and interest on the debt—no national defense, no transportation, no energy policy, no job creation, no anything else. And by 2035, the deficit will be larger than the entire American economy, growing to 185 percent of GDP. This level of debt is obviously unsustainable.

The fact that China is the single largest holder of our debt is a further cause for concern. As retiring Chairman of the Joint Chiefs of Staff Admiral Mike Mullen has warned, because our debt makes us beholden to our creditors—especially in other countries—it is the most significant threat to our national security. With the right strategies, economic growth can account for part of the solution because an expanding economy generates greater tax revenues that can be used to reduce debt. But there's no doubt that government spending on programs that are not essential to growth must stop.

Michigan has led the way in tackling this problem. In nine years, we had to grapple with $14.8 billion in cumulative deficits, cutting a greater percentage of spending than any state in the nation—and as the law required, we balanced the budget every year. We cut more government jobs at all levels than any other state. By the time I left office, we were forty-eighth in the country in the size of government relative to population. We left my successor with a balanced budget and a $600 million surplus in the school aid fund. And the Pew Center on the States twice named Michigan among the best-managed states in the nation (2006 and 2008).

Making these changes was painful, but it taught us two important things. First, it's essential to collaborate with a wide range of stakeholders to create pragmatic solutions, rather than impose preconceived plans based on ideology or political favoritism. Working cooperatively with organized labor (rather than simply bashing it as some politicians are doing) allowed us to achieve $700 million in employee concessions and $1.1 billion in other savings. Union leaders identified the ways to save they found most palatable, including pay freezes, furlough days, and benefit reductions. Thanks to retirement incentives and hiring freezes, by the time I left office our state workforce was 15,000 persons smaller than when the decade had started. We were able to make essential cuts while avoiding needless rancor and minimizing service disruptions.

Second, we borrowed ideas from creative private-sector agreements between labor and management. For example, we adopted a UAW approach to benefit reductions by creating a second tier of obligations for new employees. Where Wisconsin, for example, tried to unilaterally foist a 6 percent cost-sharing program on state employees and faced bitter opposition as a result, we worked with the unions to double the health care contributions of existing employees (from 5 to 10 percent) while imposing a 20 percent health care premium cost-sharing plan on new employees.

Michigan is also one of only two states with a defined contribution retirement plan for state employees. The 3 percent contribution we required of all employees (currently in litigation) would save us $300 million in the first year. Similar pension reforms for public school employees saved another $515 million in the first year after their adoption and will save billions in the years to come. The battles over these changes were contentious, but we resolved them amicably. I came into office with tremendous support from organized labor, and I think I left with its respect. Most importantly, we left the state in better fiscal condition than it had been in for years.

Our two-tiered solution to the benefits and retirement conundrum points the way to reform of such national entitlement programs as Social Security and Medicare. Steps like phasing in benefits, lifting the salary cap on contributions, and requiring tomorrow's seniors—the ones who are now merely kids and who haven't even begun paying into the system—to operate under a different set of expectations are both logical and politically feasible.

We couldn't always create collaboration. Sometimes, ideological rigidity prevented us from reaching agreement. I repeatedly proposed cuts to costly and obsolete business tax credits, such as on oil wells or on tobacco for hand-rolled cigarettes, which reduced revenues while producing few jobs. But because these adjustments were labeled "business tax increases," the Republican leadership reflexively refused to consider them. Our efforts to improve the state's fiscal health would have fared even better if our colleagues across the aisle had been more flexible.

Just as important as *how* we cut government spending was *what* we cut. We fought consistently for three key priorities: protecting the vulnerable, investing in job creation, and investing in human talent and skill. Thus, even as we eliminated a quarter of state departments and three hundred boards and commissions and eliminated funding for the state fair, arts grants, adult education, and government planes, cars, and general fund employee travel, we avoided cutting a single person off health care—this despite a whopping 78 percent increase in our Medicaid caseload between 2000 and 2011. At the end of the decade, we still had the second best record in the country for insuring kids. Sick children suffer—and sick children don't learn. Moral sense and common sense dictate their protection.

We shut thirteen prison facilities, more than any state in the country. The costs of overincarceration were twofold: We paid approximately $30,000 per prisoner annually to keep them detained, and we lost their financial contributions to their families and the tax rolls. So we threw a huge emphasis behind our Prisoner Reentry Initiative, which focused on triaging prisoners based on risk and then preparing them for success upon release. The program produced a 36 percent reduction in the recidivism rate, generating enormous savings we could invest in economic essentials. Without the support of rational pragmatists in the legislature, including some levelheaded Republicans, we never would have been able to accomplish this.

Over and over, we learned that we had to focus as much on the *speed* of government as on its size. This is a matter of economic competitiveness in a global marketplace. In Hunan Province, for example, according to the *New York Times*, Sunzone, a solar panel manufacturer, received all of its permitting within three months, purchased land at one-third the market price, and received expedited bank loans with the interest paid by the provincial government. In the United States, it often takes more than twenty months just to get a decision from the federal bureaucracy, and many states and localities drag out their processes even longer.

So we undertook a full-scale effort to streamline government processes. We enlisted experts to perform "value stream mapping" that enabled us to eliminate needless steps from the environmental permitting process, with the goal of reducing decision time for an air permit, for example, from eighteen months to thirty days. We eliminated scores of permits and processes that were anachronistic, duplicative, or just unnecessary, and we created an online center where businesses could more quickly and easily conduct all of their government business: permit applications, change of business licenses, registrations, tax payments, and so on. We established a business call center and an ombudsman's office staffed with experts who could explain and clarify any transaction. As a result, the Center for Digital Government ranked Michigan the top digital state in the country. Similar steps at the federal level would remove obstacles to growth as well as save taxpayer dollars that could be better spent elsewhere.

In an era when cutting government spending is both fiscally and politically unavoidable, the emphasis must be on *smart, targeted* cuts that protect investments essential to future growth.

3. Develop National Strategies for Economic Growth

In other countries, citizens expect the government to intervene to help spur growth, build and preserve industries, and create jobs. Nations like Singapore, China, and India rely on active governments to stimulate the economy. They offer companies in targeted industries such incentives as tax holidays, free property on which to build plants and headquarters, substantial financing, and capital grants for equipment and materials. Government agencies in these fast-growing countries are building infrastructure, funding research, and, perhaps most importantly, supporting education. How can we compete against rivals like these when we insist on government passivity?

Kishore Mahbubani, dean of the Lee Kuan Yew School of Public Policy at National University of Singapore, forcefully argues that America's antigovernment mentality is causing it to lose ground relative to other nations and that the United States must become more engaged in economic planning. "Such a notion," he writes, "remains taboo in an American discourse still held prisoner by the old Ayn Rand and Alan Greenspan economic mindset. Yet, in a ruthlessly

competitive global marketplace, only prudent and judicious government intervention can help an economy change course and adapt."

The truth is that we are already practicing government-led
economic development, but doing it inefficiently and haphazardly,
at the state, rather than the national, level. Make no mistake about
it. Governors and politicians who constantly proclaim that "government should not pick winners and losers" are doing precisely
that, and for good reason: Virtually every state is locked in head-
to-head battle with other states for business siting decisions. To
survive such competition, state governments are forced to practice
economic policy, whether they choose to admit it or not.

Governor Mitch Daniels of Indiana may proclaim his fealty
to laissez-faire on the campaign trail, but his state's tax code
boasts eight different credits, including those for industries like
media and alternative fuels, that the administration has chosen as
"winners." Governor Chris Christie's New Jersey Economic
Development Authority favors specific "business sectors critical
to the State's economy." In Governor John Kasich's Ohio,
twelve different tax incentives and credits are offered to businesses in particular sectors from manufacturing to technology. In
Texas, in addition to the usual targeted tax incentives, Governor
Rick Perry has doled out over $250 million to emerging busi-
nesses in five specific industry clusters.

I'm proud that Michigan was repeatedly named by *Site Selection* magazine as one of the top three states in the nation for new
businesses. But there's a big problem with this system. Each of
the fifty states is competing in a global marketplace yet lacks the
necessary tools to win in that competition. When giant nations
like China, India, and Brazil are on the opposing team, how can
Michigan, California, Florida, or Texas—to say nothing of small
states like Vermont, Montana, Tennessee, or Hawaii—hope to
emerge victorious?

We need to discard the cold war–era taboo against "economic
planning" and develop a uniquely American approach to economic

policy—one that assesses our nation's strengths, weaknesses, opportunities, and threats and executes a national strategy based upon that analysis, wisely targeting our limited resources and leveraging the resources of others in order to allow America to compete on a global scale.

Let's begin with a Jobs Race to the Top—a national program to reduce our country's long-term employment problem.

President Obama's educational Race to the Top was the most dramatically successful component of the Recovery Act. Using a modest amount of money, $4.5 billion, it stoked unprecedented competition among states to develop creative ideas for education reform. Only 11 states and the District of Columbia won the competition for federal money, but all forty-six state applicants implemented major educational improvements that will produce greater benefits than the grant money itself.

I urge that we borrow the Race to the Top concept to fuel regional job creation. The goal: To create 3 million jobs in three years. Here's how it could work:

- Fund the program by repurposing a percentage of the money the United States currently spends on economic development. To have real impact, the Jobs Race to the Top should be comparable in size and scope to its educational counterpart.
- Launch a competition focused on a critical national need with job-creating potential—for example, clean energy technology.
- Incentivize and reward the most effective locally formed public-private partnerships, involving businesses, universities, and foundations. Define "effectiveness" in terms of numbers of lasting jobs created quickly.

The Jobs Race to the Top would reward regions that build on their strengths, partner with the private sector, and change public policy to drive job creation. For example, in Arizona or New Mexico states might streamline the permitting process for solar farms, partner with private-sector solar energy producers, and bolster demand through a robust renewable energy standard. Regional governments might offer land tracts for lease at low rates or public lands available free, while public utility commissions might offer ways to partner with the Federal Energy Regulatory Commission to streamline siting off the electric grid. Federal investment dollars could thus drive technological advances that might otherwise take shape in another country.

The same kind of analysis could be done for the nation's high wind areas, for the best places to manufacture clean energy or energy efficiency products, and for areas with the potential to develop clean coal solutions, biofuels, nuclear, hydro-energy, or waste-to-energy technologies. Every region of the country has something to offer to our clean energy future; every region of the country could be creating clean energy jobs for its citizens. And a little competition can go a long way in stimulating big results.

· · · · ·

AT THE SAME TIME AS WE DEVELOP NATIONAL POLICIES TO promote business growth here at home, the United States must become more aggressive about defending American companies doing business abroad. Many have documented the flimsy support businesses have had from the U.S. government in the face of unfair foreign competition. When China requires a U.S. company to build a factory there in order to sell products in China, it's a violation of international fair trade rules. When Chinese companies steal the designs and the intellectual property of American companies, it's another violation. When Korea tacks on tariffs and taxes designed to make U.S. products impossible to export, and when companies anywhere in the world violate the energy, environmental, and labor rules that our companies abide by, the playing field tilts against us. American businesses shouldn't have to fight such one-sided battles alone.

Labor has taken some powerful stands in this struggle. For example, on September 9, 2010, the steelworkers filed a petition opposing unfair Chinese practices at the World Trade Organization under Section 301 of the Trade Act of 1974. It was the first large-scale enforcement action filed on behalf of U.S. businesses. The petition described over eighty Chinese laws, regulations, and practices that seek to benefit Chinese manufacturers of clean energy technology to the detriment of their American competitors.

America needs to get behind this enforcement action, even as it negotiates new agreements that are in the interests of the nation. Companies like General Electric are calling on the United States to get involved in negotiating an environmental goods and services agreement, separate from other trade agreements, solely for the purpose of promoting clean energy products across nations. The U.S. Department of Commerce also has the authority to initiate antidumping and "countervailing duty" cases, and it should use this power where appropriate.

The choice is simple: Either we energetically advocate on behalf of American workers and businesses, or we become the victims of rival countries that are more aggressive in defending their interests.

4. Educate or Die

"Government has never increased the standard of living of one single human being in civilization's history. For some reason, that simple truth has evaded everybody." Steve Wynn, casino mogul, threw down that gauntlet to begin our debate on economics on *Fox News Sunday* with Chris Wallace.

I nearly leaped out of my chair. Wynn's statement was most remarkable not for its sheer absurdity, but for the degree to which so much of America today would endorse it.

Wynn argues that, without businesses creating wealth, government would have nothing and could do nothing. Where Wynn is badly mistaken—and where America must wake up—is that he did not follow the causal chain to its beginning. Businesses don't create jobs; people do! Jobs exist because of a salesperson with great character who offers superior service and wins a client for life; or a smart engineer who invents a better way, making life easier for customers and creating enormous value for the business owners; or a team of software developers that opens up a whole new market by designing an innovative game, a creative tool, or a useful mobile app. Business, especially twenty-first-century business, is fueled by knowledge, character, drive, initiative, honesty. And these elements of talent reside in *people*.

Although businesses organize these people, there are three essential inputs for that human talent: genetics, upbringing, and education. Take Steve Wynn himself. Aside from the imponderable qualities contained in his genetic code, he must have learned a lot from his dad, who ran a chain of bingo parlors. And surely young Steve's experiences in primary school and at the Manlius boys school in Connecticut played a further role in shaping the entrepreneur he became. Business training can enhance human talent, and well-run companies increasingly see people development as essential to their success. But let's be clear: The major input for knowledge workers is schools. And 90 percent of American students are in public schools. If we really want to create jobs, we need to create thinkers, creators, innovators, collaborators, sacrificers—great workers of every kind. And schools are the major place we create them.

So even if government *doesn't* directly create most jobs, it does have the enormous responsibility—in a fiercely competitive, global, technology-driven world—to develop the talent to create jobs.

This is not just theory. It's reality that can be measured in numbers, as I discovered when I compared Michigan to Massachusetts. In the earlier part of the last century, Michigan and Massachusetts had similar levels of income and industrialization. But beginning in the 1980s, as both were losing manufacturing prowess, income in Massachusetts started heading up, while income in Michigan headed down. By 2008, per capita income in Massachusetts was a whopping 47 percent higher than in Michigan. Why the difference? It's not taxes. Michigan has the nation's seventeenth-best business tax climate, while Massachusetts ranks thirty-second. The real explanation is quite straightforward: Massachusetts has the most educated population in the nation.

We saw the writing on the wall in 2005. Only one-third of adults in Michigan had a college degree. More disturbing, only 27 percent of parents felt that it was essential for their children to get a college education.

We needed to create a culture shift. In the face of global competition, Michigan needed to get serious about education.

We started with the kids. We overhauled the standards for education, significantly increasing the learning standards (technically known as "grade level content expectations") in every single grade at every single school. As a result, every year since 2005, the reading and math scores on state assessments for every grade, K through 8, have increased.

We took a close look at expectations in high schools, too. To my utter amazement, before 2006 the state had only one statewide high school education requirement: a class in civics. In 2007, I signed into law our high-standards high school curriculum. Now teens in every high school in the state have to take a college prep curriculum: four years of math through algebra II, three years of science, four years of English, a foreign language, an online learning experience, the arts. Critics argued the new requirements would cause a spike in the dropout rate. Instead, it declined, from over 15 percent in 2007 to just over 11 percent in 2010.

We did more. We required every student to take the ACT college entrance exam. Once the standards were in place, the test scores began to rise. They're still far from optimal, but they show progress. We've also seen a 70 percent increase in the number of kids taking Advanced Placement courses.

Finally, we set what business strategists refer to as a Big Hairy Audacious Goal—a daring objective that is both daunting and energizing, challenging individuals to exceed their own expectations. Our goal: to double Michigan's number of college graduates. The people of the state rose to the challenge. Since 2003, we've seen a 35 percent increase in enrollment in community colleges and a 6 percent increase in enrollment in universities.

But all this was still not enough.

In Michigan today, 35.6 percent of our citizens have college degrees, well below the national average. Twenty-five percent have some college, but no degree. We viewed these adults as "low-hanging fruit"—people motivated to try college but in need of help to finish the job. Many had been flattened by the new knowledge economy and realized they needed to upgrade their skills.

I'd learned a thing or two about reaching out to the unemployed from my experience in Greenville. We created No Worker Left Behind for those directly hit by layoffs. The program offered financial support for two years' training or certification at a community college—$5,000 per year, for a total of $10,000 per worker. We repurposed federal workforce training money provided under the Workforce Investment Act and the Trade Adjustment Assistance Act to allow us to retrain unemployed workers while they collected their unemployment checks. The catch: They had to agree to be retrained in an emerging sector, such as health care or entrepreneurship. (No way we would pay for people to study either of my two college majors, political science and French. They had to earn degrees in something *useful!*) Glenn Voisin and over 150,000 other citizens enrolled in training, giving Michigan an adult retraining rate four times the national number. At last count, 75 percent of those who had completed the training had retained or landed a new job; 83 percent of those with new jobs found work in the new field they had trained for.

Our experience can be taken national. The federal Department of Labor could launch a second-to-none retraining initiative by repurposing workforce retraining funds allotted under the Workforce Investment Act and Trade Adjustment Assistance to allow unemployed or underemployed workers to be retrained at community colleges while they are collecting unemployment. The Obama administration has taken an important step in this direction by expanding Pell grants for access to community college. The nation should go further by developing a system for technical education and onsite apprenticeships, modeled after the successful German system. A government-industry partnership to train young workers for specialized jobs requiring hands-on skills would help out-of-work youth and develop the talent necessary to keep jobs in America.

Access to schooling isn't the only issue we face. Overall reform of our education system is also badly needed. The United States was once the world's leader in science and math education; now we rank fifty-second. We've fallen from first place to sixteenth in the number of college graduates, and 40 percent of the doctorates awarded in the United States today are to foreign-born students.

What can we do as a nation to up our education game?

First, we should set one national set of standards and a unified testing program. Currently, every state has its own system. Even though the Obama administration's Race to the Top initiative has improved and equalized high school educational standards in many states, we need to continually add rigor and look for opportunities to standardize testing nationwide—for example, by using the National Assessment of Education Progress tests and the ACT college-entrance exams with all high-schoolers.

Many governors and state legislatures resist the national standards movement, arguing that it weakens states' rights and local control of schools. The Race to the Top competition represented a brilliant response to that argument. By offering cash incentives in exchange for improved educational standards, it motivated heretofore-resistant state legislatures to get on board with the nationwide drive for school reform.

The success of the Race to the Top model ought to be repeated and enhanced. The next phase should require the following changes to state education policies:

- Establish minimum 90–90 goals for every school, requiring that 90 percent of the kids graduate and 90 percent of the graduates go on to college or postsecondary education.
- Require longer school days and years in academically challenged schools and districts.
- Use data to evaluate everyone in schools based upon learning progress and terminate ineffective teachers and principals.
- Financially reward the most effective schools.
- Financially reward teachers who agree to teach in the most challenging schools.
- Encourage flexible, site-based management of local schools, enabling schools to add early childhood programs, double math or science classes, and so on.
- Foster talented and gifted schools and students, encouraging and nurturing genius in every form.

Today America still has a creativity advantage. We're the only nation in the world so solidly built upon diversity, with a glorious hodgepodge of people from all nations and cultures. Our diversity, our openness, is our strength. We need to open our doors to global brilliance, inviting academic geniuses from all corners of the planet to bring their gifts to America. And we must strive to produce more Thomas Edisons and Bill Gateses, Maya

Angelous, Stevie Wonders, Stephen Spielbergs, W. K. Kelloggs, Gertrude Belle Elions, and Stephen Chus—as well as millions of smart, well-trained, creative men and women who are ready to run the factory floors, program the computers, and design the high-tech machinery that will power the knowledge economy of the twenty-first century.

5. Create Fairer, More Flexible Labor-Management Partnerships

The global economy presents a creative opening for organized labor. Germany, for example, has lost its share of low-skill manufacturing jobs to low-wage countries, but it has successfully kept its advanced manufacturing plants and infrastructure, even during the recession. On an April 2010 investment mission to Mannheim, I saw why.

We visited Daimler's Mercedes Benz Truck Engine operations and toured the 102-year-old plant where Carl Benz invented the automobile. At the helm of the German facility was the mustached Herman Doppler.

"My one goal," he told our delegation, "is to keep manufacturing jobs in Germany. We know that China and Eastern Europe are our competitors. But in Germany we have figured out how to make it work . . . in *partnership* with the unions."

"How?" I blurted out. "That's the question we've been trying to answer for a decade!"

"Two ways," said Doppler. "First, during downturns, our government allows companies to employ their workers on something called *Kurzarbeit*—short-time work. They work reduced hours, which costs companies less. But about 60 percent of the salary shortfall is made up by the Federal Employment Agency—the government. So instead of paying people for being on unemployment full-time, the government subsidizes their part-time work during the recession." This plan, Doppler told us, helps companies keep skilled people on board. And during the last recession, it helped the families of 5,100 people at Doppler's plant alone.

"And your second secret?" I asked.

"Our collective bargaining agreement with the unions allows us to adjust working hours and wages to match order levels. Workers can bank their extra regular-time hours. During the recession, workers could take advantage of positive balances on working-time accounts. Paid overtime plunged, so we reduced overtime costs significantly because workers used the hours in their banks. This arrangement saves, on average, about 17 percent on our payroll."

"So," I said, "you have a heavily unionized workforce—"

"Yes, very much so," he nodded.

"And you have labor representatives on the management boards of the companies?"

"Yes."

"And labor agreed to these kinds of flexible laws and contracts?"

"Not only did they agree, but they worked with us to craft them," he said.

There are important lessons here for American business and labor leaders. Most American labor laws date from the 1930s and 1940s. They were relevant and groundbreaking at the time, but today many of their features are anachronistic. And the new breed of labor leaders understands the need for change.

In June 2010, Bob King was elected president of the UAW. Raised in Detroit in the 1960s, King is well versed in the storied history of Local 600, the auto union he worked for—the 1935 hunger march for jobs and unemployment compensation during which the Detroit police killed five marchers, and the famous 1937 Battle of the Overpass, where thugs led by Harry Bennett, Ford's notorious security chief, beat back the UAW's attempts to organize the massive Rouge River factories complex. He honors that history. But King knows that a new era calls for new strategies.

On August 2, 2010, he gave the keynote address at the Center for Automotive Research's Management Briefing Seminar. Addressing the leadership of the car companies and suppliers, King declared, "The UAW of the 21st Century must be fundamentally and radically different from the UAW of the 20th Century. The 20th-Century UAW tried to find ways to achieve job security, such as job banks, that in the end did not achieve the results we were seeking. The 21st-Century UAW knows the only true path to job security is by producing the best quality product, the safest product and the longest lasting product at the best price."

King candidly acknowledged the union's past mistakes: fighting clean air efforts, single-mindedly opposing global trade, fostering an adversarial relationship between union and management, and creating "a litigious and time-consuming grievance culture." It was time, he said, for "a new UAW."

This was no overnight conversion for Bob King. As the UAW's VP for Ford, he had become a partner, negotiating contracts that increased productivity and shared risk fairly between workers and management. When UAW workers in Chicago expressed concerns about the quality of the new Ford Taurus, King and his people understood that it was *their* reputation, as much as the company's, that was at stake. They convinced Ford to slow the launch and address the quality concerns. After its thorough redesign, the new Taurus won the J. D. Power quality award for large cars, beating out an excellent Buick Lucerne, as well as competing vehicles from Hyundai, Toyota, and Nissan.

If King's vision is fully realized—a big "if"—the UAW will become the auto industry's key partner in its pursuit of global competitiveness. Rather than being an anchor that drags a company under with inflexibility and unrelenting costs, the UAW will be the trainer and broker of the world's greatest talent for manufacturing the world's most technologically complex mass-produced product. That would be a welcome paradigm shift.

In Dundee, Michigan, the UAW has already negotiated a contract that embodies this fresh vision. The Global Engine Manufacturing Alliance, owned by Chrysler, is producing the new engine for the Fiat 500 that hits showrooms in the fall of 2011. To ensure maximum flexibility, the UAW contract has only one job classification. The objective is to ensure that "anyone can do any job, anywhere, anytime." A visitor to the floor of the new plant would have trouble telling managers from union members; management and labor work in teams; and every person working there has a college degree or technical certification.

Partnership. Quality. Competitiveness. Flexibility. Teamwork. Innovation. Productivity. Continuous cost-savings. Respect. These are the values of the new UAW and the new auto industry—and hopeful harbingers for the future of manufacturing in America.

6. Make Smart Government Investments in Industries Crucial to Growth

America requires a job policy focused on knowledge-economy industries in which America can compete effectively. Such a policy should include smart investments by government in sectors that align with important national or regional goals.

In Michigan, we diversified our economy by expanding sectors tied to our unique assets (our advanced manufacturing skill set and our geography) and by training our citizens to attain the skills needed for success in those new sectors. Both strategies require a long-term, sustained commitment to restructuring and investment. Despite the overwhelming washout of traditional manufacturing jobs from America, our policies enabled us to attract or retain almost 4,000 businesses and, directly or indirectly, about 653,000 jobs.

We made our mistakes, but we also made great inroads. What follows are the actions that worked and their implications.

Saving the auto industry. There is no doubt that the federal government's intervention saved the auto industry, the manufacturing backbone of America. Without that involvement, there would be 1.4 million more Americans unemployed and Michigan's unemployment rate would be over 20 percent. The taxpayer costs from the increased demands on the social safety net—unemployment insurance, health care, food stamps, housing, homeless shelters, community losses in property taxes, foreclosures, and so on— would have bankrupted Michigan and, potentially, other states.

Instead, all three domestic automakers are reporting profits and hiring thousands of people for the first time in a decade— during May 2010–2011, 55,000 workers were added to the automotive sector. The companies used bankruptcy as an opportunity to change management, clear out excess capacity, streamline operations, achieve more nimble and less expensive labor contracts, and address their legacy costs. GM successfully went public and is paying back the U.S. Treasury well ahead of schedule. Chrysler will be going public in 2011 and, in May 2011, paid its loans back—six years sooner than anticipated. Ford decided not to borrow any more money from the U.S. government but continues to shrink its long-term debt and grow its profits and expand its workforce.

The Obama administration's decision to intervene to rescue the American auto industry was controversial. As the meltdown unfolded, leading Republicans scrambled to denounce the idea of government support for the industry. On Wolf Blitzer's CNN show, Utah Governor Jon Huntsman called the rescue "a big mistake" (November 20, 2008). On Fox's Neil Cavuto Show, Minnesota Governor Tim Pawlenty said the Obama administration's actions on the auto companies, health care, and energy would make America look "like some sort of a republic from South America circa 1970s" (June 3, 2009). And on Greta Van Susteren's Fox program, Newt Gingrich called President Obama "the most radical president in American history" (April 12, 2010), with the auto bailout as his chief piece of "evidence."

Events proved all these denunciations wrong and left the conservative politicos tongue-tied—or scrambling to rewrite history. When, on May 24, 2011, Chrysler announced that it was repaying the loans years ahead of schedule, the same Mitt Romney who'd used the pages of the *New York Times* to declare "Let Detroit Go Bankrupt" boldly sought to claim credit for the auto industry's turnaround. "Mitt Romney had the idea first," said Eric Fehrnstrom, a Romney spokesman. "You have to acknowledge that. He was advocating for a course of action that eventually the Obama administration adopted."

This was doubly wrong. In the first instance, without the government's investment, which Romney condemned, there would have been no auto industry left to save. Second, it was the government's intervention and the high-speed bankruptcy orchestrated by the Treasury Department that saved GM and Chrysler. A traditional bankruptcy without the U.S. government's participation would likely have meant liquidation and the loss of the backbone of American manufacturing.

The auto industry bailout was an extraordinary effort demanded by a once-in-a-lifetime confluence of troubles. But there are many more routine, less risky ways the federal and state governments can partner productively with the private sector.

Energy. The turbulence in the Middle East early in 2011 demonstrated again that it's time to reduce our dependence on foreign sources of energy. Add in the environmental costs of fossil fuels, and it's no wonder that the emerging clean energy industry—dubbed "the mother of all markets" by venture capitalist John Doerr—has attracted so much worldwide attention. Since 2004, private investment in clean energy has risen globally by over 630 percent. By 2030, the clean energy sector will employ 37 million people. One in four new jobs will be related to clean energy.

The question is, where will those jobs be? In Michigan, we made a commitment to ensure that our state would capture its fair share of those jobs. The United States should do the same.

New energy suppliers need customers, so we passed a renewable portfolio standard (RPS), which required that the state acquire a modest 10 percent of its energy from renewable sources by 2015. The new standard ensured that solar, wind, and other providers would find a ready market for their offerings. The new law also rewarded energy companies for helping customers to use less energy through deployment of energy efficiencies such as insulation, programmable thermostats, efficient appliances, and LED bulbs. The RPS also allowed "net-metering," encouraging people to become energy entrepreneurs by deducting from their energy bill any renewable energy generated through small wind turbines or solar panels installed at their homes or businesses. In this public-private partnership, we aligned interests—our state's interest in creating new energy goods and services with the suppliers' interest in ongoing profit—to create a system of mutual benefits that will spur job and business growth for decades to come. A federal clean energy standard would create a national market for renewables—and it wouldn't add a dime to the deficit.

Under President Obama, the federal Department of Energy also offered competitive grants for renewable energy manufacturing as part of the Recovery Act. I asked our legislature to create irresistible state tax credits for wind, solar, and biofuels, as well as for advanced energy storage systems (such as the lithium-ion battery used in an electric car). Expanding our private-public partnerships, we created thirteen Centers of Energy Excellence to help commercialize universities' breakthrough technologies in clean energy. In Singapore, they call such three-way partnerships among government, academia, and industry the "golden triangle"; in Sweden, the "triple helix." Whatever they're called, the idea is the same—and it's powerful.

A unique strength that only government can provide is the capacity to think systemically about the entire value chain and seek opportunities to strengthen each link in that chain through incentivizing "clusters" of related companies. For example, an electric vehicle lithium-ion battery has essentially four parts: anode, cathode, electrolyte, and separator material. We attracted to Michigan eighteen companies supplying these parts to form a manufacturing supply chain; they're projected to create 63,000 jobs in the state.

Similarly, in the wind sector, even though we had many auto suppliers who could make parts for wind turbines, we did not have a foundry to make the large castings necessary. We convinced URV, a Swiss/Swedish company, to build the world's largest foundry for such castings in Eaton Rapids, Michigan. We partnered with two auto suppliers, MAG and Dowding Industries, to enable quick machining of wind turbine blades with lightweight carbon fiber materials. We partnered with Oak Ridge National Laboratory to research the best wind turbine materials, and we teamed with Dow to manufacture those materials. Finally, we partnered with another auto supplier, Merrill Technologies, to build the state's first huge, utility-scale wind turbine hubs. Federal and state incentives mutually leveraged each step of the process in the creation of the wind cluster.

In the solar sector, we had a terrific anchor company—Hemlock Semiconductor (HSC), the world's largest producer of polycrystalline silicon, the purest human-made substance and a significant foundation for the building of solar panel cells. We decided to use HSC as our recruitment arm, compensating it with an "anchor tax credit" if the company convinced its suppliers to come to Michigan.

As a result of the creative tools we deployed, by 2010 we had 120 solar companies and 121 wind companies providing 28,000 jobs and investing nearly $3.8 billion in our state. Combined with battery companies, in just two years Michigan had cultivated 159 clean energy companies with plans to invest over $9.4 billion and create more than 90,000 jobs over the next decade.

The steps Michigan took to attract new industry were effective. But again, states can't fight these competitive battles alone. Countries around the world, starting with China and India, are marshaling their resources to become more attractive to industries of all kinds. The U.S. government needs to help foster partnerships with the states and businesses in key industries like energy, manufacturing, information technology, and health care.

America can do a much better job of creating robust incentives for job creation through credits or deductions that are auditable and tied to specific U.S. economic activity. Our current incentives are weak. Sixteen other countries offer significantly better innovation tax incentives than the United States does. In Australia, for example, as Dow CEO Andrew Liveris observes, a company can deduct a whopping 125 percent of its innovation expenses, a significant factor in deciding where to locate. Furthermore, in America the R&D incentive is temporary and must be renewed by Congress. This creates a disincentive for companies to invest because most major investment decisions are based upon a thirty-year horizon. Credits, deductions, and competitive grants can all help our companies to compete and create quality jobs here.

Access to capital. In the wake of the financial market meltdown, the banks became extremely risk-averse, choking off loans to many small and midsized businesses. These companies desperately needed access to capital in order to survive. This is a challenge that governments can help address—and in Michigan, we did.

American Gear is a machine shop in Westland, a working-class suburb of Detroit. The company's customers build very large objects, from autos to ships or mining equipment, and the gears are often enormous, requiring tooling equipment that is large, heavy, and incredibly expensive. Some of the massive machines that shape and grind the iron and steel parts are over seventy-five years old, oft-tweaked yet still functioning.

I visited Jeff Emerson, owner of American Gear, in October 2010. He was animated in telling me his story.

When the 2008 recession hit, orders fell. For the first time, Emerson's business started losing money. He has twenty-five employees, most of whom have been with him from the start, and as in many small businesses, his employees are like family to him.

National City, his bank of many years, had been acquired by PNC. The new bank imposed new, stricter rules and was threatening to pull Emerson's line of credit. He had always made payroll. He had never defaulted in twenty-five years in business. Although his company lost money in 2009, Emerson made all loan payments on time. It didn't matter; the bank refused to make badly needed capital available.

Emerson was spitting mad. "I couldn't believe they would turn their back on me after all these years."

He turned to the state for help. Michigan found him a willing partner, Comerica Bank, and the state capped off his loan with funds from our Supplier Diversification Fund to make the deal work. Using moneys from our state's settlement with the tobacco companies over the health risks from smoking, the Supplier Diversification Fund made a deposit in Comerica to buy down the bank's risk of loaning to a company with depreciated capital assets. Jeff was thrilled, Comerica was happy, and the state's contribution is getting paid back steadily. Jeff's payments into the Supplier Diversification Fund make more money available to small manufacturers seeking to remake themselves. It's the kind of self-sustaining economic development program the feds could replicate and greatly expand.

The Obama administration has been watching and learning from Michigan—and offering its help. In the midst of the auto supplier financial crisis, I invited the president's economic advisor Larry Summers to visit Detroit to hear from the business owners themselves. He heard how factory doors were closing, workers were being laid off, but suppliers were eager and scrambling to diversify and find new customers for new lines of business.

But we didn't simply complain about the problem. We presented Summers with our solution—a supplier diversification fund to help companies like these gain access to desperately-needed capital. With the help of advocates like Gene Sperling and Brian Deese, it became the basis for the Small Business Lending Act, signed into law by President Obama on September 27, 2010. This brought Michigan an infusion of $79 million, which banks and other private-sector lenders would leverage at a ten to one rate, thus freeing up almost $800 million in loans for small businesses.

To help meet the capital needs of start-up companies, we "securitized" our tobacco settlement fund to create the 21st Century Jobs Fund. In other words, we borrowed against the revenues tobacco companies had agreed to pay out over future years and made that capital available for other venture capital partners to leverage against. Every tobacco settlement dollar is augmented by 2.5 private dollars invested. The combined result is a $2 billion, ten-year commitment to diversifying our state's economy into strategic growth sectors through access to early venture capital. Over five years, this program has helped 1,500 companies, created or retained 26,000 jobs, and stimulated $2.3 billion of investment in Michigan in the sectors we were targeting for growth. We also invested $350 million of pension funds directed to early-stage Michigan companies looking for investors.

Under ideal circumstances, private sources of funding would be abundantly available to support economic growth, job creation, and technological progress. When that's not the case, we mustn't allow ideological constraints to render us helpless. Sometimes only government has the capacity to jump-start growth—and then it has the moral obligation to act. Every day we delay, America loses more jobs.

7. Face Down Threats—Become the Change

The best strategy for overcoming a threat is to face it down, to "steer into the wind," as I like to say. Michigan didn't always see it that way.

Michiganders had long feared globalization. The reasons were understandable: Our economy had consistently been eroded by manufacturers leaving for cheaper countries. As I've noted, I continue to believe we must fight every unfair tilting of the playing field. But I have also tried to lead *into* these fierce global winds. Instead of being victims of globalization, we need to embrace it and take advantage of it, not by promoting outsourcing but by encouraging *insourcing*.

In my terms as governor, I made twelve international trips to recruit businesses. As a result, our state attracted forty-eight companies and $2 billion in investment, with more than 20,000 jobs generated. It was surprisingly easy to get midsized companies in other countries to invest in Michigan. These companies were interested in the American market, but many lacked the multinational global staff to help guide them through the process. Because of their smaller size, relationships were important. My message to them: Let Michigan be your gateway to the United States—we'll help you.

My experience as governor led me to conclude that international recruitment is the lowest-hanging fruit of job creation. Every governor and our president should set specific targets for foreign direct investment (FDI) in America. Other countries have done so; we should be much more proactive, focused, and methodical about such efforts. Ambassador Michael Wood in Sweden, a Michigan native, modeled what's possible. His business background ensured he could speak the language of those he was targeting to recruit to America, and his personal knowledge of Michigan's situation generated an attitude of active partnership. In turn, he helped us understand the Swedish business landscape. His assistance helped us recruit Swedish Biogas to Flint, a city desperate for jobs. There's no reason the president and the Departments of State and Commerce couldn't set specific FDI goals for every U.S. ambassador to help our states grow jobs in America.

Michigan learned to steer into the wind in other ways as well. For years, the auto industry and our congressional delegation had fiercely resisted CAFE standards and fuel efficiency guidelines. When our auto world collapsed, we realized it was time to stop resisting. Instead, we got in front of the movement to help lead the nation toward independence from foreign oil. Where in 2004 the Detroit headlines were screaming, "CAFE Mandates Will Hurt Big Three," by 2010 the stories crowed, "Chevy's Electric Volt to Get 93 Miles Per Gallon." We *became* the change instead of fighting it.

Sometimes, in business and in life, a shock is required to make change possible. A person who is gaining weight yet resists diets and exercise finally has a heart attack. Suddenly, a healthier lifestyle becomes not just a challenge but also an opportunity for a new way of life. The auto industry bankruptcies helped shock Michigan policymakers into a whole new mind-set. Will it take another massive recession to shock America into seeing the global economy and the energy-environment threats as opportunities?

8. Practice Do-It-Yourself Leadership

The job of reconfiguring an economy hollowed out by globalization is too big for any one leader. No president or CEO can do it by himself or herself. Change must come from individuals everywhere and in every walk of life. When Dan urged me to "give the work back to the people," this is what he meant.

I like to refer to this as DIY leadership—do it yourself. It's a change that millions of active citizens have already embraced, in forms as diverse as the "social entrepreneurship" movement that has led to the founding of thousands of small, creative nonprofit organizations; creative projects like Wikipedia that pool the knowledge of thousands of people to benefit everybody; and decentralized social networking systems like Facebook and Twitter that connect the ideas and interests of millions around the world.

Governments have a long way to go to grasp the full implications of the DIY movement, but I'll mention a few of the powerful ways we've already begun to make government more efficient and help people to lead their own change efforts.

Sometimes it takes an infusion of cash to encourage people to do it themselves. One example is the way we jump-started the alternative energy industry with incentives that encouraged private companies to innovate, develop new products, and create jobs. The distributed generation of energy—encouraging cities, companies, and individuals to produce their own energy and sell the excess back to the grid—is classic DIY.

We played a similar role in several other industries, including advanced manufacturing, life sciences, defense, and tourism, and made a major effort in film production. (Before we developed aggressive new incentives for moviemakers, three films per year were made in Michigan. In the two years between 2008 and 2010, the film industry spent $648 million in Michigan's economy, created 10,000 jobs, and made 120 films.)

Education, of course, is the ultimate form of DIY work. In Michigan, we have an amazing education story to tell that highlights DIY leadership.

Kalamazoo is a community of 75,000 people in southwestern Michigan that has more than its share of poverty—62 percent of school kids qualify for free lunch. In 2005, a group of anonymous benefactors promised a scholarship for every student in the Kalamazoo Public Schools. The Kalamazoo Promise offered full college tuition and fees for every student in the school district who graduated and attended college in Michigan.

It was a game changer. Three-quarters of the school staff reported improvements in school culture. More students have stayed in school, and far more are going to college. Record numbers of students and parents are turning out for college nights—which now begin in elementary schools. The Promise reversed the average annual 8.7 percent decline in enrollment; as families began moving into the district, public school enrollment increased by 12.1 percent, more than 1,000 students.

The Promise also has given impetus to school improvement efforts at all grade levels. Kalamazoo's Central High School, for example, has already increased the number of students taking Advanced Placement courses by over 200 percent. The proud students competed for, and won, President Obama's presence at their 2010 commencement, where they sang the praises of the Promise.

Not every community of 75,000 has a group of wealthy benefactors with such powerful charitable instincts. But Chuck Wilbur, my education advisor, came up with a way to spread the Kalamazoo idea around the state. We convinced the legislature to authorize the ten poorest districts to capture part of their share of the local education tax. This sum, when combined with fundraising from local community foundations, enabled those communities to begin offering Promise Scholarships to kids in those public schools. We're hoping the impact on local education will be comparable to what happened in Kalamazoo.

Our No Worker Left Behind retraining effort was one of the most fascinating ways we strove and schemed to create a DIY revolution. We knew workers had to "upskill" themselves if they were to participate in, and help remake, our economy. But many workers in their forties, fifties, or sixties were daunted by the prospect of going to college. No Worker Left Behind jump-started them by dangling the offer of free tuition. Some colleges went further, setting up shop in local union halls to offer remedial classes and test prep for workers. Within two years, over 150,000 adults enrolled in community colleges and training programs across Michigan. They simply would not have done that if we hadn't reconfigured policy and if local people hadn't stepped up with DIY leadership.

Our state IT department mounted a similar effort to remove barriers between citizens and their government, making it easier for people to help themselves rather than relying on administrators to help them. The department created the Michigan Business One-Stop, putting every possible permit, process, and business service online and creating a simple one-stop business portal to access all of it. By the time I left office, over two hundred permits had been put on line, and by letting businesses do it themselves, we were reducing staff numbers and customer frustrations.

We were especially focused on entrepreneurs, the paragons of DIY leadership. Instead of sitting in offices waiting for them to come to us, we went to them. In 2010, we teamed with the Kauffman Foundation to pay for 1,000 would-be entrepreneurs to be trained at entrepreneurship "boot camps" across the state, further decentralizing leadership by teaming them with a mentor and a credit union to support their business plans.

When the economy crashed and our human services staffs were overrun by the sheer volume of needs to be met, we told our IT folks to take what they did with the business one stop and bring it into human services, too. We surveyed our services to determine which ones could be put online. To help sign people up, we enlisted other agencies, such as local community action agencies, United Way, local libraries, and other partners that could give the community access to computers. Foundations helped fund the start-up costs. By the time I left office, over 280,000 Michigan citizens were signing up for food stamps, home heating assistance, or unemployment benefits online. Instead of requiring struggling families to come to a distant, central Department of Human Services office to take a number and wait in line for help, we piloted a decentralized approach.

We also brought the services to the people by placing DHS offices inside the local schools with the highest number of kids in poverty. We called them Family Resource Centers (FRCs). They provided wraparound services—food assistance, rent assistance, home heating, connection to unemployment insurance and job training—to the families whose kids attended the school the centers were housed in. By 2010, we had fifty-two FRCs in high-poverty schools. The results: Attendance in those schools improved by 12 percent. School performance and graduation rates also improved. Parents were more likely to come into the schools instead of being leery about going inside. Employees both of schools and of our Department of Human Services were happier. And families got help like never before.

Michiganders, like other Americans, have a long history of self-reliance. They don't want to be dependent on government, or anyone else, to make their lives better. Our experience shows that when people are given the tools to help themselves, they're eager to step up and exercise DIY leadership.

· ·

MICHIGAN HAS JUST EMERGED FROM THE MOST GRUELING DECADE in living memory. In parallel, ordinary citizens around the United States are still struggling to recover from the Great Recession of 2008–2009, our worst economic downturn since the Great Depression. While stock prices have climbed and corporate profits have soared to record levels, employment still lags, and incomes for millions of American families continue to stagnate.

Economists are crunching the jobs data and scratching their heads over why America seems to be in a "jobless recovery," but we know why. The country's economic structure has changed; globalization and technological change are eating away the foundations of the old economy. The nation needs to actively intervene to create jobs in America, for it won't happen on its own.

True economic recovery, when it comes, won't be reflected merely in a rising stock market or the exploding profits of big companies; it won't be found only in improved consumer confidence figures or the price of oil per barrel. Economists and politicians need to step outside of their offices and visit the communities where people are living tough, where people measure recovery in terms of one crucial data point: the real unemployment rate. Who cares if the big companies are making enormous profits, if they're not reinvesting those profits back home? Who cares if consumers are buying more, if almost every product for sale is manufactured overseas?

A bullish stock market doesn't reflect the fact that many Michiganders, and millions of other Americans, are still grappling with the transition to a new world where their old skills and aspirations feel obsolete. We know why the country's job growth is anemic. We don't need an economist to explain it. Our neighbor whose job was moved to Mexico, our friend who was laid off by GM, and our recently graduated niece who's still looking for a full-time job can explain why. Our nation's economic recovery is jobless because we haven't intervened to defend our businesses from unfair trade, haven't partnered with them to create good new jobs here, and haven't invested strategically in education and retraining to prepare workers for today's knowledge economy.

Michigan's experiences, bad and good, should be a battle cry for America. We're far from the end of our journey, and there are many challenges ahead, but the single most important measurement—job growth—has started to improve. No doubt some of that improvement can be traced to the gradual recovery of the national and global economies. But there's also no doubt that our recovery was greatly accelerated by federal and state government action to assist our private sector. We've tried lots of things. Some worked and some didn't. Now that Michigan's jobs recovery is under way, we can see that America doesn't have to resign itself to a jobless recovery. The scary prospect is that failure by government to respond aggressively will make chronic joblessness inevitable in this new global world.

Hands-off, laissez-faire, free-market economics will only ensure that other governments step into the void. America can either take action on behalf of its citizens or watch passively as our people and businesses lose to more determined foreign competitors. *America needs to wake up.*

We must be as aggressive as our global competitors. We must craft a uniquely American manufacturing and industrial policy to create jobs and economic growth for our people. I have offered ideas on policies that have begun to work in Michigan. Countless others are being experimented with in states across the country, the laboratories of democracy. But states alone don't have the tools to compete against China or India. The federal government must act.

Change is hard, and we went first. Michigan is changing. The American auto industry is changing. The UAW is changing. Glenn Voisin and millions of workers like him are changing. Now America must change if we are to win the battle for jobs and economic growth in an ever-more-competitive, global world.

Will we rise to the challenge? I know that we can. And three hundred million Americans are depending on it.

ELEVEN MONTHS OF HOPE

A Michigan Timeline: June 2010–May 2011

July 15:
LG Chem breaks ground on new battery factory in Michigan.

July 20:
General Electric announces expansion in Grand Rapids.

July 21:
Whirlpool announces it will build a new global headquarters in Benton Harbor.

July 22:
High school test scores in Michigan rise to highest on record.

July 27:
Michigan Motion Picture announces it is converting old GM factory in Pontiac into a film studio.

June 26:
John Deere announces it is opening three wind farms in Michigan.

July 30:
Chrysler announces plans to hire 900 workers in Detroit.

August 10:
Business Facilities magazine ranks Michigan in top three in nation for alternative energy investment.

September 13:
A123 opens America's largest electric vehicle battery plant in Livonia.

September 20:
Magna e-Car Systems opens an electric vehicle testing lab in Auburn Hills.

September 22:
Johnson Controls, Inc. and Ford partner to build all-electric Transit Connect in Livonia.

September 24:
Dow announces it will open its PowerHouse Solar Shingle factory in Midland.

September 29:
Dow Chemical and Tata announce $45 million services center in Midland.

October 7:
The Orion factory, once slated for closure, will be saved, and will make small, fuel-efficient vehicles for GM.

October 13:
Michigan is ranked fourth in nation in solar jobs, after Texas, California, and Pennsylvania, according to Solar Foundation.

October 20:
URV to open the nation's first large-scale wind turbine castings foundry in Eaton Rapids.

June 2010	July 2010	August 2010	September 2010	October 2010

June 2010:
Unemployment in Michigan drops to 13.2% from 14.5% six months before.

July-August 2010:
Unemployment in Michigan drops to 13.1%.

September 2010:
Unemployment in Michigan drops to 13%.

October 2010:
Unemployment in Michigan drops to 12.8%

January 1:
State school fund has $500 million surplus entering into new administration.

January 10:
Volt named Car of the Year at the North American International Auto Show in Detroit.

November 7:
Michigan job postings up 55% over one year ago.

December 2:
Brookings Institution reports that Detroit is the seventh-fastest growing region in the country.

January 14:
Economists predict net job growth in 2011, the first job growth in a decade.

May 2:
Chrysler reports $115 million profit, first since bankruptcy.

November 9:
Comerica Bank's Michigan Economic Activity Index rose two points in September to the highest rate since June 2008.

December 6:
Chrysler announces that the Sterling Heights Assembly Plant, once slated for closure, will be saved and is adding a second shift.

January 17:
Michigan auto industry expected to add 45,000 jobs in Michigan by 2012, and nearly double the number of cars and trucks produced. This prediction rivals the creation of modern mass production and the World War II conversion to military production.

May 5–11:
GM reports $3.2 billion profit and announces it will invest $2 billion to upgrade 17 plants and hire 4,200 new workers.

November 30:
General Motors launches the Volt, and announces it is hiring 1,000 more engineers.

December 7:
Michigan lands first large wind turbine assembly plant.

February 28:
Gallup Job Creation Index proclaims Michigan had the best job creation improvement in the nation in 2010.

April 26:
Ford reports $2.6 billion profit, largest in 13 years.

May 16:
Economists predict $429 million surplus in current year and 60,000 new jobs each year for the next two years.

November 2010	December 2010	January 2011	February 2011	April 2011	May 2011

November 2010:
Unemployment in Michigan drops to 12.4%.

December 2010:
Unemployment in Michigan drops to 11.7%; Michigan's unemployment in one year has dropped by 20%. The nation's drop in that same time: 4.8%.

Now, that's the way it's supposed to be.

ACKNOWLEDGMENTS

MANY PEOPLE HELPED US IN SHAPING THIS BOOK, AND EVEN more played crucial supporting roles in helping us deal with the challenging events recounted in these pages—too many to thank them all. Mentioned here are but a few of them.

To our wonderful children—Kate, Cece, and Jack—who have experienced and endured much over these past twelve years, and who have grown into generous and passionate souls: we love you so. Thank you to our parents—Dan's beautiful and faithful mom, Mary Mulhern, and his dad, the late Jack Mulhern, who would have thoroughly enjoyed the ride; and Shirley and Vic Granholm, who instilled in Jennifer the strength and values she carries with her. We are grateful to our siblings, who give us humor, humility, and love: Jen's brother, Bob Granholm, and Dan's sisters and brothers—Kathy Rizzo, and Ann, Mary, Pat, Jim, and Sheila Mulhern; and our fellow "out-laws" Paul Rizzo, Ray Maturo, Cam Dilley, Kathy Shaw, and Jeanne Mulhern.

Our literary agent, Carol Franco, delivered us to a superbly talented and committed team at PublicAffairs. Thank you to our editor at PublicAffairs, Clive Priddle, whose keen observations shaped and sharpened the book, and to our consulting editor, Karl Weber, for an incredible yeoman's job of helping us polish the manuscript. Great thanks go to those who, along with Carol, read drafts and commented on the manuscript, including Jill Alper, Chuck Wilbur, Genna Gent, Fred Hoffman, and Kent Lineback. We thank Phil Revard for painstaking fact-checking. To Cathleen Carrigan, a.k.a. wizardkitten: you're the smartest cat in the blogosphere.

A profound thank you to our friends and the members of our professional team: to Dave Katz and Jill Alper, the dynamic duo who have been both friends and advisors to us; to the greatest political partner a governor could have, Lieutenant Governor John Cherry; to Liz Boyd, Pearl Dekker, Karen DeMott, and Carole Polan of our administrative and transition teams, who tended to countless subtle but important details; to Sherry Hicks, Jennifer's closest assistant for nearly 15 years; to Alex Edwards, Pat Costick, Jerome Marks, Oralya Garza, Steve Lyon, Gayleen Gavitt, and Kelly Brennan, who helped hold our lives, family, and friendships together as the economic bombs were detonating around us; to the men and women of the Michigan State Police governor's security detail who protected us and grew to become part of our family; and to those who led our political and campaign efforts—Dave and Jill, Howard Edelson, Trisha Stein, Mark Mellman, Joe Slade White, Cheryl Bergman, Carrie Jones, Gary Torgow, and David Baker Lewis.

We're also very grateful to Jennifer's stellar Executive Team members, who carried Michigan on their backs and in their hearts through the battles and triumphs described in these pages, including—among others—Rick Wiener, Mary Lannoye, John Burchett, Dan Krichbaum, Nate Lake, Teresa Bingman, Lisa Webb-Sharpe, Tim Hughes, Regina Bell, Dana Debel, Steve Liedel, Kelly Keenan, JoAnne Huls, Liz Boyd, Chuck Wilbur, Genna Gent, Lynda Rossi, Kim Trent, Leslee Fritz, Mary Zatina, Fred Hoffman, Beth Bingham, Chris Priest, Maxine Berman, Susan Corbin, Jim Stokes, Jennifer LeFevre, Jeff Dutka, Sarah Garcia, Greg Roberts, Tim Kovacik, Elva Revilla, Robert Davis, Rick Martin, and Walt Herzig. Thanks to our clean energy team: Greg

Main, Jim Epolito, Skip Pruss, Doug Parks, Andy Levin, Joe Dooley, and Brandon Hofmeister. Thank you to every one of the members of the cabinet, many of whom served shoulder to shoulder with Jennifer for the entire eight years, battling on the front lines for Michigan day in and day out.

We are grateful to Julie Yapp, our children's caregiver for the past nine years, whose pure goodness and selflessness have been an inspiration to us.

A special thanks to our "pre-governor" friends (you know who you are), who continued to nurture our friendship through thick and thin: the U.S. Attorney Amigos, the Harvard Law School Villains, the Woodside neighbors, the Wayne County team, Desiree Cooper and Butch Hollowell, and Marianne and Larry Talon.

We owe a debt to Jim Kouzes and Ronnie Heifetz, the leadership scholars and friends who guided us into and through the maelstrom.

Thank you to our priests, Father Mark Inglot and Father Joe Krupp, for their support, prayers, and advice, and to the people of St. John Student Center and to so many others who prayed for us and for Michigan.

Finally, thanks to our mentors, the late Ed McNamara, Judge Damon Keith, and Congressman Sander Levin, for teaching us three key things: to always do what's right and let the chips fall where they may; to fight for the underdog; and to remember that when you do good policy, the politics will take care of itself.

Jennifer Granholm
Dan Mulhern
Haslett, Michigan
May 2011

APPENDIX: 99 REASONS (PLUS 17 MORE) WHY TAX CUTS ALONE ARE NOT THE KEY TO ECONOMIC GROWTH

CONSERVATIVE LAISSEZ-FAIRE DOGMA TENDS TO TREAT government spending as *the* enemy of economic growth, with the corollary that tax cuts can serve as a magic elixir any time the economy falters. Michigan proves it's not true. The Granholm administration favored a lean, efficient, and targeted tax regime, as evidenced by the following list of 99 business tax cuts (plus 17 individual tax cuts) signed into law during our two terms in office. But lower taxes alone didn't jump-start our state's growth. It took the comprehensive growth program described in this book to help Michigan recover from the recession of 2008–2009. Today, policy makers at the national level are struggling to learn the same lesson.

A. Business Tax Cuts Approved by Governor Granholm (2003–2007)

	Tax Cut	Public Act	Effective Date
1	Tax Abatement for Bio-Diesel Manufacturing	2003 PA 5	4/24/2003
2	Doubled Number of Tax-Exempt Agricultural Renaissance Zone	2003 PA 93	7/24/2003
3	Removed Health Cares Costs from Single Business Tax Base for 2004, 2005, and 2006	2003 PA 240	12/29/2003
4	Removed Health Cares Costs from Single Business Tax Base for 2007 and After	2003 PA 241	12/29/2003
5	Authorized Michigan Economic Growth Authority (MEGA) Tax Credits for Qualified High Technology Businesses	2003 PA 249	12/29/2003
6	Extended Eligibility MEGA Tax Credits through 2009	2003 PA 250	12/29/2003
7	New Single Business Tax Credit for Distressed Businesses	2003 PA 251	12/29/2003
8	New Tax-Exempt Tool and Die Recovery Renaissance Zones	2003 PA 266	1/5/2004
9	Doubled Single Business Tax Credit for Apprenticeship Training	2003 PA 273	1/8/2004
10	Personal Property Tax Reductions for Special Tools and Standard Tools	2003 PA 274	1/8/2004
11	Personal Property Tax Reductions for Special Tools	2004 PA 4	12/31/2003
12	Expanded Boundaries of Coldwater Renaissance Zone	2004 PA 16	3/4/2004
13	Personal Property Tax Exemption for Pharmaceutical Companies	2004 PA 79	4/21/2004

	Tax Cut	Public Act	Effective Date
14	Expanded Eligibility for Single Business Tax Credits Approved by Michigan Economic Growth Authority for Multi-Site Facilities and Businesses with Leased Employees	2004 PA 81	4/22/2004
15	Single Business Tax Exemption for Start-up Businesses	2004 PA 126	5/28/2004
16	Property Tax Exemption for Business Incubator Personal Property	2004 PA 244	7/23/2004
17	Property Tax Exemption for Business Incubator Property	2004 PA 245	7/23/2004
18	Exemption from Obsolete Properties Specific Tax for Start-up Business Facilities	2004 PA 251	7/23/2004
19	Property Tax Exemption for Start-up Business Property	2004 PA 252	7/23/2004
20	New Single Business Tax Deduction for Research Programs and Grants	2004 PA 258	7/23/2004
21	New Single Business Tax Credit for Automobile Donation	2004 PA 302	7/23/2004
22	New High-Technology and Manufacturing Job Creation Single Business Tax Credit	2004 PA 319	8/27/2004
23	Technology Park Facilities Tax Exemption for Start-up Business Facilities	2004 PA 321	8/27/2004
24	City Utility Users Tax Exemption for Start-up Businesses	2004 PA 322	8/27/2004
25	Industrial Facility Tax Exemption for Start-up Businesses	2004 PA 323	8/27/2004
26	Exemption for Start-up Businesses from Tax on Lessees and Users of Tax-Exempt Property	2004 PA 325	8/27/2004
27	Expanded Eligibility for Single Business Tax Credits for Businesses Making Capital Investments	2004 PA 398	10/15/2004

	Tax Cut	Public Act	Effective Date
28	New Tax-Exempt Redevelopment Renaissance Zone	2004 PA 430	12/20/2004
29	Reduction of Property Taxes for Erroneously Uncapped Assessments	2005 PA 23	5/23/2005
30	New Property Tax Abatement for Qualified Logistical Optimization Centers	2005 PA 118	9/22/2005
31	MEGA Tax Credit for Job Retention at a Rural Business at Risk of Closure	2005 PA 185	10/24/2005
32	Commercial Redevelopment Property Tax Reduction	2005 PA 210	11/17/2005
33	Venture Capital Investment Income Tax Reduction	2005 PA 214	11/21/2005
34	New Property Tax Abatement for Qualified Commercial Activity Property	2005 PA 267	12/16/2005
35	Expanded Tool and Die Renaissance Zones	2005 PA 275	12/19/2005
36	Manufacturers' Personal Property Tax Credit for 2006	2005 PA 289	12/20/2005
37	Manufacturers' Personal Property Tax Credit for 2007	2005 PA 290	12/20/2005
38	Manufacturers' Personal Property Tax Credit for 2008	2005 PA 291	12/20/2005
39	Manufacturers' Personal Property Tax Credit for 2009	2005 PA 292	12/20/2005
40	Insourcing Credit for Jobs Transferred from Another State or Country to Michigan for 2007 and 2008	2005 PA 293	12/20/2005
41	Insourcing Credit for Jobs Transferred from Another State or Country to Michigan for 2009	2005 PA 294	12/20/2005
42	Modify Tax Base Apportionment to Reduce Single Business Tax Liability	2005 PA 295	12/20/2005

	Tax Cut	Public Act	Effective Date
43	Special Single Business Tax Reductions for Delphi/Visteon	2005 PA 296	12/20/2005
44	Sales Tax Exemption for Aircraft, Parts, and Materials Temporarily in Michigan	2006 PA 17	2/9/2006
45	Use Tax Exemption for Aircraft, Parts, and Materials Temporarily in Michigan	2006 PA 18	2/9/2006
46	Authorized MEGA Tax Credits for Vaccine Laboratory Sites	2006 PA 21	2/14/2006
47	Expanded Historic Preservation Single Business Tax Credit	2006 PA 53	3/9/2006
48	Expanded Eligibility for Obsolete Property Tax Exemption	2006 PA 70	3/20/2006
49	Expanded Eligibility for Tool and Die Recovery Zone Tax Exemption	2006 PA 93	4/4/2006
50	New Brownfield Tax Credits	2006 PA 111 2006 PA 112 2006 PA 113	4/10/2006 4/10/2006 91 days
51	Expanded Renaissance Zone in Benton Harbor, Berrien County	2006 PA 116	4/11/2006
52	Expanded Renaissance Zone in Carson City, Montcalm County	2006 PA 116	4/11/2006
53	Expanded Renaissance Zone in Montcalm County	2006 PA 116	4/11/2006
54	Authorized Renaissance Redevelopment Zone in Wixom, Oakland County	2006 PA116	4/11/2006
55	Authorized Renaissance Redevelopment Zone in Ostego County	2006 PA 116	4/11/2006
56	Authorized Renaissance Redevelopment Zone in Midland, Midland County	2006 PA 116	4/11/2006
57	Authorized Renaissance Redevelopment Zone in Walker, Kent County	2006 PA 116	4/11/2006
58	Expanded Renaissance Zone Tax Credit Eligibility for Pharmaceutical Companies	2006 PA 116	4/11/2006

	Tax Cut	Public Act	Effective Date
59	Expanded Rural Businesses Qualified for MEGA Tax Credits	2006 PA 117	4/11/2006
60	Expanded Eligibility for MEGA Tax Credits in Ontonagon County	2006 PA 117	4/11/2006
61	Expanded High-Technology Businesses Qualified for MEGA Tax Credits	2006 PA 188	6/19/2006
62	Reduced Property Taxes for Farm Operations Involving Cervidae	2006 PA 214	6/21/2006
63	Extended and Preserved Brownfield and Historic Preservation Tax Credits	2006 PA 240	6/27/2006
64	New Renaissance Zones for Renewable Energy Facilities	2006 PA 270	7/7/2006
65	Exempted Leaded Racing Fuel from Motor Fuel Tax	2006 PA 277	1/1/2004
66	Reduced Property Taxes for Hunting Preserves	2006 PA 278	7/7/2006
67	Expanded Eligibility for MEGA Tax Credits for Full-Time Job Creation	2006 PA 281	7/10/2006
68	Expanded Eligibility for MEGA Tax Credits	2006 PA 283	7/10/2006
69	Increased Number of Agricultural Processing Renaissance Zones	2006 PA 284	7/10/2006
70	Created New Forest Products Processing Renaissance Zones	2006 PA 304 2006 PA 305	7/20/2006 7/20/2006
71	Research and Development Compensation Tax Credit	2006 PA 323	7/20/2006
72	Reduced Property Taxes for Horse Boarding Stable Operations	2006 PA 376	9/22/2006
73	New Property Tax Exemption for Qualified Forest Property	2006 PA 378 2006 PA 379 2006 PA 380	9/27/2006 9/27/2006 9/27/2006
74	Reduced Commercial Forest Tax for Sustainable Forest Conservation Easements	2006 PA 381	9/27/2006

	Tax Cut	Public Act	Effective Date
75	Use Tax Exemption for Delivery Charges	2006 PA 428	10/5/2006
76	Sales Tax Exemption for Delivery Charges	2006 PA 434	10/5/2006
77	Expanded Eligibility for Plant Rehabilitation and Industrial Development Property Tax Abatement	2006 PA 436	10/5/2006
78	Expanded Authority for Designation and Expansion of Renaissance Zones	2006 PA 440	10/5/2006
79	Increased Alternative Energy Renaissance Zones	2006 PA 476	12/21/2006
80	Authorized Renaissance Redevelopment Zone in Kent County	2006 PA 476	12/21/2006
81	Authorized Renaissance Redevelopment Zone in Jackson County	2006 PA 476	12/21/2006
82	Authorized Renaissance Redevelopment Zone in Midland County	2006 PA 476	12/21/2006
83	Expanded Eligibility for MEGA Tax Credits	2006 PA 484	12/29/2006
84	Authorized Rural MEGA Tax Credits in Kent County	2006 PA 484	12/29/2006
85	Authorized Mega Tax Credits in Northern Michigan	2006 PA 484	12/29/2006
86	New Property Tax Exemption for Methane Digesters	2006 PA 550	12/29/2006
87	Expanded Sales Tax Exemptions for Athletic Event Organizing Entity	2006 PA 590	1/3/2007
88	Expanded Alternative Energy Tax Credits and Exemptions	2006 PA 632	1/4/2007
89	New Motion Picture Production Sales Tax Credits	2006 PA 657	1/9/2007
90	Nonprofit Hospital and Housing Construction Sales Tax Credit	2006 PA 665	1/10/2007

	Tax Cut	Public Act	Effective Date
91	Nonprofit Hospital and Housing Construction Use Tax Credit	2006 PA 666	1/10/2007
92	Expanded Eligibility for Obsolete Property Rehabilitation Property Tax Abatements	2006 PA 667	1/10/2007
93	Expanded Use Tax Exemptions for Corporate Sponsors of Athletic Event Organizing Entities	2006 PA 673	1/10/2007
94	New Industrial Development Property Tax Abatement for Strategic Response Centers	2007 PA 12 2007 PA 13	5/29/2007 5/29/2007
95	New Industrial Development Property Tax Abatement for Motorsports Entertainment Complexes	2007 PA 12 2007 PA 13	5/29/2007 5/29/2007
96	Exempt Industrial and Commercial Personal Property from Local School Property Taxes	2007 PA 37 2007 PA 39 2007 PA 40	7/12/2007 7/12/2007 7/12/2007
97	Exempt Industrial Personal Property from State Education Tax	2007 PA 38 2007 PA 39	7/12/2007 7/12/2007
98	Expanded Eligibility for MEGA Tax Credits	2007 PA 62	9/19/2007
99	Michigan Business Tax Deferred Tax Liability Deduction	2007 PA 90	9/30/2007

B. Tax Cuts for Individuals Approved By Governor Granholm (2003–2007)

	Tax Cut	Public Act	Effective Date
1	Use Tax Exemption for Personal Property Brought into Michigan	2003 PA 27	3/30/2004
2	Income Tax Credit for Police, Fire, and Advanced Life Support Special Assessments	2003 PA 28 2003 PA 29	6/26/2003 6/26/2003
3	Use Tax Reductions for Implementation of Streamlined Sales Tax Agreement	2004 PA 172	9/1/2004
4	Sales Tax Reductions for Implementation of Streamlined Sales Tax Agreement	2004 PA 173	9/1/2004
5	Sales Tax Exemption for Automobile Transferred to Individual by Charitable Organization	2004 PA 301	7/23/2004
6	Use Tax Exemption for Automobile Transferred to Individual by Charitable Organization	2004 PA 312	8/27/2004
7	New Income Tax Credit for Donation of Automobile to Charitable Organization	204 PA 313	8/27/2004
8	Use Tax Exemption for Donation of Motor Vehicle to Individual Eligible for Public Assistance by a Church	2004 PA 435	12/21/2004
9	Expanded Historic Preservation Income Tax Credit	2006 PA 52	3/9/2006
10	Expanded Eligibility for Principal Residence Property Tax Exemption	2006 PA 114	4/10/2006
11	New Income Tax Credit for Stillborn Birth	2006 PA 319	7/20/2006
12	New Michigan Earned Income Tax Credit	2006 PA 372	9/22/2006

	Tax Cut	Public Act	Effective Date
13	"Pop-up Tax" Exemption for Land	2006 PA 446	12/8/2006
14	New Individual Family Development Account Contribution Income Tax Credit	2006 PA 514	12/29/2006
15	Reduced Sales Tax for Charitable Auction Purchases	2006 PA 577	3/4/2007
16	Property Tax Exemption for Nonprofit Single Family Homes and Duplexes	2006 PA 612	1/3/2007
17	New Income Tax Exemption for Disabled Veterans	2007 PA 94	10/1/2007

SOURCE NOTES

1. The Bounce

19 *It wouldn't be easy*: The line, "Only challenge produces the opportunity for greatness" is quoted from James S. Kouzes and Barry M. Posner, *The Leadership Challenge*, 3rd ed. (San Francisco: Jossey-Bass, 2005), p. 76.

23 *Dan and I shared a mantra*: "Accept, adjust, advance" is from Joe Caruso, *The Power of Losing Control* (New York: Gotham, 2003), p. 215.

3. A Different Kind of Crisis

45 *A report from the global accounting and consulting firm KPMG*: KPMG's Auto Executive Survey 2004, at http://us.kpmg.com /jnet/English/Archives/2004/MarApr/AutoSurveyEng.pdf.

50 *They interviewed Greenville's genteel Mayor Walker*: Quoted on Fouroboros (blog), November 12, 2004, at www.alchemysite .com/blog/outsource_anorexia.html.

55 *It's their work, too*: The words "give the work back to them" are adapted from Ron Heifetz, *Leadership Without Easy Answers* (Cambridge, MA: Harvard University Press, 1998), p. 128. Dan

and I studied under Professor Heifetz at the Kennedy School of
Government at Harvard University.

56 *The commission worked throughout 2004*: Lt. Governor's Commission
on Higher Education and Economic Growth, *Final Report of the Lt.
Governor's Commission on Higher Education and Economic Growth*
(Lansing, MI: December 2004), at www.cherrycommission.org/.

4. Landing in a Hurricane

72 *By the time Toyota decided*: "Toyota's Powerful Friends in Washington," Associated Press, February 8, 2010, at www.msnbc.msn
.com/id/35293626/ns/business-autos/t/toyotas-powerful
-friends-washington/.

75 Business Week *summarized the strategy*: David Welch, "Go Bankrupt, Then Go Overseas," *Business Week*, April 24, 2006, at www
.businessweek.com/magazine/content/06_17/b3981068.htm.

76 *At one press conference in New York*: Keith Naughton, "Motown
Mechanic," *Newsweek*, October 24, 2005, www.newsweek.com
/2005/10/23/motown-mechanic.html.

5. Blown Away Yet?

93 *Just in case my sense of urgency*: Jeffrey McCracken and Joseph
B. White, "Ford Will Shed 28% of Workers in North America," *Wall Street Journal*, January 24, 2006, p. A1; quoted at
"Brad DeLong's Grasping Reality with Both Hands" (blog),
http://delong.typepad.com/sdj/2006/01/covering_the_ec
_8.html.

6. Blowing Up Taxes, Budgets, Mind-sets . . . and Mattresses

119 *After adopting a cut-laden budget*: The following graph indicates
the severity of the budget gaps our administration had to resolve
in each of the nine years we were in office.

Budget Gaps Resolved
Over $14.8 billion in shortfalls in 9 years

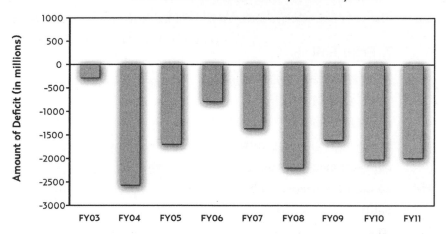

122 *My morning news clips*: Charles Slat, "The China Connection," *Monroe News*, May 6, 2007, at www.monroenews.com/apps /pbcs.dll/article?AID=/20070506/BUSINESS/105060027.

123 *According to a survey*: Eric Scorsone and David Zin, *The Michigan Economy and State Revenue: A 10-Year History (1999–2009)* (Lansing, MI: Senate Fiscal Agency, April 2010), at www.senate .michigan.gov/sfa/Publications/Issues/StateRevenueTenYears /StateRevenueTenYears.pdf.

125 *At a National Governors Association meeting*: Carly Fiorina, quoted in Richard Florida, *The Rise of the Creative Class* (New York: Basic Books, 2002), p. 6.

125 *CEOs like IBM's Lou Gerstner*: http://wyldtv.blogspot.com /2010/10/cnn-former-ibm-ceo-lou-gerstner-on.html.

126 *Canadian-generated tax competitiveness reports*: Duanjie Chen and Jack M. Mintz, *Ontario's Fiscal Competitiveness in 2004* (Toronto: Institute for Competitiveness and Prosperity, November 8, 2004), at www.competeprosper.ca/images/uploads/ChenMintzReport _241104.pdf.

131   *The same Andy Dillon*: Peter Luke, "Some Democrats Cringe at Service Tax; Frosty Reception Spells Trouble for Granholm's Plan," *Grand Rapids Press*, March 15, 2007.

7. Free Fall

150   *Now, eight years later, Romney's message*: "Gov. Romney Will Turn Around Michigan's Recession," at Mitt Romney, Road to the White House (campaign blog), January 10, 2008, http:// mittromneyroadtothewhitehouse.blogspot.com/2008/01 /gov-romney-will-turn-around-michigans.html.

150   *McCain's message*: Michael Levenson, "Staking Out the Next Battlegrounds," *Boston Globe*, January 10, 2008.

165   *Within days, in an act many saw as treasonous*: Mitt Romney, "Let Detroit Go Bankrupt," *New York Times*, November 18, 2008, at www.nytimes.com/2008/11/19/opinion/19romney.html?scp=1 &sq=romney%20let%20detroit%20go%20bankrupt&st=cse.

168   *In January 2006, Bush had been quoted*: Christopher Cooper and John D. McKinnon, "Bush Plays Down Bailout Prospects for GM and Ford; President Says Market Forces Are Important for Industry; A Hard Line on Hamas," *Wall Street Journal*, January 26, 2006, p. A1.

168   *With voice cracking, the normally tough*: "Rattner on GM, Chrysler Turnaround Plans: 'They Were Delusional,'" *Detroit Free Press*, December 15, 2009, at www.freep.com/article/20091216 /SPECIAL04/912160355/Rattner-GM-Chrysler-turnaround -plans-They-were-delusional-.

8. The Unthinkable

192   *I kept trying to make time*: Steven Covey, *The 7 Habits of Highly Effective People* (New York: Free Press, 2004).

9. Green Shoots

202   *The theme of John Kotter's*: John Kotter, "Leading Change: Why

Transformation Efforts Fail," *Harvard Business Review*, March-April 1995; reprinted in Harvard Business Review, *HBR's Must-Reads on Change* (Boston: Harvard Business Publishing, January 2007), pp. 4–11, at www.nimbusconsultinggroup.com/files/HBRs _Must_Reads_on_Change.pdf.

204   *The most common ego identifications*: Eckhart Tolle, *The Power of Now: A Guide to Spiritual Enlightenment* (Novato, CA: New World Library, 2004), p. 46.

205   *He worked it spiritually*: St. Augustine, *Confessions*, I (i) 1.

207   *I thought of the prayer*: Known as "The Romero Prayer" because of its association with assassinated Archbishop Oscar A. Romero of San Salvador, the prayer is widely available online. The story behind the prayer and a complete text can be found at the Web site of the Office of Justice, Peace, and Integrity of Creation (JPIC) Congregation of Notre Dame in Montreal, Canada: www.jpic-visitation.org/reflections/prayers/romero.html.

225   *The ultraconservative* Wall Street Journal: Sharon Terlep and Jeff Bennett, "Carmakers Stabilize Year After Bailout," *Wall Street Journal*, April 22, 2010, at http://online.wsj.com/article /SB10001424052748704133804575197990349307652.html?mod= WSJ_Autos_AutoIndustry3.

225   *As* U.S. News & World Report *then commented*: "GM Pays Back Government Loans 5 Years Early," *U.S. News and World Report*, April 22, 2010, at http://usnews.rankingsandreviews.com/cars -trucks/daily-news/100422-GM-Pays-Back-Government -Loans-5-Years-Early/.

10. Cracking the Code

232   *And we began to get results*: Metropolitan Policy Program, *Global Metro Monitor: The Path to Economic Recovery* (Washington, DC: Brookings Institution, December 2010), at www.brookings.edu /~/media/Files/rc/reports/2010/1130_global_metro_monitor /1130_global_metro_monitor.pdf; Dennis Jacobe, "North Dakota

and Washington, D.C. Best Job Markets in 2010," Gallup Job Creation Index, February 28, 2011, www.gallup.com/poll/146402/North-Dakota-Washington-Best-Job-Markets-2010.aspx.

234   *He asked whether we had seen the stories*: Nick Summers, "How Chinese Suicides Could Hurt Apple," *Newsweek*, May 28, 2010, at www.newsweek.com/2010/05/28/how-chinese-suicides-could-hurt-apple.html.

235   *In his memoir, George W. Bush recalls*: George W. Bush, *Decision Points* (New York: Crown, 2010), p. 256.

235   *Jack Welch, former CEO of GE*: Quoted in, for example, "Where America's Jobs Went," *The Week*, March 18, 2011, at http://theweek.com/article/index/213217/where-americas-jobs-went.

236   *When Delphi filed for bankruptcy*: David Shephardson, "Slimmer Delphi, with no UAW workers, files for IPO," *Detroit News*, May 26, 2011, at http://detnews.com/article/20110526/AUTO01/105260426/Slimmer-Delphi—with-no-UAW-workers—files-for-IPO#ixzz1NW7ni4by.

236   *Between 2003 and 2008, as Michigan was leading*: Roya Wolverson, "Outsourcing Jobs and Taxes," Council on Foreign Relations, February 11, 2011, at www.cfr.org/united-states/outsourcing-jobs-taxes/p21777, citing www.bea.gov/international/di1usdop.htm.

237   *The Congressional Budget Office has projected*: An Analysis of the President's Budgetary Proposals for Fiscal Year 2011 (Washington, DC: Congressional Budget Office, March 2010), at www.cbo.gov/ftpdocs/112xx/doc11280/03–24-apb.pdf.

237   *As retiring Chairman of the Joint Chiefs of Staff Admiral Mike Mullen*: "Mullen: Debt Is Top National Security Threat," CNN US, August 27, 2010, at http://articles.cnn.com/2010–08–27/us/debt.security.mullen_1_pentagon-budget-national-debt-michael-mullen?_s=PM:US.

238   *We cut more government jobs*: Jackie Headapohl, "Michigan Sheds the Most Government Jobs in the Past Decade," mlive.com

(website), May 28, 2011, at http://www.mlive.com/jobs/index
.ssf/2011/05/michigan_shrinks_the_most_government_job.html.

240 *In Hunan Province, for example*: Keith Bradsher, "On Clean Energy, China Skirts Rules," *New York Times*, September 8, 2010, at
www.nytimes.com/2010/09/09/business/global/09trade.html
?scp=1&sq=hunan%20province%20solar%20panels&st=cse.

241 *Kishore Mahbubani, dean of the Lee Kuan Yew School*: Kishore Mahbubani, "U.S. Needs to Shed Its Taboo on Economic Planning,"
Financial Times, May 5, 2011, at http://mahbubani.net/articles
%20by%20dean/Us%20needs%20to%20shed%20its%20taboo
%20on%20economic%20planning.pdf.

246 *It's reality that can be measured*: Randy Albelda and Marlene Kim,
"A Tale of Two Decades: Changes in Work and Family in Massachusetts, 1979–1999," *Massachusetts Benchmarks* 5(2) (2002):
12–17; Charles L. Ballard, *Michigan's Economic Future: A New
Look* (East Lansing: Michigan State University Press, 2010), pp.
60–62.

253 *On August 2, 2010, he gave the keynote address*: Bob King, "A
UAW for the 21st Century," August 2, 2010, at www.uaw.org
/articles/uaw-21st-century.

INDEX

JENNIFER M. GRANHOLM was elected governor of Michigan in 2002 and reelected in 2006. Born in Vancouver, Canada, and raised in Southern California, she is an honors graduate of both the University of California at Berkeley and Harvard Law School (where she earned her JD). She began her career in public service as a judicial clerk for Michigan's Sixth Circuit Court of Appeals. She became a federal prosecutor in Detroit in 1990, and in 1994 she was appointed Wayne County corporation counsel. Granholm was elected Michigan's first female attorney general in 1998.

DAN MULHERN, a graduate of Yale and Harvard Law School, is an expert in leadership development and practice. He has worked in the public, private, and not-for-profit sectors. Since 1999 he has been working as a public speaker, consultant, radio personality, and writer in the field of leadership. His radio show *Everyday Leadership: Making Work Work* is broadcast across most of Michigan on the Michigan Talk Network. He is the author of *Everyday Leadership: Getting Results in Business, Politics, and Life*. For ten years, he has been writing an acclaimed blog, "Reading for Leading," which is received directly by thousands of readers.

Granholm and Mulhern have three children.

PublicAffairs is a publishing house founded in 1997. It is a tribute to the standards, values, and flair of three persons who have served as mentors to countless reporters, writers, editors, and book people of all kinds, including me.

I. F. STONE, proprietor of *I. F. Stone's Weekly*, combined a commitment to the First Amendment with entrepreneurial zeal and reporting skill and became one of the great independent journalists in American history. At the age of eighty, Izzy published *The Trial of Socrates*, which was a national bestseller. He wrote the book after he taught himself ancient Greek.

BENJAMIN C. BRADLEE was for nearly thirty years the charismatic editorial leader of *The Washington Post*. It was Ben who gave the *Post* the range and courage to pursue such historic issues as Watergate. He supported his reporters with a tenacity that made them fearless and it is no accident that so many became authors of influential, best-selling books.

ROBERT L. BERNSTEIN, the chief executive of Random House for more than a quarter century, guided one of the nation's premier publishing houses. Bob was personally responsible for many books of political dissent and argument that challenged tyranny around the globe. He is also the founder and longtime chair of Human Rights Watch, one of the most respected human rights organizations in the world.

•　　•　　•

For fifty years, the banner of Public Affairs Press was carried by its owner Morris B. Schnapper, who published Gandhi, Nasser, Toynbee, Truman, and about 1,500 other authors. In 1983, Schnapper was described by *The Washington Post* as "a redoubtable gadfly." His legacy will endure in the books to come.

Peter Osnos, *Founder and Editor-at-Large*